Bogus
Allegations

The Injustice of Guilty Until Proven Innocent

Michelle Lombardi Gesse

JOHNSON BOOKS
BOULDER

LIBRARY OF CONGRESS CATALOGING-IN-PUBLICATION DATA
Gesse, Michelle Lombardi.
Bogus allegations : the injustice of guilty until proven innocent /
Michelle Lombardi Gesse.—1st ed.
p. cm.
ISBN 978-1-55566-450-3 (alk. paper)
1. Gesse, Steven—Trials, litigation, etc. 2. Trials (Offenses against the person)—
Colorado—Boulder County. I. Title.
KF225.G47G47 2012
364.15—dc23

2012003204

Published by Johnson Books
a Big Earth Publishing company
3660 Mitchell Lane, Suite E, Boulder, CO 80301
1-800-258-5830
E-mail: books@bigearthpublishing.com
bigearthpublishing.com

9   8   7   6   5   4   3   2   1

Printed in the United States of America

"It doesn't take any guts
to bring a case to prosecution,
if there's any kind of case at all,
but it takes some guts and smarts
to look at the evidence and see
that it's not enough for a conviction."

—STUART WOODS, *Strategic Moves*

To Steven—
I never suspected marriage would be such an adventure.
Though I don't regret any moment of the journey,
there's no doubt some adventures were more fun than others.
Who would want life to be boring?
I love you.

To Trip—
Thank you for believing in us and saving our lives.
Thank you for being such a good and thorough lawyer.
And thanks for being nice, too.

To all of our good friends—
you know who you are.
You believed Steven was innocent from the
beginning and supported both of us.
You were at the trial if you could be there.
And you flooded the heavens with your prayers.
Thank you!

Chapter 1

I used to think the innocent had nothing to fear. Now I know this is not true. The innocent may have more to fear than the guilty. I assume the guilty have at least had a chance to think about what they would do if they were arrested.

Chapter 2

April 4, 2009

It was Saturday, and my husband, Steven, and I had arrived back home from Texas only the previous Thursday evening. Home was our house in the foothills outside of Boulder, Colorado—as we liked to say, "In Boulder County but not in the city limits." This was our way of saying that we didn't consider ourselves "typical Boulderites." We had lived in our home for over sixteen years, longer than we had lived anywhere else. That tells you that we liked living there.

Our home was set on approximately four acres at 7,300 feet elevation, or about 2,000 feet above Boulder and Denver. You could look out our east facing windows and actually see the Denver airport almost sixty miles away. On a clear day (which was most of the time), I think you could see Kansas. Even though our lot was not that big, our home was situated in a way that we couldn't see any of the neighboring homes, and they couldn't see ours. The privacy meant that we didn't have any window treatment on the window in our bathroom, and never closed any of the blinds in our house. The only way someone could look into our windows was with a telescope. And at that point I would hope they weren't too disappointed after going to all that trouble!

Though we liked our privacy, we also liked entertaining and sharing a bottle of wine and maybe dinner with friends. We were fortunate that we had good friends who lived on our lane and who enjoyed the same things. Tom and Jean had lived in their home for about five years and we had become good friends. They would water our plants and pick up our mail when we were gone. We would feed their cats and pick up their mail when they were gone. They would come over a few times a week to join us for a bottle of wine and dinner at the spur of the moment. I didn't like to plan ahead, and found cooking for four no more work than cooking for two. And we enjoyed the company. They were the first ones I would call if we needed help for some reason and I suspect we were the first ones they would call.

Tom and Jean were both retired military. Tom was Steven's age; Jean was about ten years younger. Tom's background was as a meteorologist, though now most of his work was consulting. Jean was a nurse practitioner who worked two days a week. She had lots of interests that kept her busy the rest of the time. When Tom was traveling we tended to see Jean even more, as we often invited her to join us for dinner if we knew she was alone. It was a short walk from our home to theirs along our driveway. Though Tom and Jean's politics differed dramatically from ours, we considered them very good friends and certainly the closest to our home geographically.

We had left Texas hill country on March 31, after spending two months there in our motor home. My husband, who was sixty-three and retired, had been on a quest for the last few years to find a place where we could begin to establish roots and make friends in anticipation of retiring. I wasn't retired yet. I was fifty-nine and owned a small manufacturing company headquartered in Boulder. Plus, my Type-A personality would have made retiring difficult. This was our second year of wintering for a few months in Texas. It hadn't been a good trip and we both agreed that we weren't retiring there. I didn't even want to visit there again.

Part of the problem had been the lack of amenities in the area. There were no good restaurants near the campground. One of the reasons we enjoyed Boulder was that we both liked to eat and drink, and there were a number of excellent restaurants in Boulder—more than you would usually find in a much bigger town. Marble Falls, Texas, didn't have any in 2009. There had been a few the prior year, but they had failed by the time we arrived on February 1. Ironically, the weather had been even better in Boulder than in Texas for much of the two months. And the folks in the campground weren't really interested in outdoor potlucks or drinking some good wine with us. We were glad that Steven's brother and his wife had been there with us, as they supplied our social interaction for the two months. By 8:00 p.m. the picnic tables in the campground were empty (except perhaps for ours), and the TV lights illuminated the inside of most of the motor homes. It was a pretty boring campground to be honest.

The other issues with the two months were more personal. Steven (I call my husband Steven, everyone else calls him Steve. His legal name is actually Mark Steven, but no one besides phone solicitors call him Mark.), his brother Gregg, and our sister-in-law Jane all had horrible colds for the first three or four weeks we were there. I'm not sure how I avoided catching the cold, but I did. I had three business trips out of Austin during those first four weeks though, so I was actually gone a lot. I know the colds weren't Texas's fault, but the three of them being under the weather made them reluctant to do much.

The saddest part of the trip was that we had to put our eleven-year-old Newfoundland, Samson, to sleep. He was pretty old for a Newf, but he was doing okay when we left Boulder with him and our other Newf, Bella. Bella was only four. Her job had been to keep Samson active and happy, and to make him live longer, which she probably did. Everyone thinks their dogs are special, but I am sure Samson was. He was massive—a hundred and seventy-five pounds in his prime with a huge, beautiful head. And he was gentle. But he was old.

I was at the airport in Cincinnati waiting for my return flight on the last Thursday in February when I called Steven. He was in tears. Apparently Samson's breathing had become labored that day. It was apparent that he wasn't going to last long. I wanted to be with Samson at the end. Steven wanted Samson to wait for me and, in reality, Steven didn't want to make this decision alone. I called Gregg and Jane and they said they would go to the Austin airport with Steven so he wouldn't have to drive there alone. My flight wasn't scheduled to arrive in Austin until after 10:00 p.m. that evening, and I was worried about Steven driving safely so late at night, given how distraught he seemed. All of them were in the Suburban to pick me up: Steven sitting in the back with Samson and Bella, Gregg and Jane in the front seats. Steven was holding Samson's head out the window so the breeze would help him breathe. Bella was confused. Everyone was crying.

The next morning Samson was worse. His breathing was even more labored and he wouldn't accept any water or a treat. We knew it was time. So we made an appointment and took Samson to the local veterinary hospital where they administered the drug to him in the car, while we cradled his head. Samson went off to the Rainbow Bridge to wait for us. When they took him out of the car, Bella tried to follow him into the veterinary hospital. If you've ever had a dog that was with you almost all the time, you know how hard losing him can be. It was very hard on all three of us. Gregg and Jane felt the loss, too, as they had known Samson since he was a puppy. They had lost dogs over the years, so empathized with us and cried with us.

Bella was a different dog after that. She still ate, but she didn't want to play with any of the other dogs. She didn't want to go for walks. She just wanted Samson back. So did we.

Then at the very end of our visit, Marble Falls experienced the worst hail storm in its history. Our motor home was severely damaged, as was our trailer, our Miata sports car, and our Suburban. (When the Gesse's leave home for two months, they take a lot of their home with them.) The damage total, which was mostly covered by insurance, was over $50,000. It was a dismal end to a pretty disappointing two months.

So it wasn't a great trip. Steven and I were both happy to be home. I think Bella was, too, though she walked through all the rooms looking for Samson when she first got home. Our home was a fairly typical mountain home. The entranceway, family room, and two guest bedrooms were on the lower level. Our entranceway opened to both levels with a staircase leading to the upper level. The kitchen, family room, and dining room were all one great room upstairs. Our bedroom, the master bathroom, and a study were at the other end of the upper level. After two months in a thirty-four-foot motor home with my beloved husband and dog(s), it was good to be home. It was going to be a luxury to not have full-time visual contact with my husband. Togetherness is good, but two months of seeing one another all the time could test the best of marriages.

I was actually enjoying being close to "my things" again. I took my time looking at all the family photos that lined the walls throughout the house. I didn't have any surviving family. I was an only child and both my parents were gone, so I enjoyed looking at their photos—some of which went back to their wedding in 1947. I took time to enjoy the "family" portrait we had taken a few years earlier with Samson and Bella, and to think about how glad I was that we had done that.

Perhaps surprisingly, I was looking forward to going back to work. I had a great management staff that ran the place very competently while I was away. As long as they could access me daily via e-mail and cell phone, and send reports via FedEx when necessary, the place ran smoothly. I usually worked two to three hours a day out of our motor home when we were traveling for long periods like this. But after a certain amount of time, I felt out of touch by not being there. I needed to walk around the plant and talk to people. It was time for me to be physically present again.

The first day home, I groomed my house plants and moved them from the kitchen counter where they had been relocated to make watering them easier on our neighbor, went grocery shopping, and made unpacking (and laundry) a priority. Because we lived in the mountains and the road to our house was a mountain road, we didn't keep our motor home at our house. It's amazing that although we have an attached three-car garage and a 990-square-foot outside garage, we were lucky to keep one or two cars in a garage at all. People would ask what we had in there. Well, the correct answers would have included the phrases, "It depends," and "A lot of very priceless junk that neither of us can part with." Also, on occasion our vintage BMW race cars and our motorcycle might be in the garage.

My focus for Saturday and Sunday was going to be sorting and washing clothes, bedding, and towels from the motor home. Steven's was going to be emptying the motor home of anything that might freeze when the temperature dropped again. On Saturday, it had begun to snow. The snow made everything look clean and good. I was happy sorting clothes and exercising the washing machine. Bella was happy to be home. Steven was busy making trips back and forth to the motor home. Pretty much an average day.

Chapter 3

April 4

Actually my first priority on Saturday morning was to get a haircut and, to be perfectly honest, colored. Let's face it, I'm fifty-nine years old. That grey streak was cute at thirty-five. But not now, not at fifty-nine—especially since I guess it's no longer a streak but an epidemic of white hair. (I wasn't really sure, as it had been a very long time since I had seen a whole head of natural hair color on me.) I had gone over eight weeks without a haircut or color. My short brown hair was longer than I could remember it in years, and it was white at the roots. The funny thing was that I have my hair dyed brown with blond highlights, but keep some white in the front so it will look natural. But obviously I didn't really want it natural or I would have saved a lot of money and time and just left it alone. I had scheduled a hair appointment for this Saturday before I left town. It was a haircut and color emergency.

Okay ... I am somewhat vain. I color my hair. I exercise. I work out with free weights. I get facials. I even get my eyebrows colored. I do all of this in a rather successful effort not to look younger, but to look as good as a fifty-nine year old could without resorting to cosmetic surgery. I admit that I had gained ten-plus pounds in Texas (actually fourteen, but ten-plus sounds better). In my defense, the food choices in restaurants weren't that healthy, and the routine at the gym we went to most days didn't work as well as my home routine. And since I was working out of the motor home and had my hubby around all the time, we tended to eat three full meals a day—no yogurt lunches, no oatmeal or cereal breakfasts. These were three real meals every day for two months. But my five-foot seven-inch frame wouldn't have been considered "fat" by most people even at a hundred and thirty-eight pounds. (I can't believe I actually told you that!)

My hubby had also gained weight in Texas. Unfortunately he had gained about twenty-plus pounds that, when added to his already generous five-foot ten-inch frame, did make him look heavy. We were both resolved to get back in shape when we got home. I do love my husband. We'd been married for thirty-seven years and I still find him sexy and good looking. He has these beautiful green eyes with laugh lines around them that I find irresistible. But he hasn't had six-pack abs in a long time and his waist size has gotten larger over the years.

Steven has naturally curly hair, which he typically fights. I had talked him into letting it go natural before we left for Texas. That meant he had curls. By the time we got back, he had unruly long curls. It made him look somewhat like a mad scientist. His haircut appointment was scheduled for the following week. We had no idea he would be almost as desperate for a haircut as I was. But his hair was light brown and though tinged with grey throughout, he didn't have the color issues that I did.

After my haircut that morning, I returned to the house and focused on getting laundry done and putting stuff away.

As Steven walked in the house from one of his afternoon trips, he said, "I ran into Ward in the driveway."

On our lane, the home between ours and Tom's was occupied by an older couple, Lee and Ellie. Lee was in his early eighties, while Ellie was in her early seventies. Lee was a retired emergency room doctor, and Ellie was in her last year of teaching graphic arts at the University of Colorado. We didn't have a lot of social contact with them. Lee tended to avoid any social interaction (and he didn't drink at all), and Ellie hadn't been the same since one of her sons died a few years earlier. We tried to be friendly—we delivered cookies at Christmas and food packages when someone was ill or had died. Steven also used their plow to plow our driveways, as Lee has had problems with his back in the past. Our contact was limited to conversations in the driveway when we saw one another or phone calls to coordinate plowing.

Ward was Ellie's son, a forty-six-year-old active Navy Seal. "The truck battery was dead. I think Lee or someone left the lights on, so I took him our charger so he could start it. I told him I'd plow, but he seemed to want to do it." Steven chuckled and added, "I couldn't tell if he thought plowing was going to be fun, or if he just wanted an excuse to get out of the house."

"How long is he in town for?" I asked.

"He's leaving on Monday, so I invited them for a drink tonight."

"Great," I said, looking at the piles of laundry still in the living room and the piles of stuff all over the house. "Did you tell them the house was still a mess from our unpacking?"

"Yeah, but he didn't seem to care. He jumped at the invitation, so I think he'd like a little company other than his folks for a few hours."

That's my husband, I thought. He would feed the deer when it snowed at our house; he would buy special feed for the wild turkeys; he'd give workmen a beer when they were done at the end of the day; and he'd invite anyone he met to our home for dinner or drinks.

Steven and I decided to make one final trip to the motor home since I wanted to check the freezer and the fridge to see what shouldn't stay there much longer. When we got home later that afternoon I checked messages. There was a message from Ellie saying, "Ward said you invited us over tonight. We're actually going to Lee's daughter's house for dinner. Can we make it tomorrow night around 4:00 p.m.? I have something going on in Denver and Lee won't come, as you know, but Ward would like to come over around four. That was really nice of you to invite us. We really appreciate it."

I returned her call, and in the usual game of message tag said, "Tomorrow afternoon at 4:00 p.m. is fine. Tell Lee he sure is welcome to come over with Ward. And you should plan on stopping by when you return from Denver. I'll fix some dinner. See you tomorrow."

That was a much better idea since it gave me a chance to reduce the piles of dirty clothes in the living room. Our focus during the evening and the next morning was on getting "stuff" put away upstairs, since that's where the kitchen was and where we entertained.

We were still tired from the return trip, the trips up and down the stairs with "stuff" and cleaning. Our usual routine when we were home in the evening was to take a steam bath and then soak together in our jetted tub before going to bed. I think the water routine got established during the first few years we were married. Our first apartment in Chicago didn't have a shower; instead we had an old claw-foot bathtub. So each evening we would take turns sitting in the tub and talking while the dry party sat on a rug next to the bathtub. It became so much a part of our usual evening ritual that we still do it almost forty years later, though now we have the luxury of sitting in the tub together and having jets that soothe us. Who says getting older is all bad? So that's what we did that evening, Saturday April 4. All was well with the world. We still missed Samson terribly but we were happy. We slept soundly.

Chapter 4

April 5: The Beginning

I got up and decided to exercise first thing while Steven looked at the news on his computer. We had a small enclosed deck downstairs off the family room that had free weights and some equipment. I used it more faithfully than Steven did, usually about three times a week. I knew my "regular" routine would be somewhat painful after two months of time off for bad behavior. I was right.

While exercising, I noticed a couple of pistols that Steven had brought with him to Texas that had been placed in the downstairs family room waiting to be put away. He and Gregg had planned to go boar hunting with a friend, but never did. There was also a shotgun in a case leaning against the wine cellar waiting to be put back in the gun vault. But I put them out of my mind because they weren't in my way and they wouldn't interfere with our casual dinner that evening. Besides, it was Steven's job to put them away.

I had met Ward a few times before. He was a Navy Seal now based in San Diego. His stepfather, Lee, had told him years ago that Steven was a hunter and a gun collector, so Ward had come over years before to look at some of Steven's guns and to look at our mounts. Both Steven and I used to be avid hunters, and we had a number of deer and antelope heads mounted over the fireplace and along the stairway. For some reason, however, with age came a lack of enthusiasm for the sport. We had always eaten anything we shot and used to live on venison and antelope. But neither of us had done any game hunting in over ten years. Steven still went pheasant hunting, though not with the frequency he did when he could talk his dad into accompanying him. Hunting always seemed to me to have a couple of aspects. One was certainly the hunt itself—the search, the skill, the focus it took. The other was the camaraderie. We enjoyed the time spent outdoors with one another, with the guide, and the other hunters in the lodge.

Steven walked in while I was exercising and said, "I'm going to call Tom and ask him if he wants to join us for dinner tonight. I think Jean is still out of town and he'll be alone."

"No problem," I responded. There wasn't any difference to me in making dinner for four or five, assuming that Ellie would join us after her event in Denver.

"I should also call Diane and Roger and tell them we aren't going to meet them for dinner tonight," Steven said. I had forgotten all about Roger and Diane. We were leaving for Italy with them for a week on April 16. This Sunday evening was supposed to be a planning session for that trip.

"See if they can reschedule for another night this week. We really don't have too much to talk about. I know Diane has been doing a lot of research," I laughed. "And we'll want to coordinate our wardrobes to make sure we bring the same kind of clothes."

The trip to Italy was planned in celebration of my sixtieth birthday. My mother was born in a little town outside Lucca in Tuscany, and we were going to stay in Lucca, rent a car and take day trips to various towns in Tuscany, including San Ginese where my mother was born and my great grandparents were buried. Diane and Roger had never been to Europe and had decided to go with us even though their first grandchild was due right around that time. They had decided they couldn't pass up the opportunity to travel with us since my somewhat deteriorated Italian language skills were always useful and we had some ideas for the day trips.

In anticipation of that evening's dinner, I took some salmon out of the freezer that we still had from a fishing trip to Door County, Wisconsin, the previous summer. It was one of the last filets and I wanted to use the remainder of the salmon before too long. I was going to open some bottles of bruschetta toppings for bread that I had from Trader Joe's (tomato and artichoke), boil some pasta with Brussels sprouts that I had bought the previous day, and toss a salad. That would be a good, healthy, and easy meal.

The rest of the day passed quietly. I finished doing laundry. I packed up some Texas food items we had purchased for Tom and Jean as a "thanks for picking up our mail, watering our plants, and forwarding the important stuff to us" gift into a basket to give to Tom that evening.

I had also set four places at the kitchen counter for dinner that evening. The salmon was seasoned and waiting for Steven to grill it; likewise the asparagus, which he would cook on the grill; the Brussels sprouts were cleaned to add with the pasta to the boiling water at the appropriate moment, and appetizers were set out.

About ten to four, Steven said, "Are you ready for a drink? We have some gimlets left in the freezer if you want one. I think I'm going to have one." I had read a novel while we were in Texas where the "hero" mixed vodka 4:1 with Rose's lime juice and put it in the freezer to make the perfect gimlet. We tried that in Texas and found it to be pretty good. Even with the four of us, we hadn't finished the bottle of vodka, so we brought the almost empty bottle back from the motor home yesterday.

"I think I'll just have a glass of red wine," I said. There was one bottle of red wine on the kitchen counter that I had opened the previous evening and from which I only had one glass. I had two new bottles on the counter—a Seghesio Old Zinfandel and Seghesio Defiance, a blend. That was one of my favorite California wineries, as their wine was excellent, moderately priced, and the family was Italian.

Steven opened the bottle of Zinfandel and poured me a glass. He also poured himself a gimlet. Before either of us had a chance to even take a sip of our drinks, I heard the front doorbell. In our house, I was the one who heard the doorbell. Samson used to bark when he heard someone approach our house, but Bella didn't—I think maybe because that had been Samson's responsibility when he was alive. She never thought she needed to bark at anyone approaching our house. Steven was slightly deaf (he said it was from working in a factory during high school and college) so he never heard anything subtle.

"Would you get the door, babe?" I asked Steven.

"Oh, I didn't hear it." *Big surprise,* I thought. "Sure."

It was 4:00 p.m. exactly. Steven went downstairs and let Ward into the house. I hadn't seen Ward in a number of years. Steven had run into him at a gas station the prior January, a few days before Lee was going to have his back surgery. At that time Ward told Steven about the impending surgery, gave him his card, and asked him to call him immediately if he became aware that Lee or Ellie were having serious issues. Apparently Ward wasn't going to be able to stay around during the surgery.

Once we knew about the surgery, I brought them some cranberry bread. Steven invited Ellie to go out to dinner with us the evening after the surgery assuming everything was successful, and we offered to do whatever we could to help them. We did take Ellie out to dinner the evening of Lee's surgery once he was out of recovery. Ellie called before dinner that evening and asked me to go to their home and retrieve some underwear, pills, and a cell phone charger from her house. I had never before been in Ellie and Lee's bedroom and felt strange rummaging through her drawers and in her medicine chest, but eventually found what she needed. Before we left for Texas I also brought them dinners for the first few nights that Lee would be home, which wouldn't happen until after we left. We never saw him after the surgery, but we did keep posted on his progress with updates via e-mail from Jean.

I heard a few pleasantries exchanged in the entrance and as they walked up the fourteen steps to the upper level. I heard Ward say, "Any new guns since I was here last?"

I couldn't see them, but imagine Steven must have pointed to the guns still in their cases in the family room downstairs, as he said, "I think you've seen the Thompson Contender there."

To which Ward replied, "I've seen that. So nothing new?" Since I didn't hear a response I assume Steven nodded or mumbled a response indicating that he didn't have anything new to show Ward.

I had forgotten how imposing Ward could be. He gave the impression of being taller than his five-foot eleven-inch frame. He was muscular with short cropped hair. If you didn't know he was a Navy Seal, you would initially guess he was either military or a coach just by looking at him. He walked in wearing a short-sleeve t-shirt and carrying a small bag. Even though it was still snowing lightly, he wasn't wearing either a coat or a sweater.

As Ward approached the counter where I had arranged four table settings and appetizers, Steven said, "Would you like a drink? Don't feel like you have to drink, but we're having one."

"I am absolutely ready for a drink," replied Ward. "We went to my sister's house last night and Lee was supposed to be the designated driver. But I don't trust him to drive at night so I limited myself to one beer. After almost a week with Lee and Ellie, I am absolutely ready to relax and have a few. What are you having?"

"I'm having a gimlet, that's basically vodka with some lime juice. Michelle is having red wine. But we have beer, too. What would you like?" Steven answered.

"I'll try a gimlet," Ward said. "Want to see what I bought my little girl?" We both nodded and he pulled out two little t-shirts with Boulder logos on them. "What do you think?"

"They're adorable," I said.

"Cute," Steven said, as he handed Ward his drink. What did we know about t-shirts for little girls? We never had kids and it had been a long time since we had bought anything for little girls. But I thought they were cute.

"Lee didn't want to come?" I asked. "Is he home alone?"

"Yeah, but you know Lee. He doesn't really like any social contact. He's become more like a hermit over the years, so he's happy there. And I was ready to get out for a few hours."

"How's his back doing?" Steven asked.

"Pretty good. But he hates getting older and isn't doing it very well. But you know that. Thanks, by the way, for everything you did for them when Lee had his surgery. I know Ellie really appreciated it. She doesn't get out much since Lee won't do anything, so just going out to eat in Boulder was really a big deal for her. And she said you wouldn't let her pay for anything, so that was really nice."

"It wasn't anything. We were just glad we could do something," Steven said.

There was a bit of a lull in the conversation, which I tried to fill. "It's been awhile since you've been here," I said. "We've redone our bathroom since then. Want to see it?" I figured if I had to look at the t-shirts, he could look at the bathroom.

The three of us walked down the hall to our bathroom. It was a short trip and an even shorter inspection. "Nice," Ward said and then we walked back to the kitchen. I guess remodeled bathrooms weren't his thing. As we approached the kitchen, Tom walked in. As was his custom, he came through the unlocked front door without ringing the bell. As was Bella's custom, she didn't bark or otherwise let us know that anyone was approaching the house. But since she knew Tom and liked him (of course, Newfs like everyone), she stood at the top of the stairs as Tom walked upstairs and barked at him then. The barking wasn't a warning bark or a scary bark, it was a "Boy, am I happy to see you. You know where my treats are kept and you are going to give me one, aren't you" bark.

"Hey guys," Tom said, opening the pantry door that gave him access to the treat jar and handing Bella a treat. Despite a full head of dark hair, Tom's lined face made him appear older than sixty-two. He was small of build but fit from lots of bike riding, spinning classes, and work around the house.

Steven said, "Tom, this is Ward, Ellie's son."

"Pleased to meet you."

"Likewise," Ward said.

"Ward is a Navy Seal, a captain," Steven said, addressing Tom. "Tom is retired air force," he said, now addressing Ward.

Tom lifted a bottle of white wine that he had been holding. "I think it might be buttery. Want to try it?" Steven was on a perpetual search for a chardonnay made the way they used to be made in the '80s with a very buttery, oaky taste. Most chardonnays now have a more fruity flavor. It had been a quest that kept a lot of our friends who knew (or thought they knew) wine searching for a suitable old-fashioned chardonnay.

"Sure, I'll try that when I finish my drink," Steven said. "What about you, Tom? What would you like? We have some open red wine or the white you brought? Or something else?" Then Steven noticed that Ward had already finished his drink. As I followed Steven's gaze and spotted the empty glass, I was surprised that anyone could drink a glass of vodka that quickly. But I figured Ward was one big guy, and a Seal, and no one was driving anywhere that night. "And what about you, Ward? What would you like next? Another gimlet? Wine? Something else?" I heard Steven ask.

Both Ward and Tom opted for a glass of red wine. I continued sipping my glass of red wine and Steven continued with his gimlet. I moved to the other side of the counter and busied myself with dinner preparations. Ward stood at the end of the counter, Steven on the kitchen side of the counter, and Tom sat in one of the stools positioned by the counter. Everyone helped themselves to appetizers.

Once Tom arrived, much of the conversation involved Tom and Ward discussing their military careers. They exchanged grades, secret handshakes and postings. Perhaps I exaggerate, but I was busy with dinner and didn't have an interest in much of the conversation. It was background noise to me and didn't require much participation by me or even by Steven.

"My next promotion would be to admiral," I heard Ward say.

"That requires a congressional appointment, doesn't it?" Tom asked.

"Affirmative," Ward replied.

"What happens if you don't make admiral?" Steven asked.

"If I stay in the navy, I might have to jump again. Or I could retire," Ward replied.

"Would you consider retiring?" Tom asked.

"I don't know," Ward said. "I'd like to spend more time with my little girl. I never used to worry about coming back during a jump before she was born, but I do now. But I don't know how I'd fit into civilian life after twenty-five years in the navy. My wife likes being the captain's wife. She likes entertaining and being the senior officer's wife. We're happy with the schools in San Diego. We like our lifestyle. I like to give orders. I don't know if we could afford to move or how either of us would like it. I don't know if I would fit in anymore. I'm not sure what I would do and I can't afford to do nothing."

"Tell us about your missions," one of the guys said.

"I can't say a lot, but ..." and then followed some anecdotes that could have formed the basis for at least a few Steven Segal movies—jumps into

African countries and Afghanistan, as well as other locations. Tom and Ward continued to drink red wine. At some point, the second bottle was opened and I had my second glass. Steven poured himself a glass of the white wine that Tom had brought as a gift and pronounced it, "Not bad— but not oaky or buttery." *Oh good, the quest was still on!*

"I'm tough," I heard Ward say. Was it my imagination or was he standing taller and puffing his chest out even more? And then he ran through the details of his physical regime—running, weights, strength training, more cardio. I thought, *Pretty impressive for a guy in his mid-forties.*

"You know, my godson is the strength coach at the University of Illinois in Chicago," I mentioned proudly. "He won the amateur strong man competition in Colorado when he was here in school. He doesn't have an ounce of body fat on him." Since Steven and I both have body fat, Nick and his physique was something we had always been proud of. Plus Nick was a good kid and promised when he was nine never to allow either of us to be put into a nursing home and to always take care of us.

"He's not strong like me," replied Ward. *All right already,* I thought. *Don't personalize it.* "He's not tough here where it counts," he said, pointing to his head with his index finger. "There are guys stronger than me and bigger than me, but they're not as tough. They can't think quick and react like I can, even though I'm older than them. They worry about things. I can beat up someone with a telephone book and leave no scars, no evidence of what I did. And I don't worry about it after I do it. I am tough and can do things younger officers won't or can't do."

Okay, okay, I thought. *You are one mean son-of-a-bitch. No arguments from me.* And right then I was thinking that I didn't like Ward quite as much as when I just ran into him briefly in the driveway. But he was at my house and at my table and I was going to be nice.

"Steven, what about putting the fish on the grill? The water's boiling and I'm ready to drop the pasta and the vegetables into the water." And maybe get this evening over with. It's not turning out to be as much fun as I thought.

"Where's the olive oil?" he responded. Olive oil was Steven's grill secret. You put enough olive oil on anything on the grill and it would be good. So we coordinated the time for the pasta, fish, asparagus, and salad to all get done at the same time. Normally I would have served the pasta first, but I didn't think Ward would either know the difference or care at this point.

"Why don't you call Ellie?" I suggested.

"Yeah, I probably should," Ward said. "But I don't have her cell phone number with me."

"I do," I said, "from when Lee was in the hospital."

I handed Ward our house phone and read him Ellie's number. "The phone's not working," he said.

"That happens sometimes up here when the weather's bad," I said. "Let me get my cell phone, it should work." So at 5:09 p.m., as my cell phone would later confirm, Ward called Ellie and told her to come by our house on the way home, as he was still there.

As Steven and I put food on the counter, Steven, always the gracious host, said, "We need more red wine," as he looked at Tom and Ward's empty glasses.

"Here use this," I said, handing him the bottle of red wine that I had opened the night before. "It's fine," I responded to his questioning look. At this point, I figured it really was fine.

So we put some of everything on each person's plate. "I shouldn't eat," Ward said. "I promised Ellie I would have dinner with her when she got back."

"Go ahead and have some dinner," I said. "There's plenty and Ellie can eat when she gets here."

A few minutes later I heard the doorbell. Steven went downstairs to let Ellie into the house. Ward picked up his plate with his food almost untouched and put it next to the sink. "I don't want her to think I was eating," he said.

So I set a clean dinner service at Ward's place for Ellie as she walked upstairs with Steven. I heard Steven saying, "You look really nice, Ellie. No really. Better than I've seen you look in a long time. That's a great dress. You really do look nice. Healthy, too."

"Why thank you, Steven," I heard Ellie say. "I actually got the coat at the PX the last time we visited Ward in California."

You might think this was excessive complimenting and it probably was. But Ellie hadn't looked or felt very good since one of her sons died a number of years before. This was the best she had looked to either of us in a long time, so both Steven and I were happy to see her looking healthier and happier, at least on the surface.

"Sit down, Ellie," I said. "What can we get you to drink? Red wine?"

"I don't drink red wine," she replied. "Do you have any white wine?" So Steven poured her a glass of white wine from the bottle Tom had brought. It must have been about 5:30 p.m. when Ellie arrived. I prepared a plate with a little of everything on it and gave it to Ellie.

"This is really nice," she said. "I didn't expect dinner. I thought I was going to have something when we got home. I really do like salmon, this is great."

"Ellie, you really do look good," Steven said once again. "I can't believe your male students aren't making passes at you all the time." My husband thinks that compliments need to be extreme to be appreciated. He doesn't realize that sometimes they become so ludicrous that they lose credibility. But he tries.

"I'm happily married, Steven. That would never happen." Ellie replied.

"I'm not saying you're not happily married. I'm just saying that they are probably imaging you in a thong and thinking that you're hot." This comment was unfortunately typical of my husband. Anyone who knew him would not have been either surprised or offended by it. They would have laughed it off as "typical Steven" and gone on with the evening.

"Steve, why would you even say that? I'm happily married." Ellie was upset. For whatever reason, Steven's intended compliments were not being taken as compliments, but had been offensive to Ellie. I thought her reaction was a bit extreme, but didn't really focus on it too much.

"I'm sorry," Steven said. "I didn't mean any offense."

And the conversation moved on to the showing Ellie had been attending in Denver and Lee's back and some other mundane but safe topics.

At some point, Steven said to me, "Is there another bottle of white wine?" Ellie's glass was empty. So I went downstairs and found that our wine cellar contained a lot of red wine, but only two bottles of white wine. They were

cult wines from Sine Quo Non. I had waited for four years to get an allot-
ment of wine from this very small, cult vineyard. So I had a quandary. Should
I share a bottle of this very special and fairly expensive wine with some folks
who I didn't think would appreciate it (Ward and Ellie) and who I thought
had already had too much to drink to appreciate it (Ward and Tom), or
should I pretend to be a bad host that has run out of white wine? Gracious-
ness won out and I brought the bottle of wine upstairs.

When Steven saw the wine, he said, "WOW! This is really good stuff.
How do we warrant this?"

"Simple. It's the only bottle of white wine we have, if you can believe
that." I wasn't going to give away that we had a second bottle.

"You are all going to have to have a taste of this," he said, reaching for
five clean white wine glasses and pouring the contents of the bottle equally
into the five glasses and handing them to everyone. I sniffed and sipped
and smiled. It really was a splendid white wine.

The conversation continued and Ellie had finished her second glass
of white wine. "Do we have another bottle?" Steven asked. "No," I quickly
replied. "We're all out of white wine." *And perhaps the evening should be
ending,* I thought.

But my husband, being who he was, went downstairs in search of yet
another bottle of wine. What the hell, no one was driving. We have a certain section of our cellar where we keep what we refer to as one-off bottles.
These are single bottles not suitable for a dinner party because there was
only one such bottle, but appropriate for the two of us to share with dinner. Steven apparently looked in that section and came up with a 1991
Silverado Reserve Cabernet. Not white, but fairly rare and excellent. And
it was our only bottle of that vintage.

"They don't want any more wine," I said. "You don't want to open
that bottle right now, it's special." I wasn't trying to say that our guests
weren't special (which they weren't), but at this point in the evening I
didn't think this special bottle was going to get the respect it deserved.

"What better time is there to open it?" asked Tom.

"We're together now. Who knows when we will be together again?
Let's open it," shouted Ward, moving and waving his arms as he spoke.

So Steven opened that special bottle of wine. Because of its age, he decanted it through a piece of cheesecloth. Ward said, "Geez, I've never seen anything like that. What are you doing?"

To which Steven replied, "I'm just making sure no sediment or cork gets into the wine. With a wine this old, you can't be sure there aren't some particles in there that would affect the taste of the wine. In fact, we can't really be sure that this wine will be that good—though it has been cellared since we got it." With those comments he poured the decanted wine into yet another four clean red wine glasses. Ellie declined the red wine and had an empty glass in front of her.

Steven said, "I'm really sorry, Ellie. I don't think this has ever happened before, but we are out of white wine. Is there anything else I can get you?"

Ward piped up, "Try a gimlet, Mom. You'll really like it. It's a pretty mild drink actually." I had never heard of a drink that was almost all vodka described as mild, but didn't disagree. Ellie agreed and Steven poured her a gimlet from the bottle in the freezer.

Tom took a sip of the 1991 Silverado Reserve and pronounced it, "Awesome. The tannins are mild. It sure has aged well." Everyone seemed pleased. I took my glass of red wine and set it aside to enjoy later after I finished my excellent glass of white wine. I noticed Steven did the same. Our guests drank theirs as conversation continued.

I was determined not to open another bottle of wine, as they kept getting more expensive and rarer the later it got. As the momentum of the dinner party faded, I found myself having to work at enjoying the company. When I noticed that both Ward and Tom had finished their last glass of red wine, I turned to Ellie and said, "It's getting late. Would you like some leftovers for Lee?" It wasn't much past 6:30, but it felt late to me. Ward had been there since 4:00 p.m.—I was ready for the evening to be over and our company to leave.

"That would be nice," she replied. So I put some salmon and asparagus into one plastic container, some pasta into another, and the leftover salad into yet another, and said, "Lee's probably worried about you. You should think about getting back to him." I was clever, wasn't I?

So we walked them downstairs trying to keep Bella from rubbing against Ellie's dark dress. Steven helped her on with her coat. Ward asked Steven and Tom if they wanted to go jogging with him for five miles the next morning. Both gentlemen declined—Steven looked like he might have been asked if he wanted to eat live eels.

We walked outside. I left Bella inside as Ellie had a car and I didn't want the dog walking around while Ellie drove away. Black dogs can't be seen very well on a dark night. Ward asked Tom if he wanted a ride home, but Tom declined preferring instead to get some fresh air. Ward and Ellie each hugged me and Steven, thanked us for the evening and then left in Ellie's car to drive the short distance to Ellie's home. Tom left carrying the basket of food from Texas to walk the short distance to his house. It was snowing lightly and there was little moonlight. It was the type of late winter storm that we often got in Colorado in April.

I was glad to see them leave. Ellie wasn't normally much fun, and Ward had become boorish as he drank more and commanded center stage.

I opened the front door to let Bella out as they drove away. She came out and began to sniff the edges of the driveway looking for that perfect spot to relieve herself. Steven turned to me and said, "I'm glad we had them over. I think they had a nice time."

You would have to know my husband to understand how important it is to him that our guests have a nice time. Everyone has ways they measure their "worth," and for Steven, one of those measures was his ability to entertain and make our guests feel well treated and special. This was very important to him—more so than even to me. He received a lot of satisfaction in serving our guests a good meal accompanied by fine spirits and good conversation, while giving the impression that it wasn't a lot of effort. This was one reason he continued to invite Ellie and Lee to our house or to share holidays when they might have been alone. As we closed the door, cut the lights, and went back inside the house, Steven was very satisfied that once again Ellie, Tom, and Ward had indeed "had a nice time."

I didn't respond to his comment. I was glad they had left, as they had not been an enjoyable bunch for the last hour. Ellie never demonstrated any sense of humor, and she had been true to form that evening. I had come to realize that Ward was self-centered with an unjustified sense of his own importance. And Tom would get quieter the more he drank, so he was very quiet by the end of the evening. It wasn't near as important to me as it was to Steven that they had had a good time. They ate our good food, drank our good wine, and even took leftovers home. They should have been more than satisfied with the evening. I wanted to get some dishes done and go to bed. I was still tired from the trip and it had been a long evening.

Chapter 5

April 5: Evening

When we reached the upper floor, Steven walked into the laundry room to fold a load of clothes that was in the dryer. (Now can you understand why I love him so much?) I began cleaning up the food and plates in the kitchen. When he was done, he walked into the kitchen and filled the sink with soapy water. Though I was filling both of the dishwashers and this had been a simple dinner, there were still a lot of dirty dishes and glasses. Steven started washing the wine glasses and knives that I wouldn't put in the dishwasher. We were both quiet as we saw to our chores. The CD player was still quietly playing '60s rock'n'roll selections.

Steven was very particular about the counters and didn't think that I had cleaned them adequately, so he began spraying the counters with a cleaner, wiping them thoroughly, and then running his hand across them to make sure they were smooth and clean. (What in the world would have been my incentive to do it better?!)

When we were getting close to being done, I asked, "Do you want me to fill the tub?" It wasn't very late—perhaps 8:00 p.m. "Sure, if you're up to it," he replied. So I walked down the hall to our bedroom and master bath and started filling the tub. Then I walked back into the kitchen and started drying some of the glasses.

We were still finishing up in the kitchen when I thought I heard the doorbell. Steven was facing away from me when I walked to the walkway overlooking our entrance and thought I saw someone outlined in the front door's glass panels. We had turned out all the outside lights after everyone had left, so I couldn't be sure. Without saying anything to Steven, I went downstairs and opened our front door.

To my surprise, Ward was standing there. I don't remember saying anything to him when he spoke first. "Is Steve home?"

"Yes," I replied, while thinking, *Where else would he be?*

"Can I speak to him?" Ward asked.

"Sure." So I walked upstairs with Ward following close behind me.

When we got upstairs, Steven was still at the sink with his back to us. Ward started to walk up to him from behind. Steven must have caught movement in his peripheral vision because he turned around. He looked as surprised as I was to see Ward returning after what must have been close to an hour. Holding a dishtowel in his hands, Steven said, "Did you forget something?"

Ward moved to within inches of Steven and said, "If you ever talk to my mother like that again, I will rip your head off and shit down your neck." I was standing by the kitchen counter—speechless. Steven looked stunned. It wasn't just the words—it was the way they were delivered. Ward didn't shout. He didn't yell. He sounded like a soldier telling someone exactly what he would do if that person didn't follow directions. "You can't talk to a woman like that. You are going to come with me right now and apologize to my mother. Now. Move."

I was shocked. I'm sure Steven was, too. Remember—he thought it had been a nice evening. So did I. I was standing at the kitchen counter like an understudy for the part of Helen Keller before she learned to speak—mouth open, trying to figure out what the hell was going on. My mind was not processing the conversation—if you could call it that, since so far Steven hadn't said a word. I remember reading about folks who were caught in a shooting at a Lubby's cafeteria in Texas years ago. One survivor said she was shocked that some folks just stood there and didn't take cover or try to run away. They just looked on as if they couldn't believe what was happening to them. That was how I felt.

Steven looked at me, and as he dried his hands on the kitchen towel, and said, "Okay." As he walked in front of Ward, he said, "How about if we wait until morning to do this? We've all had a bit to drink and it's late. Let's just handle this issue tomorrow."

Ward said, "Now. You are going to apologize to my mother now."

"I didn't mean to offend her. I'm sorry if she took something I said wrong. I was only trying to compliment her," Steven said, in another failed attempt to diffuse the situation. It didn't work.

"You're going to our house and you're going to apologize now," replied Ward.

Steven led the way down the stairs with Ward close behind. I moved to the walkway where I could look down into the entranceway. Steven said, "Let me put on some boots and grab a coat." It was only then that I realized that despite the snow and the cold, Ward had walked to our house wearing only a t-shirt. Steven's boots were still in the entrance from when we had followed folks outside, so he slipped his feet into them and grabbed a jacket. I hadn't said anything the whole time.

Ward said, "Let's go."

Steven looked up at me and said, "I'll be right back. Don't worry."

Ward held our front door open and followed Steven outside.

• • •

In hindsight, I realized there were a number of things that I should have done at that point—or even before. There was no reason for me not to have allowed Ward in the house, as I didn't know the purpose of the visit or his mindset until after he was upstairs. But I should never have let Steven leave the house with Ward. I think it would have been hard to stop them, but I should have tried. Steven said later that he was worried that Ward would turn violent in the house and didn't want to do anything that would have upset him further. But in retrospect, being the direct victim of physical violence at Ward's hands would have been better than what happened. I should have called the police immediately when they left the house and explained the situation. At that point my husband had been threatened and forced to accompany an irrational, violent person into the night. But I had no experience with this type of situation—so I did nothing.

And though I hate to admit it, I was more inclined to blame my spouse at that point for the situation than someone I hardly knew. Maybe his comments to Ellie that were meant to be a compliment were in poor taste. One could certainly argue that. Just because I had not found them offensive, and Steven hadn't meant any offense by them, didn't mean that they couldn't have offended Ellie. And Lee and Ellie had been our neighbors for seventeen years and would continue to be our neighbors. So maybe a "Sorry" wasn't such a big price to pay for peace in the neighborhood.

I walked into the bathroom and turned the water off in the tub. Who needed an overflowing tub at this point in the evening? Besides, by then the tub was full. I'm not sure what I did for the next ten minutes or so, but I did start to get really worried. *What was going on? Where was Steven? Had Ward turned violent? Had Steven been hurt? Should I do something?* Less than fifteen minutes had passed, when I put the leash on Bella and started down our driveway toward Ellie and Lee's home. (You had to put the leash on Bella to get her to walk, since she was not a fan of exercise and was basically afraid of the dark. The leash gave her some comfort and meant she couldn't run home without pulling me with her.)

As I started up the hill on our driveway, perhaps a hundred feet from our front door, I saw Steven walking back. As we got closer I said, "What happened?"

His response was quick and to the point. "They're crazy. They are all fucking nuts."

He went on to say, "I got there and Lee and Ellie were cowering together in a corner. I didn't know if they were scared of me or Ward. Ward said to apologize, so I did. I told them I was sorry if something I said offended them. Lee started going on about how he had never liked us since we moved into the house, how they weren't comfortable with us, how I can't talk to women the way I talked to Ellie. I think he is really losing it. Then Ellie says she loves us but she doesn't like us or something. They are all crazy."

"Are you okay?" I asked.

"Yeah," Steven replied. "I tried to talk Ward into waiting until tomorrow, but he kept pushing me up the hill. Said he'd break both my legs if I didn't keep walking. He kept pushing me. He is absolutely a lousy drunk. And he's a bully. Thinks everyone has to do what he says. And I told him that."

"You didn't!" I said.

"Sure did," Steven said. "When I was through apologizing and they were through rambling, I asked Ward to come outside with me. I told him, 'Thanks for your service to our country. I really appreciate it. But you are a bully and a lousy drunk. If you ever come onto my property and threaten me or my wife again, I will shoot you. I will ruin your military career. I will sue you, your parents, your family, the military, and anyone else I can think of. Your career will be over. Do you understand? Do not ever come near me, my wife, or my property again.'" Steven delivered this little speech to me with some pride.

I couldn't believe it. He had threatened a Navy Seal—not just any Navy Seal, but a drunken Navy Seal who had demonstrated some very serious violent behavior. A Navy Seal who had bragged about killing folks with his bare hands. A drunk, violent Navy Seal who was only a few hundred yards away from where we were standing right now. *Was my husband nuts, too? What was with the testosterone?*

The look on my face as we walked into the house must have told Steven more than my words had (since I hadn't said anything besides "You didn't" after his speech). "Don't worry," he said, "they'll be fine in the morning and we won't have to see Ward again." I wasn't sure about any of this. My stomach was in a knot and I was very scared. "Is the tub still full?" he asked. When I nodded, he simply said, "Let's get in the tub and go to bed. We can both use a good night's sleep."

Steven put the short, waist-length carhart jacket he had been wearing on the railing in the entranceway and slipped out of his boots. I took Bella's leash off of her and we walked upstairs to our bedroom together. Steven acted like everything was okay. Two rational guys had a little conversation and everything was going to be okay. I wasn't so sure. I was afraid. I kept thinking, *What if Ward comes back and is even more violent? What are we going to do?* I knew the front door was locked, but the door wasn't really that secure. It never bothered me much before, since we live in such a private place, but it bothered me that night.

"Stop worrying," Steven said, "everything is fine." We had both forgotten about the glasses of the Silverado Reserve that we had saved for the tub. As we soaked in the tub I peppered him with questions.

"Did you suggest putting this little confrontation off?"

"Yes, of course I did. You heard me suggest that at the house before we left."

"Why did they come to our house for dinner if they hadn't liked us for seventeen years?"

"How do I know?" he shot back.

"Why did Ellie let us take her out to dinner in January when Lee was being operated on if they never liked us?"

"Drop it, Michelle. It's over. They're crazy. We don't have to have a lot to do with them. They're neighbors. Just wave from now on. Forget tonight ever happened."

"Why did you have to threaten Ward?"

"What the hell was I supposed to do? The man walked into *my* house, threatened me, forced me to go to his folk's house, all the while threatening to break my legs, insulting me—all after eating dinner at our house. Just what exactly did you want me to do? Thank him for the experience? He's a bully and he shouldn't be able to get away with doing something like that. He's damn lucky we didn't call the police." Steven was getting mad now. Perhaps he was right. At a minimum we could discuss it further in the morning.

Steven took two Tylenol PM so he could sleep. Our tub has a twenty-minute timer, but I was too upset to stay in there for that long, so I got out after about ten minutes. Steven stayed in the full twenty minutes and then got in bed. He was probably asleep within five minutes after a kiss and an "I love you." I laid awake for much longer, but finally fell asleep.

It should have been the end of a really weird night. Instead, it was the start of the scariest night of my life.

Chapter 6

April 5: Crisis Point

At some point after we had both fallen asleep, our phone rang. Steven picked it up, but it still wasn't working and he couldn't hear anyone, so he hung up. When it rang a second time, he answered and said, "Our phone isn't working. I can't hear you. If this is important, call my cell phone" and recited the number. Because Steven's father was ninety years old at the time, we always answered the phone when it rang in the middle of the night.

When his cell phone rang, I heard Steven say, "There isn't anyone outside. I'm asleep. I'm going back to sleep. I am not going anywhere."

"Who was that?" I asked.

"I don't know, someone saying there were police outside."

Oh, my god, this wasn't good, I thought. "What are you talking about?" is what I actually said.

The cell phone rang again and Steven answered it a second time. "I have no idea what you are talking about," he said. "I was a volunteer fireman. I'll call you back." This didn't seem to be a coherent conversation. Between the wine, soaking in the tub, two Tylenol PM, and being asleep, I wasn't sure Steven understood what was going on. I certainly didn't.

"What's happening?" I almost screamed in frustration.

"Nothing, hold on," he said as he dialed, then he said, "Is this the Comm center?" Steven had the Comm center phone number in his cell phone from when he was a volunteer fireman. He gave his name and address and said, "Someone called up here a few minutes ago." Apparently that was the same operator to whom he was speaking.

"There was no gun," I heard him say. It was then that I began to panic. "We had some neighbors over for dinner a few hours ago and they left. Nothing happened."

At that point I got out of bed and put on sweatpants, a sweatshirt, and a pair of slippers. Steven had already walked to the windows in our bedroom, which overlooked the front of our house. He said, "I am looking out our windows right now and I can't see anything. If there are police out there, tell them to turn their lights on."

Oh my god, what was going on? What has happened? Police at our house? For some reason, I started down the stairs to the front door. When I reached the entranceway, I turned on the outside lights and walked outside into nothing. I couldn't see anyone or anything, even with the lights on. Bella stopped at the middle landing on the stairs. She wasn't brave enough to walk outside with me.

Suddenly, there was a swarm of police officers with rifles, shotguns, and handguns aimed at me. I saw one officer with a German Shepherd. It was surreal. This kind of thing didn't happen to people like me. Nothing in my life had prepared me for this moment. It was like a very bad movie. One of the officers shouted, "Get over here. Get behind the car." We had two 1999 Suburbans and a 2002 Suzuki, and they were all parked in the driveway. The officers must have been behind our cars when I came out of the house. I wouldn't move. I actually don't think I could have moved. Afterwards, when someone asked me why I didn't do what the officers told me to do, I said the answer was simple—I knew exactly what was in the house. It was my husband of thirty-seven years. I wasn't afraid of what was in the house. I was terrified of what was outside the house. I did not obey their commands.

One of the officers grabbed me by the arm and tried to force me away from the house. I wouldn't move. A female officer approached me—gun drawn—and patted me down. In hindsight, I assumed they wanted to make sure I had no weapons hidden under my sweats.

Steven walked out in a bathrobe with his cell phone to his ear. I heard him saying, "I am not going to put this phone down. Are you recording this? I want it recorded if they shoot me."

Oh my god, what was going on here? Why were we surrounded by police with weapons? Were we both going to be shot? I stepped between Steven and the cops. If they tried to shoot him, they would have to shoot me first. Surely they wouldn't do that? Actually, there was little thought going on in my mind at that time. It was emotion and reaction. No thinking. Just reaction. I stood between Steven and the guns.

An officer yelled, "Drop the cell phone. Drop the cell phone." Steven didn't let go of the phone. So they yelled at me, "Take the phone. Take the phone."

I walked up to Steven and took the phone.

Someone yelled, "Are you armed?"

Were they crazy? We weren't armed. We weren't even dressed. We had been asleep. So Steven opened his bathrobe to show them that he was not concealing a weapon—hard to do when you're stark naked. They surrounded him, put handcuffs on his wrists, and began walking him to a squad car parked at the very end of our drive, close to what we called the outside garage.

I heard Steven saying, "What am I being arrested for?"

I said, "Can I get him some shoes? Some clothes?" All he had on was his bathrobe. It was about thirty degrees outside and still snowing lightly. Our driveway was gravel once you left the cement apron in front of the house, so it would be painful to walk on that barefoot.

"Yeah but be quick," an officer responded. So I ran upstairs and grabbed sweatpants and a sweatshirt off the hooks in our closet. On the way back outside I grabbed the boots Steven had on earlier in the evening and handed them to him. He slipped his feet into the boots while an officer took his clothes.

It seemed like there should be something profound to be said at a time like this but I couldn't think of anything to say. It was like being dropped into a play and not knowing the script. As Steven walked toward the police car, I said the only thing I could think of, which probably came from every cop show or movie I ever saw. "Don't talk to anyone until we get a lawyer." It was the only thing I could think of to say. It didn't really occur to me at the time that we didn't know a lawyer to call—especially at that time of night.

During this whole confrontation—with our front door open—there was absolutely no sign of our dog. She was apparently not on protection duty that night. All one hundred fifty–plus pounds of her were safely tucked into her crate. It was safe there. As the police car with my husband drove away, I saw even more officers appearing from behind our house and garage. Apparently they had surrounded our home. I was in total bewilderment in front of my house while at least half a dozen police officers still surrounded me with their guns drawn. I didn't comprehend what had just happened or why. I began asking, "Why did you arrest my husband? What is going on?" This became a mantra I kept repeating, though no answers were forthcoming.

Finally one of the officers said, "Can we go inside?"

Chapter 7

April 5: Late Evening

I led a small contingent of six or seven officers into our entranceway. Though I didn't read their nametags, I remember one was a female officer, one was Oriental, all the others were generic white males.

"Mam, are there any guns here?" one officer asked.

I answered honestly, "Yes, we have a lot of guns. There are a couple right there," I said, pointing to the gun cases about twenty-five feet away, but visible in the downstairs family room. "And there are lots of guns in vaults. What is this about?"

At some point, I am not sure when, someone told me that a neighbor had accused Steven of threatening him with a gun. I didn't have to be a rocket scientist to know who the neighbor was. But no details were offered and no further questions were answered.

"Can we search the house?" one of the officers asked.

"Not without a search warrant," I replied quickly—almost automatically. That was amazing. I have never been in a comparable situation. Movies and novels must have prepared me to answer so quickly—we watched a lot of movies and I read a lot of detective novels.

"Do you have some place to go?" another officer asked.

"Go? Where would I go? This is my home. My dog is here. My husband is coming back here. I'm not going to leave." *Why are they asking me such a stupid question?* They probably didn't even know that I had a dog, since she had elected to retreat to her crate in our bedroom.

"We can't leave you here alone," the officer who seemed to be in charge said.

"Great, don't," I answered. Who wanted to be alone at that point in the evening? Certainly not me. *And why couldn't they leave me alone?*

"Is there anyone else here in your home?" When I shook my head, the officer continued, "We will have to check the rest of the house before we leave to make sure no one else is here." This was surreal. They were actually worried about terrorists or criminals lurking in my kitchen pantry or in my closet. But perhaps this was just protocol.

So I left three or four officers downstairs, while three other officers and I walked through the whole house. I opened closet doors to show them that no one was hiding in between hanging garments. They looked inside my kitchen pantry. They checked the linen closets. At some point I actually had the thought that I was glad my laundry had been done and folded and that my closets were neat. Amazing. My life was in the process of being destroyed and I was proud of neat closets.

When we returned downstairs the other officers were waiting. They introduced me to Officer Eric Witte, who would stay with me while they went in pursuit of a search warrant. At some point, someone handed me a card with a phone number that I could call to try to find out if Steven had actually been booked or what his status was.

· · ·

I sat down on the stairs in the entrance and started to cry.

Officer Witte said, "Is there anyone you could call?"

Who do you call in the middle of the night when your husband has apparently been arrested? We didn't have any family in the Boulder area. In fact, I didn't have any immediate family. So I got my cell phone and called Tom.

"Tom, do you know what's going on?" I asked.

"No," he lied—as I found out only later. In fact, he did know exactly what was going on.

"Steven's been arrested. I don't know what's going on. I don't know why. I don't know what to do. I'm scared," I sobbed into the phone.

"Is there anything you need from me?" In hindsight, that was a strange response. In hindsight, I realized that what I would have expected was an offer to come to my home and sit with me. In hindsight, I would have expected Tom to say simply that he was on the way down to the house. But he wasn't. He simply asked if I needed anything, like you would do if you ran into an acquaintance who had suffered a loss. You would say, "Is there anything I can do?" expecting an answer of "No, but thanks for asking."

"I might need a place to stay tonight. I don't really know what's going on." I was repeating myself, but at this point what did you expect?

"Well, let me know." And he hung up.

I was all alone in the house with Officer Witte. Witte seemed young to me, but he was probably mid- to late thirties. I was holding two cell phones—mine and Steven's at that point. I asked if I could go upstairs to get my phone book, and he said yes. I dropped my cell phone on the way back downstairs and the battery fell out. I fidgeted with getting it back together on the way downstairs and was relieved that I could still get a dial tone.

When I returned to Officer Witte, we moved into the downstairs family room. Though I didn't focus on it at the time, the gun case that had previously been upright, leaning against the wine cellar, was now lying flat on the floor in front of the wine cellar.

The only lawyer I knew was our corporate attorney, so I called his home number. We've known Chris for almost seventeen years and have done things socially with him and his wife. There was no answer. I kept trying every fifteen minutes. What I didn't know at the time was that Chris and his wife had moved earlier that week and their house phone had not been connected in their new home. So no one was answering my frantic phone calls because they weren't being put through to his home.

Steven's cell phone rang. It was Steven. I assumed it was the infamous "one phone call" he would be allowed. "I'm fine," he said. "Is there someone there with you?"

"There's a police officer here with me."

"Did you call anyone? What about Tom?"

"I called him." But I couldn't remember why he wasn't here. I had called him. "I'm trying to call Chris, but haven't had an answer. Don't talk to anyone until you talk to Chris or someone from his law firm."

"I know. I just want to make sure you're fine," Steven said. "You need to buy me some pre-paid minutes so I can call you. They said I could make a call once every hour. So go ahead and buy some minutes for me so I can call. I think it's like calling with a credit card. The minutes are for calls to a phone number, so just get them to my cell phone, okay? Do you understand? Are you all right?"

I nodded. Then added, "I'm fine. I'll get the minutes. Please be careful … take care of yourself … I love you."

"I love you, too. We'll be fine. I have to say goodbye now. I'll call you back as soon as I can."

We were both lying. Neither one of us was anywhere close to fine.

• • •

Buying pre-paid minutes was my first lesson in navigating "the system." How many minutes should I buy? How long was he going to be there? I settled on thirty minutes. I can't remember what they cost but remember thinking I could call from Europe for less. Certainly there was some sort of mistake, and Steven would soon be safely home with an apology from the Boulder sheriff's department.

After Steven's phone call and after I purchased the thirty minutes, I settled on the sofa clutching a brown throw pillow, and rocked back and forth. "Do you know anything about what's going on?" I asked.

"I don't know details," Officer Witte replied, "but I understand that someone accused your husband of pointing a gun at him."

I couldn't seem to register this. "Someone accused my husband of pointing a gun at them?" I repeated quietly. When Officer Witte nodded, I almost screamed, "That's impossible. My husband never pointed a gun at anyone. He never had a gun. That's not something he would do." My mind was reeling. Ward called the police and told them Steven threatened him with a gun. That was ludicrous. The one thing I knew was that Steven did not have time to go looking for a gun when Ward kidnapped him. I was vacillating between being terrified, scared, mad, and incredulous.

"They were here for dinner. I fixed dinner. We had some wine. They took leftovers home. It was a nice evening. Steven said they had a good time." How could someone who had just eaten dinner with us, shared wine with us, visited with us, and left on a happy note come back an hour later enraged and ready to kill my husband and then turn the whole situation around so that it sounded like he was the victim? I remained seated on the sofa in the downstairs family room clutching my furry brown throw pillow to my chest and rocking back and forth. Officer Witte was sitting in the wood rocking chair.

"I let him in the house. I can't believe I let him in the house." I kept repeating this phrase over and over again.

Around midnight, I was close to panic since I had not been able to reach Chris. I finally thought of another lawyer in the firm, a corporate litigator, whom we had worked with and had gone out with a few times. I realized I had his home number, so I called Neal. Neal answered and probably wouldn't have been more surprised to hear the Easter Bunny on the line than he was to hear me crying.

"Neal, it's Michelle Gesse. Did I interrupt anything?" What a stupid question to pose to someone you know only casually when you call him at midnight.

"We're almost as old as Steven and you, what would you interrupt?" I wasn't really in the mood for humor, but Neal didn't know that.

"Steven's been arrested and I don't know what to do."

I gave Neal a brief recap of what I knew. He replied, "Tell Steven not to talk to anyone until he has an attorney present." I didn't bother to tell him that was the same advice I gave Steven.

"I'll call our criminal litigator and get back to you as soon as I can." I felt relief. The firm did have a lawyer who could fix this. It was some progress.

• • •

Officer Witte and I sat together in the downstairs family room for a long time. Though I had told Steven not to talk to anyone without an attorney present, I didn't realize that the same advice should have applied to me. I rambled about the evening—the food, the good wine that we had all drank, the company, etc., I kept repeating, "I should never have let him in the house. I should never have let him in the house."

I learned that Officer Witte was a new father; he had an eight-year-old son by a prior marriage; this was his first night back on the swat team after his paternity leave; he also had a motorcycle; he was hungry (I offered to make him something to eat, but he declined—probably afraid of what I'd put in it); he liked to fish; he liked red wine; he enjoyed sushi; and a whole bunch of other things. Under other circumstances, I think we had a lot in common and might have enjoyed one another's company.

Since I had indicated I wanted a lawyer, and he knew I was in the process of trying to secure one, he carefully avoided asking me any questions about the events of the preceding evening. But I still talked and kept saying, "I shouldn't have let him in the house. I really shouldn't have let him in the house." In addition to that mantra, my conversation consisted mostly of comments bewailing the fact that I let Steven leave with Ward. I should have called the police. I couldn't believe that someone could take advantage of our hospitality and then turn around and accuse my husband of a crime. I talked about the wine that had been consumed that evening. I wanted him to know that Ward was drunk. All I succeeded in doing was making Officer Witte think that Steven had drank too much.

At some point Neal returned my call and said the criminal lawyer would call me first thing in the morning. He thought that Steven might be allowed bail that night, but if not, there would be a hearing the following afternoon to get him out on bail—assuming charges were being filed. And under no circumstances were Steven or I to speak to anyone without an attorney present. And I was to convey all of this information to Steven when he called on one of his hourly calls. Neal did not mention the criminal lawyer's name at the time. It wouldn't have meant anything to me, anyway. But he did assure me that he was a former Boulder County Assistant DA and that he was the most competent lawyer for the job.

Steven's calls came fairly regularly about an hour to ninety minutes apart for a while. He would tell me not to talk to anyone until we had talked to our attorney. I would tell him the same thing. He would ask how I was doing and if there was someone there with me. I told the truth about Office Witte, and I lied and said I was doing fine. He lied and said he was doing fine. We both knew we were lying. The calls were short.

Though I longed to hear his voice and was relieved each time Steven called, the calls were stressful.

I wasn't physically handling this stress too well, so I had a lot of trips to the bathroom while we waited. I would ask Officer Witte each time if I could go upstairs and use the bathroom and he always said yes. On one such trip, I remembered that we sometimes kept a gun in our nightstand or in the top drawer of Steven's dresser. I checked but there were no guns in either location. I have to admit that I would have moved any gun I found in the nightstand or dresser to the vault that was in our bedroom closet. I knew with absolute certainty that my husband did not have a gun earlier in the evening when Ward abducted him, but I didn't want anyone to find something that lent any credibility to the possibility that he had.

Bella had worked her way downstairs once it was just me and Officer Witte. She laid quietly in the family room and accepted belly rubs from Witte and me whenever we were inclined to offer them. I assume she wondered where her dad had gone, but it wasn't such a bad night for her.

At some point after midnight, the doorbell rang. The woman at the door identified herself as a victim's advocate. She had missed the turnoff to Lee and Ellie's house and had ended up at our home. Officer Witte explained where she should go. Amazing—the parents of the individual who had falsely accused my husband of what I would later learn was a felony, were being visited by a victim's advocate. What crime was committed against them?

And what about me, I thought. Ward was a guy who boasted about tearing people apart limb by limb without leaving any evidence, and he's the supposed victim? Ward threatened my husband in our home and the victim's advocate was going to comfort him and his family at his house? Meanwhile, I was at home with a police chaperone wondering what they had done with my husband and clutching a pillow to my chest for comfort. Where was my advocate? Whatever happened to innocent until proven guilty? The world as I knew it no longer existed.

Hours later at about 2:00 a.m., Detective Ainsworth, accompanied by three other officers, arrived at our home with a search warrant. I tried to read the search warrant like they do on TV, but they weren't very patient. The warrant stated that Ward said he came to our house because he felt his mother had been insulted and told Steven, "If you ever talk to my mother like that I will rip your head off and shit down your neck." This was one of the few true statements Ward had made that evening. Why wasn't he in jail for threatening my husband when he apparently admitted threatening him? The warrant went on to say that Steven had threatened him with a long silver-barreled flintlock gun after returning with Ward to his parents' house and apologizing. We don't own any flintlocks. Who does?

As they walked into the house, Officer Witte assured them that Bella was no threat. Threat? This hundred and fifty pound Newfoundland was on her back with all four legs in the air hoping for more belly rubs. I wondered how they would have handled a dog with some sense of guarding home and family. The Akita we had back in New Jersey only weighed eighty-five pounds, but he would not only have barked a warning when the officer's approached our house in stealth earlier in the evening, but would have taken on the whole swat team and the German Shepherd before he would have let them take Steven away.

Detective Ainsworth, the detective in charge, had a full handlebar mustache. He looked more like an actor in an old cowboy movie, perhaps Wyatt Earp, than a member of the Boulder County Sheriff's Department. Ainsworth pointed immediately to the gun cases in the downstairs family room that were on the floor in front of the wine cellar. *Strange,* I thought, *they were upright and leaning against the cellar earlier in the evening.* Though I once again noted the change in their position, nothing registered in my mind. The detective opened the case that contained a Thompson Contender and another gun. The Thompson must weigh five pounds, with a fourteen-inch barrel and a full scope on it. It was heavy and cumbersome and could not easily be concealed anywhere. It was a single shot. It had a heavy sling used for carrying it. We have a lot of pistols in the house and any one of them would have been a better self-defense weapon than the Thompson.

Ainsworth said, "This is the gun." The detective's statement was just that—a statement. It wasn't a question and it didn't demand an answer.

This was the gun. End of conversation. *The gun that did what?* I thought. It was there all night—in the case since Thursday when we brought the guns back to the house. *Why didn't we put them away immediately?*

"Your husband says you have some gun vaults," the detective said. "Will you open them?"

"Sure." *Now that you have the search warrant.* Steven had given the detective the combinations to the two downstairs vaults housing most of his gun collection because he knew I wouldn't know the combinations, as I rarely opened them. It took me three attempts to open the vault that was in Steven's hobby room directly across from where the gun cases were laying; the vault where those guns would normally have been stored; the vault where they should have been put away days ago.

Once opened, the officers looked inside and said, "Okay."

That was all. They didn't remove any guns. They didn't handle anything in the vaults. They didn't even look inside closely. They didn't move guns around to see if there was a flintlock hidden in the back. Their inspection could not possibly have shown them anything. We could have had a small cannon in there and they wouldn't have noticed it. The same procedure and treatment was followed at the vault in a guest bedroom downstairs. No inspection, no close examination, nothing. Even more strangely, that vault was already open. Because that vault holds only shotguns, we later realized we had left it unlocked the whole time we had been in Texas. But none of the officers commented on the fact that the vault was open. Neither did they search it for the flintlock Steven was accused of using to threaten Ward.

We went upstairs to our bedroom closet that also has a vault. That vault was mostly used to store papers and jewelry, though we did keep a few handguns in there. It was the vault that I opened almost every day, but I was so nervous that it took me four attempts to open it. Once opened, the officers followed the same procedure they had used at the other vaults. They did nothing. There was no inspection of the handguns that were visible in this vault; there was no inspection to see if there were other guns hidden among the papers and the jewelry boxes; there was no apparent interest in searching for anything in any of the three vaults.

They didn't ask to look in any of the closets. They didn't look in dresser drawers or in the pantry. They didn't look in the freezers or under the bed. Their "search" consisted solely of opening the vaults, taking a cursory look in them, and opening the cases that were clearly visible in the downstairs family room.

When we were back downstairs, one of the officers, not the detective, said, "Your husband says you sometimes keep a gun in the night stand or in his dresser."

"That's right," I replied. "Would you like to take a look?" I liked asking a question for which I actually knew the answer. So we walked upstairs and looked in the nightstand and the top dresser drawer and found Steven's humidor with cigars, old magazines, and junk—but no gun.

When we returned downstairs, Ainsworth said, "Deputy Witte said a lot of alcohol had been consumed last night. Is that correct?"

I nodded a response.

"He says you showed him the bottles of wine. Would you mind showing us?"

So I opened the door to the garage that was immediately off the entranceway and pointed to the six bottles of wine that were waiting for the recycling bin.

"Can we take a picture of them?" Ainsworth asked.

I eagerly agreed, thinking this would show them that Ward had no credibility. He consumed a lot of alcohol that night—more than me or Steven—more than anyone except maybe for Tom.

I have to admit that the search wasn't what I thought it would be. On TV, searches involve opening drawers, removing items from shelves, and looking under beds. They didn't do any of that. They didn't open any drawers. They didn't look in any of the rooms except those that had vaults in them, and then their search consisted of a visual, rather cursory inspection of the vaults themselves. They didn't remove the contents of the vaults to look for anything hidden in them. They didn't look for anything that would have been hidden. They didn't look in the living room, the kitchen, the dining room, the upstairs family room, the study, the bathrooms, or the closets. They didn't look in the garage. They really didn't look anyplace. In some movies and TV shows, searches seemed to involve tearing a house apart. This search was a non-event. It was almost like they already knew what they were looking for before they began the "search."

As Ainsworth examined the Thompson, I asked, "It's not loaded, is it?" We never leave guns loaded except for a pistol in our upstairs vault.

"No, it's not loaded. But this is the gun." So he wrote out a receipt for the gun case and the two guns and handed it to me.

As the officers prepared to leave, I asked plaintively, "What happens now? I can't drive at night. What about my husband?"

Officer Witte, who had spent the most time with me, said, "I can't drive you down, that's against policy. But if your husband is going to be released, you could follow me down to the jail."

I was moved by his offer because it seemed like the first kindness anyone had offered me that evening. I called the number he gave me to see if Steven was going to be arraigned that evening, and if there was a possibility that he would be allowed to return home. I was told he would be kept overnight. Steven wasn't coming home.

It was about 3:00 a.m. when Officer Witte, Ainsworth, and the other officers left. I was alone. I went upstairs, but left every light on outside, downstairs, and throughout the house.

I crawled into bed and under the covers still wearing my sweats. I had my cell phone and Steven's cell phone on the nightstand, as well as a loaded .38 caliber revolver. Ward was a Navy Seal. I knew with certainty that he could get into our home without me (or the useless dog) even knowing it. I could be dead before my husband, who had not been allowed to post bond, was free. I was scared shitless. And I was cold. I still didn't know what to do—but I knew that sleeping was not one of my options. At this point, I was truly scared for my life. And I wanted to be able to protect myself should it be necessary. There was no one to protect me and I really felt I was in danger. I was exhausted, but wide awake and alert to any noise.

The dog, who had enjoyed being petted by every detective and policeman that came into the house, was back in her crate. Bella was scared without her dad there, and she didn't understand the light situation. Usually when we went to bed it was dark in the house, but tonight every light in the house was on.

It was predetermined that I wasn't going to sleep. I laid in bed looking down the hallway that led from our bedroom to the kitchen. How was it possible for anyone to think that my husband was able to get one of these guns when they were in the family room the whole time? Steven was doing dishes when Ward arrived the second time. He didn't do the dishes while carrying. Ward never let Steven out of his sight. How was my husband supposed to conceal a five-pound gun with a fourteen-inch barrel and a scope while being physically pushed up the hill by Ward? Why would my husband apologize first, humiliate himself, and then pull a gun on Ward? Surely someone besides me could figure out that this didn't make any logical sense.

For one brief terrifying moment I wondered whether it would have been easier to deal with an unexpected death. People were sympathetic when someone died. People died all the time. People like us did not get arrested all the time. People like us never got arrested. As I stared down the lighted but empty corridor to our kitchen, I felt more alone and terrified than I ever had in my whole life. Nothing in my previous fifty-nine years, or in all the novels I had read or the movies I had seen or the stories I had heard, was going to help me now.

That night was the first time in my life that I began to realize that the justice system did not assume innocence until proven guilty. The justice system in America assumed guilt until—at this point, I didn't know until when.

Chapter 8

Day Two: Monday, April 6, 4:30 a.m.

Monday morning I got out of bed with no sleep in my eyes or in recent memory. It was 4:30 a.m. when I took a very quick shower. I dressed in clean jeans and a sweater. This was not going to be a day that would justify makeup, so I didn't use any. It usually took me five minutes to blowdry my short hair. That morning I used only half of those minutes. No one I know would have recognized me. Then I waited for dawn to arrive. Who could I call? The answer was no one—I had to wait. I was not by nature a patient person and waiting was hard for me. I found myself just sitting and drinking coffee and staring at nothing, like I was in a stupor.

The first phone call of the morning came around 7:00 a.m. from Chris, our corporate legal counsel. Chris told me that he had spoken to Neal. Trip DeMuth was their firm's criminal legal counsel. Both Neal and Chris had spoken to Trip by the time Chris phoned me. Chris assured me that Trip was the best possible lawyer for us. He was the assistant Boulder DA on the Jon Benet Ramsey case until the governor fired him for refusing to bring charges against any family members. (That case was never solved. Was that good or bad? What did any of it mean?) I believed Chris when he said Trip was the best lawyer to help us. What choice did I have?

One of Steven's best friends, Jimmy, called about 7:30 a.m. He often called Steven in the morning on his way to work. When he asked for Steven, I started to cry.

"What's wrong?" Jimmy asked.

"Steven is in the hospital. We went to the emergency room last night. We think he has a really bad case of diverticulitis," I told him, still crying.

Steven had diverticulitis in the past, so this was the best reason I could think of for him not to be home at 7:30 a.m. I had no idea I was going to say that until I heard the words come out of my mouth. It wasn't a plan—it was spontaneous. What else could I have said? The truth wasn't an option at that point.

"Is he going to be all right?" Jimmy asked. "Should I drive over there?"

Jimmy lives about one and a half hours away, and the idea of him being willing to drive all the way to our house or to Boulder Community Hospital made me cry even harder. "No. Not now. I'll let you know if there is anything you can do."

"Is there anything you need now? Is he going to be okay?"

"It could be more than diverticulitis." How was that for an understatement? "I'll let you know. And Jimmy, thank you, I really appreciate it." At least that was what I tried to say. I'm not sure how much of that was coherent.

"Call me. Keep me posted. Anything." And we hung up.

Around 8:00 a.m., Trip DeMuth called. It was hard for me to speak coherently, as emotion caused me to cry frequently. My throat seemed to constrict and prevented me from speaking well, but I got through a summary of the previous evening's events.

Trip said, "This is very important. Could Steve have gotten a gun? Could you see him the whole time?"

I explained that I watched Steven leave the kitchen and walk down the stairs immediately in front of Ward, and that Steven was out of my sight for only a second when he passed below the walkway and he was never out of Ward's sight.

Trip said, "That's important. There was no way he could have gotten a gun without you seeing him?"

"No. No. He never had a chance to get a gun. He wouldn't have," I cried.

"But could he have gotten a gun?" asked DeMuth.

"Not without me seeing him. There weren't any guns that he could reach between the kitchen and leaving the house. No way."

Trip asked me a lot of questions, which I tried to answer. Then he explained what would happen that afternoon. Steven would be arraigned at

2:00 p.m. in front of a judge at the jail. He tried to prepare me for what I would see. Steven would be in a jail jumpsuit and would have his wrists in shackles. Trip and I would be in a seating area behind two glass walls.

"You won't be able to speak to him. It will upset you to see him like that, but you just need to stay calm."

Of course I'd stay calm. I was … usually … a very strong woman. I'd do what I had to do to get my husband safely home. We agreed to meet in the lobby of the jail half an hour before court. Strains of the old song "I am woman" began to run through my head. But in my heart, I wasn't sure how I was going to get through the day.

Before hanging up, Trip reviewed the probable conditions of bail. "Bail"—this was my new word for the day. This was not a word I ever had to use before in reference to anyone I knew. I would soon be married to someone who was out of jail on bail. Not me—no way. Trip said that one of the conditions of bail would most certainly be that Steven could not be around any guns.

"You will probably have to get all your guns out of the house before he can come back."

"I'll figure that out," I assured him.

• • •

Diverticulitis was going to be my cover story. That was what I would give as a reason for not going to work. That was why Steven wasn't home if someone called. Diverticulitis was the reason I was upset. Diverticulitis was something we could deal with. We had that happen before. But jail? Arrest? Bail? Those were not things I could describe to anyone even if I could talk.

A few minutes after talking to Trip, as I continued to sit at the kitchen counter drinking coffee, Jimmy called back.

"Are you sure you don't want me to drive over?" he said as soon as I answered the phone.

I began to sob. "Jimmy, Steven isn't in the hospital. He's in jail." This was the first time I had to say those words. "He was arrested." I could hardly say them aloud … I never had to say them before. I never rehearsed them. In fact, I had never before heard them from anyone I knew. "He was arrested" is not something that happened to people like us.

I briefly explained what had happened the night before.

Jimmy said without hesitation, "What do you need me to do?"

"Nothing right now," I replied. "But if I have to get our guns out of the house before Steven can come back, I may need help. I don't know what to do with them."

"We can put them at my house. Don't worry, I'll help. Just tell me when and I'll leave work and get over there. Anything you need, I'll help."

I was hysterical. Jimmy was ready to leave work to help us. He knew Steven would never have done anything like Ward said he did. He was a friend.

"I'll call you when I know something … and, Jimmy, thanks. And please don't tell anyone about what is going on," I sobbed.

"Not even Debbie. Don't worry, everything will turn out fine. You'll see." I hoped Jimmy was right, but I wasn't sure of anything at that point.

I called work and told them about Steven's diverticulitis. It could be more than diverticulitis I said once again. At least my lies were consistent. I probably wouldn't be in that day. I would let them know when I knew something. Yes, I was going to be fine. I was just tired and we were waiting for the doctors to tell us more. Why did lies have to get so complicated?

Then I called another good friend who lived only about a mile away and told him what was happening.

Don immediately said, "I can move the guns with you." And I cried some more. "Tell me what you want me to do and I'll do it. Anything." Two of our best friends had offered to do anything I needed or wanted, but I didn't know what I needed or wanted. I wanted my husband home. I wanted to go back to yesterday afternoon. I wished I had never met Ward. I was frightened. All I could do was drink more coffee and cry.

I asked Don not to tell anyone else what had happened. It was strange, but even though neither Steven nor I had done anything wrong, I was ashamed of what had happened. Somehow it was our fault. Somehow we must have done something wrong. Don promised not to tell anyone, not even his wife. I promised to call him once I knew what was happening and once I knew what help we needed. At that point I was naive enough to think this "incident" was something that could be resolved quietly and, hopefully, quickly.

It had been only twelve hours since Steven and I stood at the sink drying dishes together talking about getting into the tub … and now my world would never be the same. Needless to say, neither would my husband's. I had that feeling before. Three years earlier, a young sixteen year old with a driver's permit hit us while we were riding two up on our motorcycle. We should have both been dead, but we walked out of the emergency room that evening. I often thought how my life could have been over or permanently changed in the second it took that young man to decide to turn right instead of left. I had that same feeling then. Something happened and it was changing our lives. And it was my fault. I should never have let Ward back in the house. I should never have let Steven follow Ward to his parents' house. I should have called the police. We should have been the victims. We *were* the victims.

Although I was hoping for a call from Steven, I didn't hear from him that morning. He didn't know anything about my conversations or that we had engaged Trip DeMuth as his lawyer. He was showing a great deal of confidence in my ability to handle the situation. What choice did he have?

I left for the jail around 11:00 a.m. I was going to be early, but had decided to walk the dog in the park first. Besides, I was tired of being home alone and I couldn't do anything else. There was no way I could go to work, even though it was only a few miles from the jail. I drove to the park with Bella and forced her to walk around the park. She really didn't like to walk without Samson to accompany her. I felt the same way without Steven that morning.

I still arrived at the jail about half an hour before the designated meeting time. The waiting area was similar to what you might find in a doctor's office, but with a few differences. There were small lockers against one wall where visitors could secure their purse, cell phone, books, weapons, and anything else that they might have brought with them. I didn't know anything about the lockers or the protocol, so I walked into a second room with a receptionist in front of a security portal. When I explained why I was there, she advised me that I couldn't enter until shortly before the scheduled hearing time and that I needed to deposit my purse in one of the lockers. Then she loaned me the quarter I needed for the locker. Everyone else who came into the waiting area seemed to know what to do. They immediately secured their belongings if they had any. They used the phone to buy phone time or jail money for their inmate. Both sounded like prepaid credit cards that could be used for either phone access or food in prison. As I sat there, I eventually came to the conclusion that this was the waiting area for various hearings and also for visiting inmates.

Another difference between this waiting area and the waiting area in any doctor's office I had ever been in was that the other individuals who were here did not look like they would go to any of my doctors. I wasn't being mean when I arrived at that conclusion, I was being honest. They all seemed comfortable in the waiting room at the Boulder County Jail. There were whole families visiting someone. They had experience in this environment. They were natives. I was a tourist. The more I looked at people, the more I realized that they were not PLU's ("People Like Us"). I kept thinking of Tom Wolfe's *Bonfires of the Vanities* and wishing I had never read the book. We were going to pay a price because we were successful, because we had a different sense of humor, because we were conservative, for whatever reason. For some reason, someone had decided that it was time to collect their pound of flesh from our lives.

A tall, dark haired gentleman in his late forties entered. He was meticulously groomed—handsome even—and wearing the nicest suit I had seen all afternoon. In reality that compliment didn't mean much, but the suit would have been nice in any setting. He was carrying a leather briefcase. He looked around and immediately walked over to me. "Michelle?"

When I nodded, he introduced himself. "Trip DeMuth. Let's sit down over there," he said, pointing to a corner.

There wasn't a lot of privacy since all the chairs were against the three walls and facing the empty center of the room. But the two chairs he had indicated gave us a modicum of privacy.

Trip's first question was, "How are you doing?"

My response of "fine" would have been more credible if I hadn't started crying when I said that one word. I thought I might never be fine again and then a cruel thought crossed my mind. I was briefly glad my mother wasn't alive. That was awful.

I thought Trip looked competent. Hopefully that was more than just a well-tailored suit. My impression also identified him as genuinely caring. Trip seemed nice. Surely this was all good. Of course, any drowning person will assume that anything floating in the water might save them. Hopefully my lifeboat wasn't a mirage.

After about forty-five minutes we were allowed to move out of the waiting area into what I assumed was a courtroom or hearing room. I sat with the lawyer behind a glass partition. The judge's bench was in front of that partition. Trip left me and moved into the courtroom to speak to the DA about a personal recognizance bond. I learned later that this was where you didn't have to have a bail bondsman or a lien on your house to secure bail. They would let you out on your word that you would return for sentencing. When Trip returned he told me that the DA had said no. *No?* Where in the world did he think we were going to go? We had a house in Boulder—no bank accounts or homes in foreign countries. Though comfortable, we did not have a lot of cash. Our dog was here. My business was here. Our family was here. Neither of us had ever had more than a parking ticket. What did he think we were going to do? At that moment I realized with stark clarity that this was not just about Steven—it was us on trial. It was the two of us that were going to be accused of "malignant threatening," or something like that.

Steven walked into the courtroom with chains around his waist and hands. At first, I didn't even recognize him. He was one of many men in matching orange jumpsuits in a line. As I stared at the line, I recognized my husband in the middle of the group. My reaction was surprisingly flat. It was my husband, but it wasn't really. It was someone who looked a lot like my husband, but who didn't look like my husband. It was like seeing him in drag. It was him, but it wasn't him. I smiled weakly, waved a small timid wave, pointed to him and told Trip, "That's Steven." But was it really?

There were probably twelve to fifteen men in line with Steven. Many were Hispanic; most but not all were younger than my husband; most had tattoos; none looked like the retired businessman my husband was. Steven didn't actually look bad. I found myself angry that he didn't look as bad as I felt. He smiled at me from behind two different glass partitions. He looked out of place. Some of the others—with their tattoos and hard looks and long hair—looked like they belonged here. How could I make such a quick conclusion just by looking at those men?

My stomach continued to churn. There weren't actually a lot of thoughts going through my mind. What was I supposed to be thinking or feeling? I didn't know. My mind and body seemed to opt for an out-of-body experience. I was here at the Boulder County Jail, but I wasn't participating in the drama. Trip walked over and spoke to Steven briefly so he would know what was going to happen. I realized that though I had been speaking to Trip since that morning, Steven had no clue. Steven didn't even know if I had been able to get a lawyer. I'm not sure if he knew as much about what was going to happen as I did. I realized vaguely that Steven had put all of his faith and his future in my hands since last night.

When the judge walked in, we all stood. Steven's name was perhaps the second or third name called. He stood when his name was called. How did he know to do this? Trip answered "… Trip DeMuth speaking as legal counsel on behalf of Mark Steven Gesse." We had moved into a world where neither one of us could any longer answer questions directed to us. From now on until the trial, Trip would answer for us. Trip told the judge that the defendant (formerly my husband, Steven) had been married for thirty-eight years, was sixty-two years old, had no criminal record, etc., etc.—and most important—was not a flight risk. Despite the assistant DA's mild protest, Steven was released on a personal recognizance bond. He did not have a "get out of jail free" card, but he was going to be out on bail. I felt like a bit actress in a bad play. I continued to have the feeling that none of this could be happening to me.

As expected, the conditions of bail included no proximity to weapons of any kind, daily alcohol monitoring, and the requirement to stay at least three hundred feet away from Lee and Ellie. (Who in god's name would want to go close to them?) Trip and I walked back into the waiting area while Steven, still in shackles, left to be "processed." Trip said to call him when Steven got out. He wanted to meet in his office if Steven was up to it. I had no idea whether that would be in fifteen minutes or an hour, so I took a seat and waited.

I sat in the waiting room for over three hours. I didn't have a book because I had no idea I would be sitting there that long. There were no newspapers, no magazines, no old paperbacks. That was another difference from a doctor's waiting room. I probably couldn't have read anyway. I began to envision visiting Steven in jail. Could I bring him cookies? Could he have his computer and manage his investment accounts on line? If I bought him prepaid phone cards could he call me regularly? Would people be nice to him there? Would our friends visit him? How would I handle business trips and the dog? Did they allow canine visits? How would I explain his absence to his family? I began to worry about all these things as I sat waiting.

I went out periodically to check on Bella in the car. She was fine. I had almost forgiven her for not being a watch dog. She was sleeping. It was cold out so she was happy in the car—the car was her safety zone. I no longer seemed to have a safety zone.

A young woman came in carrying a small infant in a car seat and sat a few feet away from me. The baby was a little girl swathed in pink blankets and a little pink headband. She was adorable and appeared well taken care of. Her mother obviously adored her. I spoke with the young woman and learned that the baby was two months old. The mother was picking up her boyfriend (not the baby's father) for the second time since the baby had been born. *Really?* The baby was two months old and this was the second time she was trying to get her boyfriend released on bail.

The baby's mother said, "This is it. If I have to do this again, I'm out of here. But he is so good to the baby and to me. He loves her and treats her like she is his. "

I couldn't imagine being a regular here. I guess we all have to make tough choices in life. How good of a father could he be if he was being arrested regularly? But that wasn't my problem.

Other folks came and went for different court times or for visits. There were a few lawyers who arrived and met with family, but they didn't look like Trip. They reminded me of the lawyers who used to hang out outside of traffic court in Chicago when I lived there in the early eighties. They would get you out of a traffic ticket for $50—cash. I didn't see anyone I thought might be a PLU.

Some folks picked up the phone in the lobby and bought prison money or phone time for their incarcerated family member or friend. Others seemed to be visiting. What were visiting hours? How limited were they? After three hours, I picked up another phone in the lobby and said, "My husband, Mark Steven Gesse, spelled G-E-S-S-E, was being processed for bail. Do you know when he will be released?" Such basic sentences … so easy to read or write. Why did I start crying when I said these words? Why did my stomach feel like a knot? Why was I here? They told me he was being processed right then and would be out in about fifteen minutes. They didn't use the word released. The lady on the phone was very nice to me, and I was grateful. She didn't treat me like a criminal's wife.

Finally Steven came out. This was the first time I had seen him without a barrier between us in twenty-one hours. He was wearing his grey sweats and carrying a clear sack with his grey fleece bathrobe. Perhaps our world would be grey from now on. He looked tired, but otherwise looked like the same person. How was this possible? I felt like I was approaching a stranger as I walked up to him and gave him a hug. I was exhausted and didn't feel affectionate, but felt that a hug was appropriate. Underneath my exhaustion was a faint tinge of anger. How did he let this happen? Why had he made those remarks? Why did he go with Ward? Why were we even here?

There was an older fellow with him. This gentleman had wide gaps in his front teeth, grey hair, and a weathered, lined face. I am sure he was not as old as he appeared. Steven introduced me to his companion and explained that he offered this guy a ride home. I was stunned. Two days ago he was inviting Ward to our house for a nice dinner and good wine. Now he was offering a ride home to a stranger he met in lockup, if that was even the right word for where Steven had met this "gentleman." Was it possible that my life had changed this much in twenty-four hours? My husband was still being nice to folks he met accidentally—it was just that the nature of the environment had changed as well as the nature of the individuals. This gentleman did not look like someone who would normally be invited to our home. Don't get me wrong—I am the daughter of Italian immigrants. I never knew anyone who had to wear a suit to work while I was growing up. I never knew anyone except our doctor and insurance agent who wasn't paid an hourly wage. I was still more comfortable around folks like those I grew up with than those who "came from money," as my mother would have said. But this guy didn't look like anyone in my old neighborhood either. He looked like someone I might have seen walking toward the Boulder Homeless Shelter.

Fortunately or unfortunately, I had driven our small car. Since there was already a big dog in the back seat, we couldn't give this fellow a ride home. Steven's companion had to find his own way home.

Steven asked, "How are you doing?"

"Fine," I replied. "How about you?"

"Good," he said. Boy, could we both lie.

"Trip wants us to call him and stop by his office if we can. Should I call him?" I asked.

"Sure," Steven answered. "But it's already six and he's probably gone."

But Trip answered and said to come over to his office. Steven hadn't eaten or slept … but neither had I. We were already listening to Trip and doing exactly what he told us to do. It never even occurred to either of us to do anything different. I never knew I would be so good at taking instruction.

On the way to the law firm, Steven began to talk about the young men he had met and how nice they seemed. "Good looking, nice guys … really pleasant," he said. "You know, they seemed like the kind of kids I would have hired back in New Jersey. Most of them had awesome tattoos." (Was this really my husband or had they made a switch?) "But they talked about their gang affiliations and their numerous arrests and outstanding warrants like you and I would talk about what we had for dinner. Some of them said that they came to Boulder when they thought they might be arrested. Apparently in the criminal world the Boulder jail is considered a good place to be in jail—much better than Texas or Arizona according to them." The guys Steven was talking about sounded like the kind of folks who belonged in jail … not at all like my husband.

We met with Trip in the conference room adjacent to his office. There was a long wooden table with chairs around it typical of a lawyer's conference room. Trip said, "How are you both doing?" Our mutual responses of "fine" were not very convincing … when I started crying yet again.

Trip must have called Chris and Neal because they came into the conference room. I could tell by their faces that they were shocked at how we looked. I didn't even know how we looked, except that I knew neither of them had ever seen me dressed like this, without makeup, without sleep, and very stressed. Actually, both Steven and I looked and felt like shit. They both assured us we had retained a really good lawyer. They offered encouragement. They told us they couldn't believe this was happening. They couldn't understand why Ward or anyone would do something like this. At that point we hadn't figured out what could have motivated him either. I thanked Neal and apologized for calling him so late.

Without thinking, I said, "When this is all over, we'll have you and your wives over for a really nice dinner."

Chris looked startled and replied, "I think that when this is all over you should consider never having another dinner party."

But thanking folks by having them over for dinner was what I had always done. I was confused as well as tired and scared now. Maybe Chris was right and the patterns of my life were going to change. Maybe I would stop cooking and entertaining and doing the things I had always enjoyed doing. Maybe.

Trip went over the conditions of bail. No proximity to guns or weapons; daily alcohol testing; no leaving the state; regularly scheduled meetings with a drug counselor. This was the second time he had repeated this during our short meeting.

Trip said, "You have to understand how the system works. The detective and the cops have made up their mind that you are guilty. They made up their mind as soon as the phone call to 911 was made. You are now presumed guilty and will be treated that way. You have to be very careful and meet all of the conditions of the bail. We'll figure this out. I know Detective Ainsworth and can work with him. Hopefully we will get this whole thing dropped quickly but until then …" and he reiterated the conditions of bail yet again.

Unlike what we had been taught in school, Steven was not going to be presumed innocent until proven guilty. He was presumed guilty until proven innocent. Someone accused him of something. They called the police. The police came and arrested him. They were not investigating anything—they were now prosecuting. The person who made the phone call went on with his life. As we found out later, he was simply referred to in the newspaper as "the victim." We, meanwhile, had to hire an attorney. Steven was the one out on bail. He was the one who would have to defend himself. He was the one whose name would appear in the newspaper.

Amazingly it was still Monday. It seemed like weeks since guests had arrived for dinner at our house on Sunday afternoon. We scheduled a meeting with Trip for early Thursday morning. The arraignment hearing was set for Friday afternoon at what was euphemistically called the "Boulder County Justice Center."

Before we left his office, Trip went over the bail conditions once more. That was the fourth time that afternoon.

"When I was an assistant DA, we always figured that if we couldn't get someone on the charges we had, we could always convict them of bail violations. It's going to be really hard, don't underestimate it. But you have to follow the conditions of bail carefully and completely. Understand?"

We nodded. What choice did we have?

I turned to Steven and said, "We can't go home tonight." He nodded in understanding. We had guns in the gun vaults at home. I made sure they were all locked in the vaults before I left that morning, but they were still at our house. We couldn't go home. We had to get a hotel room, go to friends, sleep in the car, do something other than go home.

"We'll sleep in the motor home tonight," he said. The motor home had been winterized after our trip, and that meant there was no water … no amenities. But it was our second home and Bella (who had been in the car all day) would be fine there.

As Trip reviewed the conditions of bail once again, we seemed to finally focus on them. The alcohol testing didn't seem like a big issue at the time, though neither of us thought Steven had had too much to drink last night. Could it possibly have been only the previous evening? There had been a lot of alcohol consumed. But why didn't Ward have to do this? The limitation on out-of-state travel was going to be an issue. Our trip to Italy was supposed to begin in less than two weeks. I had actually mentioned this to Trip during our first conversation and we mentioned it again now. In hindsight, I can't figure out why I focused so much on the trip. Granted the trip was something we had planned since January and were looking forward to as a celebration of my sixtieth birthday, but I suspect there was more to it than that. I think I knew that if we canceled the trip, everyone would know why. I felt a great deal of shame, as well as terror, at what had happened. Even though rationally I would argue that we hadn't done anything wrong, I couldn't help feeling that we were somehow, someway, guilty of something. And I didn't want people to know it.

"I'll file a motion for you to take your trip at the hearing this Friday," Trip said. "But I can't promise anything. The DA seems set against being agreeable." (Asking for legal permission is called "filing a motion.")

Trip also talked about costs. This was not going to be cheap. In fact, he almost immediately began to prepare us for a decision we would have to make at some point in the future. We would most surely at some point have to decide between pleading guilty to a lesser offense or lengthening the time and the cost by opting for a jury trial. He made it very clear in this first meeting that he was not really keen on jury trials. Trip said, "How many big decisions have you made in your lives that you would want made by a jury of twelve people? Think about it. Pick twelve people randomly off the streets of Boulder and ask them to decide something that is one of the most important decisions you may ever have to make: who you should marry; where you should live; something that will affect the course of the rest of your life. Twelve perfect strangers with their own experiences and prejudices. Do you want these twelve people to decide the course of the rest of your life?"

This did not sound like civics class. This was scary. This was troubling.

My immediate response to Trip's question was, "none." I liked making my own decisions. How could folks who did not necessarily hold the same moral or political views that we did make the right decision about the rest of our lives?

What have we gotten ourselves into? I thought.

Then I realized that we had not gotten ourselves into anything. We had been dropped into something. I was stunned. It was less than twenty-four hours since Steven's arrest, and our lawyer was discussing the advantages of accepting a plea bargain. On TV, plea bargaining was an issue for the guilty. I didn't think I had ever seen a TV show where an innocent person had to choose between pleading guilty to a lesser offense versus spending their life savings in what could end up being a futile attempt to clear their name. My mom used to say, "Life ain't fair." Boy was she right.

Though it was less than twenty-four hours since his arrest, Steven had already decided that he didn't care about the money or anything else at this point. He cared about being proven innocent. He wanted justice and he already wanted revenge. He was ready to sacrifice all of our retirement accounts, our business, our home, whatever we had, to clear his name. He wanted to sue Ward, Ellie and Lee, the navy, the Boulder sheriff's department, etc. Trip expressed understanding, but basically said, "It doesn't work that way." The axis on which our world revolved had shifted.

While we were still in the meeting, but after Trip had begun to discuss the possible financial implications of defending Steven, I began thinking of how I could save money. We wouldn't be racing our vintage BMW's this year. I wouldn't buy any new clothes. I would do more consulting. What did I have in the house that I could sell? Jewelry? Since all of the jewelry I had were gifts from Steven, I wondered how he would feel about that. We had talked about a new puppy as a companion for Bella, but now I wasn't sure we could still afford one.

• • •

On the way to the motor home, we decided to rent a storage unit the next morning and put all of the guns there. We had a problem. Steven couldn't go to the house to help move the guns. We called Don and asked if he would help me the next morning. He readily agreed. After a pause, he said, "You know how you didn't want me to tell anyone? Well, the story is in the *Daily Camera,* with your name, Steve." Great—so much for my diverticulitis cover story. I had asked Trip if it would be in the newspaper, and he said he doubted it since it wasn't actually much of a story by news standards. I wondered if someone had called the paper to alert them to the story. Maybe we just had the misfortune of having this happen on a slow news day. In an innocent until proven guilty society, it was interesting that the name of the accuser was not given, but the name of the accused was. It was even spelled right. I wondered if and when Steven got acquitted, if the paper would print a story about that, but I already knew the answer. Without even asking our lawyer, I suspected the answer to that question was no. I would soon learn how many people actually read the Boulder *Daily Camera*—far more than I ever suspected.

On the way to the motor home, Steven called Jimmy and gave him a brief summary of the day's events. Jimmy wanted us to come over to his house to sleep. But we were both much too tired to make the hour and a half drive. We were exhausted and thought it would be easier to sleep in the motor home. Jimmy wanted to help the next day, but we told him that it would be easier for Don since he was closer and retired, and he wouldn't have to leave work. Jimmy wanted us to bring the guns to his house for storage, but putting them in a secured facility in Boulder seemed like a better, safer option than moving them to someone's house. Don wanted us to sleep at his house, too, but his dogs were aggressive with other dogs so that wouldn't have worked with Bella.

We stopped at a Wendy's on the way to the motor home. It was still Monday night. This was the first food either of us had eaten since our dinner party Sunday night. I couldn't eat a whole sandwich—or even a whole Frosty. Neither could Steven. We didn't have dog food, so Bella had to be satisfied with three cheeseburgers with the onions and pickles removed. She was a little confused, but happy about the hamburgers.

The motor home was cold since the furnace wasn't running. We fell into an unmade bed on top of the mattress pad and covered ourselves with blankets. I kept all of my clothes on including my socks. I was exhausted. I was numb. I was tired. I was scared.

Steven put his arm around me and said quietly, "You know I am sorry this happened. I wish I hadn't said anything to Ward."

"I know," I responded, trying not to let him hear that I was crying. "I love you." Though this was something we said each night when we got into bed, it seemed to have special meaning that night.

"Ditto," Steven said, using the shorthand we had developed when we were first married, as he tightened his hold on me. Despite the day's events, I had to smile at his word. I knew he loved me. I never doubted that. I tried not to let Steven know I was crying, but he knew and held me even tighter. Part of me blamed Steven. Part of me blamed myself. But as I laid there awake, I realized that the current situation couldn't be blamed on either of us. There was only one person to blame, and that person was sleeping in a bed at his mother's house.

For the first time in almost twenty-four hours we both fell asleep—with the help of some Tylenol PM.

Chapter 9

Day Three: Predawn

We both awoke at around 4:00 a.m. Waking up was sudden. Once awake, I didn't know where I was for a while. Neither of us had any sleep in our eyes. We were not drowsy or playful … we were simply awake. We knew each of us was awake, but neither of us spoke or moved for a while. It was like the stillness or quiet would keep us from having to confront the day and the situation. Finally when the dog whimpered, we both got up. We had a lot to do. Steven threw on his sweats and walked Bella outside.

We had no water in the motor home tank, so showering wasn't an option. Neither was making coffee. When I emptied the motor home just a few days ago, I had thrown out our old toothbrushes. I fished them out of the garbage can so we could at least brush our teeth. It wasn't so bad … I had just thrown them in and they were right on top. So our luxury was brushing our teeth and gargling with the last of the mouthwash. As I did this, I wondered at how my life had fallen apart. I'd gone from successful businesswoman to being a homeless person scrounging for a toothbrush in the trash. It was unreal to me. It seemed like I had descended into some level of Dante's hell.

Steven called Don to confirm that he would help us move the guns out of our house. Don said he'd help me load the guns into our Suburban and move them to a storage facility. Steven would rent a facility while Don and I were at our house. Since we historically left the keys in our cars when they were in our driveway, Don drove to our house, left his car there and drove our Suburban to our agreed upon meeting location halfway between our homes.

Don got out of the car, took one look at the two of us and said, "Steven, you should go to our house and take a shower. You'll feel so much better if you get cleaned up. Patricia's there and she has fresh coffee. I'll help Michelle. We'll get the guns moved, don't worry about that." When Steven didn't respond, Don repeated, "Trust me, a few minutes isn't going to make much difference and you'll feel so much better. Go. Take a shower. Have a cup of coffee. We'll take care of everything at the house."

That confirmed my suspicion that we both looked like crap. Steven reluctantly agreed.

"I'll bring you back some clean clothes as soon as we get to the house. Just wait here until I come back, then go to my house and get cleaned up," Don said.

Don and I drove the five minutes to our house. I ran into the house and grabbed Steven a clean pair of jeans, a t-shirt, and underwear. Don drove back to where Steven waited and gave him the bag of clean clothes, while I began to collect and package guns.

Strangely, there had been little conversation between Steven and me all morning. We were both operating on autopilot. We were focused on the task at hand, which was making our home safe for his return. I don't think either of us had actually processed what had happened or understood what might happen. There were things that needed to be done before we could examine the recent events, and we were trying to get them done as quickly and thoroughly as possible.

All of our guns were purchased legally. None had ever been used for anything but hunting or target practice. We had a lot of rifles that we used for hunting and target practice, and in recent years, not used at all. We had shotguns used long ago for pheasant and goose hunting and more recently for trap and skeet. We also had some handguns used for target practice, if at all. Many of these guns were very expensive. There were antique shotguns, heirlooms, and custom-made rifles.

I put some blankets down in the back of our Suburban, unlocked the two downstairs gun vaults, and prepared to move the rifles and shotguns stored there. I found some gun socks to use in packing the guns and began laying them in the car. I put towels or more blankets between layers of guns. Historically these guns would be packaged carefully in gun cases if they were transported anywhere. I tried to be careful, but found I had a sense of urgency to get them packed. I suspect I wasn't that careful— Steven could not come home until the guns were moved, and I wanted him home.

When Don returned a few minutes later, we continued moving guns into the car. While Don and I were putting the guns in gun socks or towels and loading them into the car, Steven called. "Take a shower. Don was right. I feel better after getting cleaned up. I'm going to head down the hill and look into a storage facility, so go ahead and take a shower. Get cleaned up. You'll feel better … really. I'll call you and let you know where I rent a unit and where to meet me."

I seriously doubted that anything was going to make me feel better but said, "Are you sure?"

"Yes, I'm sure. There's time. You'll feel better," Steven said.

"All right, if you're sure there's time." I don't know what I thought was going to happen. Maybe I thought the police swat team would return and find guns in the house and arrest both of us. But Steven wasn't at the house with me and Don wasn't out on bail, so I agreed to take a quick shower. I was anxious—I hadn't felt useful in the last thirty-six hours and I wanted to be doing something. Putting guns in the car was something. I wanted to keep moving. And I wanted to move fast for some unknown reason.

I did take a shower. It was quick—no bath gel, no shampoo, no shaving legs, just a washcloth and soap. But I was clean and was wearing clean clothes. This was still not a day that was going to warrant makeup or moisturizer. But I was clean.

Don waited for me while I showered and insisted on following me into Boulder in his car. I drove very carefully. I was driving a Suburban with more guns than many gun stores. None of the guns were loaded and there was no ammunition in the car, but I didn't want to get stopped by the police for any reason. I had never driven so slowly or so cautiously. I was sure that every gun that either of us owned was in the Suburban.

Don and I met Steven in the storage facility parking lot, got the key to the storage facility and then moved the guns into the facility and secured it with the padlock Steven had purchased for that purpose. We were very careful—putting blankets down and arranging the guns so that they didn't touch. We placed blankets and towels between each layer of guns.

I had very mixed emotions when we locked the storage facility door. On the one hand, I was confident that there were no guns in our home and happy that Steven and I could return there. On the other hand, I was very scared that there were no guns in our home and we had no way to protect ourselves from an intruder. I wasn't worried about a generic intruder, I was worried about Ward. It was at least a twenty-minute drive from Boulder to our home. The police couldn't get there any sooner than that if we called 911. No one was going to help us if something happened. I felt defenseless and exhausted.

I drove home alone, tired and scared. Steven was driving a second car, so I was alone in the Suburban. The overwhelming feeling I had was fear. This was an emotion I had never felt over a long period. I'd been startled before or frightened by a movie or a story. But I had never before been this afraid. It wasn't just the fear of what was happening—certainly that was part of it. But the fear at the forefront was my fear of Ward. What if the threat to his military career pushed him over the edge? What did I mean "what if"? It obviously had. The man was a Navy Seal. How would we protect ourselves if he decided to attack us physically? We might not even know he was going to attack. I was not necessarily operating rationally, I was operating on an emotional level, and I was scared.

Steven arrived home shortly after me. It was mid afternoon on Tuesday and it was the first time we had been home together in almost two days. No two-week business trip had ever seemed so long. Intuitively we both knew we needed to keep busy.

Steven gently said, "You need to stop crying. I can't take your crying. Everything is going to be all right. We didn't do anything wrong."

I hadn't realized that I had been crying since he got home. Crying had become such a normal state for me that it didn't register as unusual. When I was crying, it was hard for me to speak. "I'll stop. I'm okay," I sobbed. But there was no conviction in what I said. There wasn't much conviction in Steven's assurance that everything was going to be all right, either. I realized that for the first time, I didn't really believe my husband. Everything was not all right. Everything might never be all right again.

"Let's make a trip into town. There's garbage that needs to be dropped off and we can pick up some stuff from the motor home that we need to bring back," Steven said. He needed to do something. He needed to take some action. And making a run to the dumpster was all he could come up with.

"Fine," I replied, "I need to stop at work and just check what's on my desk."

I hadn't been to the office since the previous Friday. I was hoping that everyone would be gone by the time we got there. I had absolutely no desire to see anyone. Steven and I had not spoken about what was happening. I knew I wasn't going to talk to anyone else about what had happened. Any conversations I might have with co-workers, employees, or even friends would have to be conducted as if everything was "normal." What a charade! I figured this would be the start of my acting career.

Perhaps my childhood had prepared me for my new "role." Perhaps I had inherited my acting skills from my mother. Before she died she confided to me that she and my father had never argued, had never gone to bed mad. I think she actually believed that, but I knew the truth. When I was grammar-school age, my parents went through a tough time. They argued a lot, and my father would get mad and storm out of the house. I often suspected they would divorce. Sometimes I wished they would, just so they would stop arguing. But when I went out to play or to school, I never let on that anything was wrong at home. I pretended that everything was fine. That was what I was supposed to do and I did it well. Their marriage survived that tough period and they seemed happy after that. So maybe now if I acted like everything was okay, it would be.

We stopped at my office and all of my management staff was still there. Everyone was worried about Steven's diverticulitis. *Thank god, they must not have read the newspaper,* I thought. I said, once again, that, "It could be more than that." How was that for an understatement? "It is going to involve a whole lifestyle change." I was thinking that we were going to have to start doing background checks on everyone we invited over for a drink, but I didn't say that. Instead I said, "It's a wakeup call for Steven and our lifestyle." How's that for another understatement? I was rehearsing the phrases that I would continue to use. I was thinking that maybe it was a blessing in disguise. Our lifestyle then involved a lot of drinking and eating. Don't get me wrong—I enjoyed both and didn't think we did either to excess, but perhaps it was time for us to embrace a healthier lifestyle—no alcohol, or at least a lot less; less eating out; less entertaining; less fun. I used to think that money spent on food, wine, and entertaining was money well spent. But perhaps money well spent would now go to pay legal fees. How quickly I had adapted!

We headed home after stopping at the motor home to pick up a few things. We hadn't eaten all day, so I reheated the leftovers from Sunday night's dinner. Wasn't that ironic? We were finishing the pasta and the salmon that I had originally cooked for Ward, Ellie, and Tom. I wondered if Lee actually ate the food that Ellie and Ward brought him from our home. I found it unbelievable that he might have. I also found myself hoping that the food would stick in his throat. I was embarrassed by that thought and glad I hadn't shared it with Steven.

We weren't actually talking a lot. Both of us made occasional comments to the effect that: "Trip really does know what he's doing, don't you think?" "His contacts with the DA's office and Ainsworth have got to be good for us." "I'm sure that when they look at the facts, they will drop these charges." "There's no evidence of any wrongdoing. No one besides Ward can even suggest that you had a gun."

Toward the end of our meager dinner, Steven said, "I'm sure that when they talk to Tom, he'll confirm that the dinner party was fine and that everyone left smiling and hugging."

It hit me like a blow. Our good friend Tom had not even called since my frantic phone call to him Sunday night. He hadn't called on Monday or even on Tuesday to see how I was doing, what was going on, or if we needed any help. My first thought was that it was strange, then surprise that I hadn't heard from him or from Jean, who was supposed to have come home on Monday. I hadn't focused on it before, but as I thought about it, I was more and more surprised that we hadn't heard anything from him. I wondered out loud and said, "You know I called him on Sunday night. After they took you away and the police said 'Is there anyone you could call?' I called Tom. And he didn't come over or even call to see if I was okay or what was happening. What do you think the story is there?"

"I'm sure he's just confused and not sure of what to do. Tom and Jean are good friends, we can count on them," Steven said, as he tried to assure me. I wasn't so sure. As I thought about it, I couldn't understand their lack of response. I knew Steven and I would have been over there with Jean in a second if she had called and said the police had taken Tom away. These were two people who I would have counted among my best friends. Yet they hadn't done anything in the last two days to help Steven or me. I couldn't figure out exactly what this meant, but I had my first doubts about our "friendship." It wasn't a nice feeling.

I decided to check my e-mail and found that there had been a brief e-mail from Jean on Monday saying, "I only know what happened by way of what Ellie told Tom. …Victim's advocate says we shouldn't talk about what happened … whatever the whole story is, it really sucks and I'm really scared for you …" She was scared for me? I wasn't scared, I was terrified. Victim's advocate? The victim's advocate was talking to Jean and Tom? The victim's advocate must really be a busy person. Why was she interacting with Jean and Tom? They weren't victims of anything. What about us? We were the real victims.

• • •

Steven was trying to act normal … I didn't even try. I would just start crying periodically. I was still very frightened of Ward. Not just him, but what about other Seals that he might recruit to finish us off. When the wild turkeys that lived around us showed up in the yard, Steven said, "Boy those Seals are good … they're disguised like turkeys." Maybe his sense of humor should have gotten him in trouble, but I don't think it should have been a felony.

There were phone calls that Tuesday evening from Jimmy and Don. Steven used the phrases Trip told us to use: "We can't talk about it. Our lawyer asked that we not discuss the details of the evening or the charges with anyone, but I can assure you I did nothing wrong. There was no gun. I did nothing wrong. This will all get worked out." I didn't realize it that evening, less than forty-eight hours after Steven's arrest, but we would be repeating that mantra for months to come to friends and acquaintances and just plain nosey folks.

Both Jimmy and Don assured Steven that they knew this and they offered any help they could. "You can count on me for anything," they both said. And we knew that was the truth.

We tried sticking to our normal evening routine by taking a bath and sitting for a while in the steam shower. A soak in the tub and a steam shower would usually cause us to fall asleep quickly ... but not that night. We went to bed and stared at the ceiling marveling at how our lives had been changed. But at least we were at home in our own bed together.

Steven's good night to me was, "I love you. Please stop crying. You can't go on like this."

Want to bet? I thought. But what I said was, "I love you, too."

As I laid there trying to fall asleep, I began to pray, "Our father who art in heaven, hallowed be they name ...

"Hail Mary full of grace ...

"Glory be to the Father and to the Son and to ..."

The repetition of the Lord's Prayer, the Hail Mary, and the Glory Be to the Father—in that order—became my evening mantra to sleep. When I woke during the night I began the same recitation, in the same order, and repeated the prayers until at some point I would fall asleep again. This was a ritual that would comfort me and make me feel like I was doing something to help Steven during the whole ordeal. It's a habit that I still retain now—praying as I wait for sleep to come or when I wake up in the middle of the night. It was, unfortunately, not something I did regularly before that night. But it was something that I would continue to do regularly from then on. I knew this as I began my silent recitation.

We slept until almost 4:30 a.m.

Chapter 10

Day 6: Friday, April 10

The arraignment hearing was set for 2:00 p.m. on the Friday after Steven's arrest. We were scheduled to meet Trip in the lobby around 1:30 p.m. He had filed a motion requesting a change in the bail terms so we could go to Italy. I was still telling everyone that we had to wait for the doctor's permission for Steven to travel before we knew if we could go on our trip. Not everyone sounded convinced, but I stuck to my story. Then we found out from Jimmy that a shorter version of "the incident," or at least the police report of "the incident" had appeared in the Denver paper in addition to the Boulder *Camera*. Jimmy had been getting phone calls from folks who knew us, some only slightly, asking what the real story was—or something to that effect. My god … was there nothing else going on in the world, or had someone taken it upon themselves to try to ruin our reputations? I felt as if everyone knew within hours or days that Steven had been arrested and accused of a felony. I was sure the phone lines had been busy with the nosey wanting more details and calling our friends or those they thought might know details. Trip was amazed that the incident had made both papers on Monday morning. I didn't realize it at that time, but if it was in the paper, it was also on the web.

On the one hand it seemed as if everyone knew what had happened or at least what the paper said had happened. On the other hand some people, like my co-workers, seemed totally unaware of the real situation and believed my diverticulitis story. I didn't know who knew and who didn't. That confusion seemed to impact all of my interactions with people.

Steven thought it was important to keep busy. In all honesty I couldn't tell you what I actually did on Wednesday or Thursday except that I did get a facial that I had previously scheduled. I always thought an aesthetician was kind of like a shrink except your face looked better when you were done with your session. What was said there supposedly stayed there. But I couldn't tell anyone about this, not even Marianna. So when I started crying during the facial, she assumed it was because our older dog had died about a month and a half previously. I could still cry about that as he was a great dog, but this whole thing had cut my mourning process short. I didn't say anything that implied there was any other reason for my tears.

Whenever anyone said anything or asked about what was happening, both of us answered the same way regardless of whether it was a good friend like Jimmy or Don, or an acquaintance. We followed Trip's directions and answered, "It is an unfortunate incident. There was no gun and Steven committed no crime." My version of that being both female and Italian was, "It is an unfortunate incident. There was no gun, *we* committed no crime and *we* did nothing wrong." This was no longer about someone accusing my husband of something he didn't do. It was about someone, their family, and a whole crew of other people accusing us of doing something wrong.

On Friday I went to work early. Steven picked me up in the afternoon and we were in the lobby early. At least this time I knew the routine and had my quarter to store my purse and cell phone in a locker. I decided to leave the quarter there afterward. It was returned to you after you opened the locker and removed your belongings, but I thought that perhaps someone else like me might need it. It was the least I could do.

Trip arrived about 1:25 p.m. Once again, he was wearing a suit and was meticulously groomed. Steven was wearing a sport coat, shirt, and tie. Trip explained what motions he had filed. One motion was the request for permission for us to take our trip. Another motion was a request to get copies of all the documents and police reports. Another was to preserve the evidence—meaning the 911 tapes, conversations that may have been taped, any notes taken by the officers, etc. The final motion was to get Steven's alcohol testing moved from daily to random.

As we sat in the lobby waiting, a number of individuals stopped to make small talk with Trip. They asked what he was doing there and who he was representing. He would point to us. Certainly they could tell he was representing an innocent person. None of these individuals were criminals or being prosecuted. They were all either police officers or district attorneys or individuals involved in the criminal prosecution system. I didn't know what that meant either, but it was obvious that a lot of folks involved in this process in which we had become enmeshed knew Trip.

Shortly after 1:30 we went into the hearing room, the same one we had sat in on Monday when Steven was formally charged. It was a short and, I assumed, straightforward hearing. But then, I had never been to an arraignment before then. The judge approved the motion for our trip and advised us that Steven needed to arrange for the appropriate drug testing with his "counselor." (Should we cancel the trip to save money?) The judge also approved all of the other motions. I took these approvals as a good omen. There was no plea entered at this hearing. The judge was ruling only on the motions and scheduling the next hearing—what was called a "conference"—which was scheduled for April 30.

The three of us walked out into the parking lot. As we stood in a remote section, Steven explained to Trip that I was afraid for both of us—afraid of physical harm. This was an absolute understatement. I had been terrified ever since Sunday night. I wasn't just nervous or scared, I was truly terrified that something really bad would happen to both of us. I had told both Jimmy and Don that if anything happened to either of us to speak to Trip and to make sure there was an investigation. I was sure that Ward was either going to harm us or have someone harm us. I had seen him that night and he was scary. I had told them that even if something appeared to be an accident, it probably wasn't. I suspect now that this doesn't sound rational, but I wasn't rational. I was terrified.

Trip tried to assure me that there was no reason for this. He explained that the spotlight and the government were already focused on us. We were the assumed guilty. There was no reason for anything bad to happen to us. It did make a perverse kind of sense, but that's not how it worked in the movies. In the movies, the witnesses get killed. I wasn't convinced and told Trip that I had given his name and number to Steven's brother and to Jimmy and Don. If anything happened to us, even if it looked benign like a car accident, I wanted it investigated because I was sure it would be murder. This could only make sense to someone like me who was pretty upset. If I was dead, I wasn't going to be sure of anything much, I don't think. But what if I was sure, and not able to do anything about it? I wanted someone to follow up for me. I was assigning a spokesperson to speak on our behalf from the grave.

I abruptly said to Trip, "Do you need some money from us? A retainer?" This must have been something I had read in a novel or seen in a movie. Lawyers were supposed to have retainers to guarantee their efforts on our behalf.

"No, no, nothing like that. Don't worry about that now," Trip said. I didn't know if this was because of our long-standing relationship with his law firm or if this was simply how he operated, but it was a nice response.

At that point, a uniformed policeman came up to the three of us and began talking to Trip. He apparently knew Trip from Trip's days as an assistant DA. "Boy, its been a long time," Trip said. "How are you? What have they got you doing now?"

"I'm serving papers," the officer said. "It's okay, not much stress. Actually it's a pretty easy job."

"That's nice. Good to see you. Goodbye," replied Trip.

"Not so fast," the officer said. "I am actually serving your client. I have two sets of temporary protection orders here," he said, handing them to Trip. Both Steven and I began reading over Trip's shoulders. The orders forbid us (actually Steven, but you know how I felt about this whole situation) from coming within three hundred yards of Ellie or Lee.

"But our driveway and garage are closer than three hundred yards to their house and next to their property," I blurted.

Trip looked at me sternly and said, "I'll handle this," indicating that I should be quiet. I did eventually get the hang of letting Trip speak for Steven and me, but at this point in our relationship I still thought I should be able to speak for myself.

The officer said, "There's apparently an exclusion in the documents for use of the mutual driveway." I nodded but didn't say anything. I was a quick learner.

As the officer walked away, Trip said, "Let me look at these. I'll e-mail copies of them to you and we can discuss them and our response more afterwards."

The protection orders had me baffled, but Trip assured us that this was fairly standard after an incident like this. I was amazed that anything like this could be "fairly standard." But Steven said, "Let me drop you at work," and we parted from Trip in the parking lot.

Back at work I told everyone the doctor said it was okay for Steven to travel. I wondered if I had improved or decreased the status of the judge by calling him a doctor. Well they were both professionals, right? And then I realized they could both make mistakes. That thought wasn't very comforting.

I spent most of the evening going over sixteen-plus years of interaction with Lee and Ellie, who now seemed to think they needed protection from us. I was talking non-stop to Steven—who initially was being a patient listener. I recapped the dinner on Sunday with Ellie and her son, Ward. The fact that they stayed here, drank our wine, ate our food, took our leftovers, and left happily before their son returned to threaten to break our legs. I marveled at the apparent offense Ellie and Ward seemed to take at comments that Steven intended to be a compliment. His comments were not at all out of line for Steven. That was just what he was like. I talked about taking Ellie out to eat in January when Lee was recovering from surgery. I talked about how she asked us to stop at her house and look for pills, underwear, and a phone charger to bring to her at the hospital. In January she was asking me to look through her medicine chest and her underwear drawer and now she wanted to be protected from us. I talked about bringing her a basket of food for when Lee came home. I talked about how she confided in us with the details of her son's divorce and how the accusations made during the divorce may have contributed to his untimely death. I talked about bringing Lee and Ellie food for their whole family when Ellie's son died. I talked about trays of cookies I brought them for Christmas every year since we lived here. I talked about how Steven would plow the driveway for them because he was concerned about Ellie and Lee.

And now they need protection from us?

"Do you think Ward is still at his folks' house?" I asked Steven.

"I don't know and I don't care," Steven said. "You have to stop focusing on this. It is going to be okay. Ward isn't going to do anything. We are fine."

Sure, I thought.

• • •

We now knew that almost everyone who knew us had read or been told to read (by those vast minions of folks who we all know do not wish us well despite what they say) at least one of the newspaper accounts. I never knew so many folks actually read the Boulder and Denver papers. That explained why Diane and Roger, the friends who were going to Italy with us, and had called two or three times a day since we got back from Texas, hadn't called since Sunday night.

"Why don't you call Roger and Diane and see if they want to get together tonight. We need to let them know some of what is going on and tell them the trip to Italy is still on. Try to sound somewhat normal," Steven admonished me.

When I did call, they couldn't do dinner that night. Before we could agree on another night, Roger said, "What do I need to do to drive in Italy?" They knew. Steven was going to be our designated driver in Italy. Roger was preparing for what he needed to do if we couldn't go.

"Why don't you come over tomorrow night and we can talk about that and about Italy." They agreed. We would deal with that tomorrow night.

When I checked messages that afternoon, there was one from a friend saying, "Michelle, what can I do for you? Call me and let me know what you need. I'm here for you if you need anything."

Assuming he had heard or read about Steven's dilemma, I returned his call and left a message. "We are fine. Steven didn't do anything wrong. It is an awful mistake. He did not have a gun. We are working through the problem. I'll let you know if there is anything either of us needs, but for right now we are fine." At the end of the message my voice cracked, making a mockery of my final statement. As I hung up, it occurred to me that maybe he might be calling to see how Steven was doing with his diverticulitis. If so, my message would be one of the strangest he ever received. But a later conversation confirmed that he had read the article. He was trying to be supportive, and I appreciated it.

Trip had become our guru. Anything he told us to do, we did. At Trip's request, Steven worked at his computer documenting our interactions with Lee and Ellie and making notes about the inconsistencies in their accounts of the events of that evening. I assured Trip that Tom and Jean would be glad to come down to his office to speak to him and a private investigator. After all, they were our really good friends. They had spent holidays with us. Tom was here that night so he could confirm with Trip, just as I assumed he had done with the police, that everyone left at the same time on a happy note. They could both confirm that we had never harassed or threatened Lee and Ellie. That's what friends did. They came to your aid by telling the truth about you.

At some point after that first hearing, my fear began to turn to anger. I became really mad at Lee and Ellie and, obviously, their son Ward. For years they had allowed us to do things for them when I realized the only thing they had "done" for us was allow us to use their plow—to plow their driveway as well as ours. What had turned them against us? I was not a mother so I didn't know if this was all being done to justify the actions that their son took. Perhaps they were afraid of him and not us and were doing this to protect themselves from him. Steven said they were crouching together in the corner of the entranceway, holding hands when he entered their house that fateful night. Maybe all of these lies were intended to give Ward's story credibility.

I still cried easily—especially when someone did something really nice for us or voiced their support. But now I was also mad. I wanted this to be over. And then I wanted to get even. I used to think that it was enough for folks who did "bad" things to have to live with that knowledge. I was no longer sure that was enough. This whole "incident" was making me reconsider a lot of things.

I thought it was always best to be friendly with everyone and try to do things for them—even if they weren't exactly the kind of people you wanted as close friends. But we had tried for years to be friendly to Ellie and Lee, only to find out now that they never liked us.

I would never have shared a meal with anyone I really didn't like. For me, sharing a meal has a very strong symbolic undertone. Maybe this was because of my Catholic upbringing or my Italian heritage. I'm not sure why, but breaking bread with someone created a bond. Yet Ellie and Ward had broken bread with us, but had not hesitated to turn on us. Tom had broken bread with us many times over the years, and yet he was more silent than even casual friends.

We are changed by everything that happens to us. How exactly was I going to be changed by this? How was Steven going to be changed? I didn't know the answers to those questions.

We joined Jimmy and his wife, Deb, at their house for Easter lunch on Sunday. I was extremely grateful for the invitation and their warmth. I couldn't imagine what Deb's sister and her family thought of this strange friend who cried frequently every time someone said something nice to her or hugged her. But I couldn't help myself.

Chapter 11

Musings

Nothing in my life had prepared me for the events of that fateful night. Nothing had prepared me for the events that followed that night. By that same logic, it was safe to say that nothing had prepared our friends for that night. There was no guidebook for something like this, no precedent among our friends for them to follow. Most folks knew what to do when they heard someone was sick or had a family member die. If you were Italian like me, you made food—a cake, cookies, a basket with sauce and pasta, some wine, something edible. The quantity and the type of food depended on both the seriousness of the situation and how close you were to those impacted. An acquaintance might get a tin of cookies. A good friend would get all of the above—enough to feed the bereaved family during their entire visit.

I didn't have near the number of "girlfriends" that some women do. I'm not sure why. I had always worked in predominantly male environments and enjoyed predominantly male hobbies. I rarely went out with "the girls." I didn't have lengthy phone conversations with girlfriends daily—or even every other day. My husband was my best friend.

Two girlfriends that I might have confided in did not live close to me—one was in Chicago and one in Australia. I couldn't just call up and say, "Hi. Guess what. Steven has been arrested for threatening someone with a gun. I know that you know that is all a bunch of crap, but meanwhile my life has turned to *shit*. Did I mention that he was out on bail? And, oh yes, the lawyer has told us that this may take a long time and cost lots of money. Did I mention that I was surrounded by a swat team with drawn rifles, shotguns, and handguns when I went outside last Sunday night?" I didn't think this conversation would work that well via long distance or e-mail. So I never had it.

But we did have good friends who showed that they knew neither of us had done anything wrong and who offered to help in any way they could. They showed their support both verbally and through their actions. But there were also some disappointments. Trip asked me to ask Jean and Tom if they would speak to him so that he could ask Tom about the events of that fateful Sunday night. And I guess he would have asked Jean about our relationship with Lee and Ellie, or her impression of it. I assumed good friends like them would not hesitate to meet with Trip. It wasn't going to cost them anything but a little time—they weren't the ones paying his hourly rate.

They refused to speak to our lawyer. They said they considered this something between two neighbors and didn't want to get involved. *Excuse me!!* "Something between two neighbors" was I don't like your dog barking (although that, too, can get pretty serious), or why don't you plow your sidewalk or clean up after your dog or anything else. But *this* was not just something between two neighbors. This was one neighbor wrongfully accusing another neighbor of a serious felony … a criminal charge. Participation in this was not even something you elected. History elected it for you. I told Steven it was like living in Germany in 1943 and having a Jewish neighbor and a Nazi neighbor—the holocaust was not just something between two neighbors. Everyone had to choose sides. When you did nothing you chose to side with the Nazis and allow your Jewish neighbors to be quietly taken away. Some of you may think I am exaggerating, but I don't care. This was exactly how I felt. It is how I still feel. I was terribly disappointed and knew immediately that nothing would ever be the same between the four of us or between Jean and me again. We would become acquaintances at best, but never again friends. I would never invite them to share food or wine with us again. I couldn't.

I wondered if they would notice and miss us, but it was their choice. Maybe they could get together with Lee and Ellie. Given how boring the two of them were, that thought actually made me smile. Steven was more forgiving. Anyone could probably be more forgiving than a woman who thought her loved one had been wronged. He said they didn't know what to do, but it didn't cut it with me. If you couldn't rely on your friends in a crisis, then who exactly were you supposed to rely on? Maybe my definition of friendship was more challenging than someone else's definition—but it was my definition. And "my friends" would have to choose who to believe and who to support. They would have to be brave enough to leave no doubt in anyone's mind whose side they were on in any battle.

Initially Trip said we probably shouldn't have anything to do with them until things were settled, that it could be viewed as trying to influence them. Neither Steven nor I ever tried to influence them. We just wanted them to talk to our lawyer and tell him the truth. I didn't want to see them anymore anyway. Later Trip said it might be good for me to talk to Jean, not about the incident, but just to maintain our friendship. I think, like Steven, he was getting worried about how I was dealing with the situation. It didn't make a difference. I still didn't want to see either of them.

I always felt like there were lots of folks who pretend to be your friends but aren't really. While this was ongoing, I imagined phone calls between them talking about the newspaper articles. I envisioned a certain glee evident in their voices. I wondered if there was anyone out there who knew my husband and me who thought that this could possibly have happened. I mean think about it—in all of the hundreds of dinner parties we had, we have never had to pull out a gun. We were known as gracious hosts, and we prided ourselves on that. Gracious hosts do not do the things that we had been accused of doing.

Our life was different in many ways—some obvious and some more subtle. We locked our car doors. We had never done that in the past. We locked the house doors. We never used to do that. I looked at caller ID before answering the phone. We never used to do that. I got our house key back from Jean and Tom. I didn't want them to have access to our house while we were gone. We had always hidden a key outside where all of our neighbors and friends could find it easily. I made Steven remove the key. Trip was busy filing motions. We were supposed to leave for Italy in a few days. I felt like I should do penance, but didn't know exactly for what or how. So I went to the blood bank and gave blood. We went to church on Easter Sunday. I brought cookies to work. These were the things I could do. It was all I could think of on short notice.

I wanted to pretend that our house was a secure and safe place. I wanted to go to Italy and pretend none of this had happened. I wanted to rewind the last nine days and have another go at it. I wanted to wake up from this nightmare but knew that I was awake.

Preparations for the trip to Italy included the usual preparations for such a trip—buying Euro's, checking passports, packing, etc. And some preparations that were not typical for us, like making arrangements with Steven's substance abuse counselor for a urine test upon his return.

Chapter 12

Day 10: Tuesday, April 14

On the Tuesday after the court hearing, we received copies of the two "Motion for Civil Protection Orders" that had been filed, one each by Ellie and Lee. I was amazed. Neither of them had been present when Steven supposedly threatened Ward. Why would they be entitled to protection from us? The two motions both sought civil protection because they were the victim(s) of "Abuse of the Elderly or an At-Risk Adult," and "Physical Assault, Threat or Other Situation."

In her motion, Ellie added, "For the past ten years, Mr. Gesse has made sexist and insulting comments to me. I have reprimanded him … and have made every effort to avoid them (the Gesse's)." They were recreating history. They had stepped out of reality. I expected them to accuse us of having had human sacrifice at the dinner, that there were virgins being sacrificed for our pleasure. Those claims sounded as reasonable to me as the ones they made in the petition.

If they had been making "every effort to avoid" us, why did Ellie come to our house and stay for dinner? Why didn't she leave if she took such offense to the comments? If we have spent the last ten years making "sexist and insulting" comments to her, why would we stop now? Why come to our house and potentially have more "sexist and insulting" comments directed at her? She had come into our house and accepted our hospitality. We weren't writing graffiti on her driveway, making phone calls to her, or breaking into her home to insult her. She came into our home.

In January, she was calling up asking us to pick up Lee's prescriptions at the drugstore or asking if Steven could plow. Apparently she had been able to overcome her need to "avoid us" when she needed help. The comments Steven made could have been made unwittingly by him seventeen years ago when we first moved into our home, ten years ago, or last week. They were not out of character for him. That's just what he's like.

Did anyone actually read this stuff? Did anyone believe what she said? Did anyone look for some iota of common sense? Was this what the victim's advocate was telling them to do? Who was advising them?

I was quickly moving into the pissed column by this time—days before we were supposed to go to Italy. I felt like an actress in the theater of the absurd. Someone, someplace, had to stop and read the accusations and the inconsistencies and say this was ridiculous.

That night, over a week after the incident, when we were lying in bed trying to fall asleep and I was reciting my prayers, Steven leaned over and squeezed me. "Are we ever going to have sex again?"

"Probably," I answered, "but not tonight."

Chapter 13

April 24

I went to Italy prepared to have a terrible time. On the way over, I cried during both of the movies I watched. I can't even remember their titles, but I doubt they warranted the number of tears I shed. I usually sleep on overseas flights, but I didn't sleep at all during this trip. More surprising, neither did Steven. Steven kept saying, "We are going to have a good time." I didn't believe him.

The week in Italy was good. We always enjoyed Tuscany—I mean, who was not going to enjoy Tuscany? The week served a higher purpose than simply allowing us a good time. We were able to relax for the first time in two weeks. It was like a retreat, a respite from what was happening in our lives. It strengthened us, our relationship, and our resolve. We actually didn't talk about the incident or the terrible things we were dealing with back home. We let Italy wash over us and work her magic. This was a luxury most couples in our situation would not have had and it was priceless (to quote one of the credit cards we used). The sensual part of our relationship was restored. We weren't extravagant—no real shopping or terribly expensive meals. I realized my husband was the same person he always was. This incident hadn't really changed him. Hopefully he realized the same thing about me. This was important to both of us.

As we flew home, our mental and emotional states were better than when we left, but reality began to intrude. The closer we got to home, the greater my anxiety level. On the return flight, Steven's mantra was "We just have to get through this." I cried during the movie, *Marley and Me,* for the loss of our older dog a few months before, as well as for what we still had to face when we got home. There was an e-mail message from

Trip when we got home saying he wanted to see us the day after we returned. Nothing had really changed during our trip, but we were stronger in a way I don't think we would have been if we had canceled the trip.

In Italy, I was hoping this would be a short story. On the way home I began to understand that it might be a book—hopefully a short book. We watched the movie *What Women Want* the night after we returned and I started thinking, what if someone could hear my thoughts? *I should never have let Steven leave the house with Ward. I should have been the one to call the police ... then we would have been the victims. I want this to be over. I can't believe this is actually happening to us.* And a variety of comments similar to those. My thoughts were not exactly the sexy banter Mel Gibson was listening to in the movie.

I wanted to get a new puppy once we got back from Italy. Our house seemed empty with only the one dog—hard to explain if you are not a dog person. I had put out feelers before we left. When we returned, we had a message from a local breeder with a good reputation saying that she might place the four and a half–month old Newf puppy she had kept from a litter. The breeder said the puppy wasn't turning out to be "show stopping good looking." Steven acquiesced and agreed to go see her on the Sunday after our return. I suspect he thought the puppy would be both a good diversion for me and good therapy. Did I say go see her? Let's be honest and say go pick her up. She was cute. She was active. Bella seemed to like her immediately and to relish her new role as older sister. The first night Lola was home with us, Bella slept next to Lola's crate to keep her company. Lola was part of the prescription for keeping us busy and focused on other things. I knew Steven would have fought the idea of a new puppy if we weren't living in this nightmare. But my birthday was a week away and he was trying his best to keep me "happy" and focused on other things. So Lola joined our household, and when I woke up in the middle of the night during the next few weeks, my first thought was *I wonder if she has to go out,* which was better than the thoughts I had been having.

Meanwhile, we still had lawyer meetings; Steven still had random alcohol testing; Steven had regular meetings with his counselor; the next court date was set for the following Thursday morning; and we still had the absurd civil protection orders issue.

Chapter 14

Musings

Steven had a private meeting with Trip the day after we got back. Private meant I had to wait in the reception area. I learned afterward from Steven that Trip wanted to ask him in private if he wanted to pursue a plea bargain or proceed with a plea of not guilty. If we entered a plea of not guilty, the detective in charge would have to pursue an investigation. The result of the investigation could mean that charges might be dropped (as obviously they should) or pursued (which would be awful, time consuming, and expensive). Steven was adamant that we go forward. He did not do anything wrong and did not want to have a felony, or even a deferred felony, sentence to deal with. As I understood it, a deferred felony sentence is removed from your record once you complete the period of the deferral (a year or longer) without any "further" problems. The conditions of the deferral would be similar to those of bail. The conditions of bail were not the conditions under which we had lived most of our lives or wanted to live any future portions.

It was funny—not funny "ha ha" but funny "weird" in a way I couldn't explain. We knew the situation we found ourselves in was not of our making. We knew that we had done nothing wrong. We knew we were caught up in a nightmare. But we were still ashamed. I hadn't told anyone at work. I didn't know if they knew and were just being polite, or if they really didn't know. I thought the latter, but then I thought what I wanted to be true. Since my two best friends were not physically available to me and I hadn't said anything to them, they didn't know anything. My Australian friend was surprised and disappointed that we were not going to join her and her husband at the races in Virginia and Watkins Glen in June. They didn't know why we weren't going. We weren't going because, first of all the conditions of Steven's bail did not permit him to leave Colorado, and second of all we didn't want to spend the thousands of dollars two races that far away would cost. Cash flow, as such, was being targeted for legal bills.

If asked, I could not have explained why I was ashamed. Why do people try to rationalize why someone else has a fatal disease? We meet someone with cancer and think—they smoked, they drank, they ate junk food, they didn't exercise. There has to be a reason they are sick. Because we want to feel in control of our fate, their sickness, their disease must have been caused by something they did. Once we know what caused their disease, we won't do that so we won't get sick. That logic allows us to control our destiny. If I controlled my destiny, then I must have done something wrong that caused this to happen to us. That was logical.

Was this arrest caused by something we did? Were Steven's comments "sexist and insulting"? That's just simply dumb. Even if they were, the comments were made in our home without any bad intent. They were not a reason for violence or false accusations like this. I could rationalize all I wanted, but I still felt ashamed. Sometimes I was with Steven when he stopped at the substance abuse testing facility for his random substance testing. I would wait in the car while Steven went inside to breathe. It never took very long, but the parking lot of the center was not someplace I wanted to be seen by anyone I knew.

We were going to court. To all the world, it looked like we did something bad.

Because we were following Trip's advice, we didn't even discuss the current situation or our strategy or the events of that night with our good friends here—not even the ones who knew what was happening. We talked about it with one another. Perhaps it was making us closer. Perhaps it was making us isolated and solitary—two different sides of the same coin.

At this point in our journey there wasn't really anything for us to do. There was actually little for our lawyer to do. We had to wait while the investigation proceeded. Trip was adamant that Lee and Ellie had no grounds for civil protection orders, as they were never threatened. He was going to try to explain that to their lawyer. I was pleased that they had hired a lawyer, though I was confident their lawyer was not as good as ours. I had no other choice but to believe this. Hopefully they would drop the request for protection orders, but not before they had spent some of their money on legal fees. Neither of us had any desire to see them, but we were now on a truth quest and didn't like the implication that they had anything to fear from us or that we had ever harmed them in any way.

We were not mean folks, but the three feet of snow that fell on our home while we were in Italy and which they had to plow without our help did cause us to smile a lot. Especially when we learned that the plow broke.

During this period I focused a lot on Jean and Tom's response to the event and to us. Where I grew up, friends were those individuals who came to your aid when you needed them. Friends did not avoid you when you were in trouble. Friends did not assume the worst about you. Friends supported you any way they could. Friends were loyal to you. Maybe my definition was the old neighborhood, Italian definition of friends. Maybe waspy America had another definition for friendship. I didn't care about anyone else's definition, I was not changing mine.

I could make fewer Christmas cookies this year, as I wouldn't have to bring Ellie and Lee or Tom and Jean any. I tried to look at the bright side and told myself this whole experience was a way to sort the "real friends" column. But I was disappointed and felt a sense of loss. Steven made excuses for them. He said they didn't know what to do. I didn't care. I guess I am a no excuses kind of woman. Though I now thought Jean and Tom were fair weather friends, I understood that if this had never happened, I would have gone on considering them close friends. And I probably would have been happier ... wealthier certainly, but most probably happier, too.

Meanwhile, we had Lola and Bella to keep us busy.

Chapter 15

April 30

When Steven and I were first married, we traveled for two summers on our motorcycle across the U.S. and Canada. We were young. We were poor. We slept in a pup tent. We ate dinners prepared over our campfire. We had sex almost every night. We spent less than $1000 in total and traveled for almost twelve weeks. We were very happy. We didn't own a home or anything much, other than a used car and that bike. Life was simple.

As we got older, Steven used to joke that he was lucky if I could do Europe on $1000 per day. (I think it actually depended on the day and the city.) We were still happy, but life was not as simple. (And in case you are curious, though I think our sex life in normal times was still better than most folks our age, we weren't doing it every night anymore.)

I was learning that you couldn't defend yourself from false accusations on $1000 per day. We had yet to get our first bill, but I suspected we had spent more than that in the last twenty-six days. You might think that we were lucky we could afford it. And yes, we absolutely were. But keep in mind that the money had to come from someplace, and that someplace was our retirement funds. Between the hit we had taken in our retirement funds from the downturn in the market that occurred shortly before "the incident," and depleting these accounts for our legal bills, we have no alternative but to die earlier than we thought we would.

The conference hearing was held on April 30. Oh, you don't know what this is? Consider yourself lucky. This was the hearing where the defendant (that would be us, or more accurately Steven) typically indicates his desire to pursue his rights through the legal system as opposed to taking a plea bargain offer. Prior to the hearing, the DA typically offers you a deal—you know, the plea bargaining we are all familiar with from TV. Unlike TV, the plea bargain is typically offered to the defense attorney via e-mail or phone. Steven was offered a deal. He could plead guilty to a lesser charge that was a misdemeanor. He wanted no part of it.

Though I said nothing to Steven, I was torn. Part of me wanted this whole thing to be over. Our friends were getting pumped for information about "the incident," about us, etc. We were apparently *the* topic of conversation wherever people who knew us (no matter how slightly) were together.

I wanted the expense to stop. I wanted the emotional toll to stop, though I realized pleading guilty for whatever reason to something you did not do would not stop the emotional toll. In fact, perhaps it would make it go on even longer. I wanted someone to be able to Google my husband's name and not find the articles detailing only his charges. It didn't matter what I wanted. We were going forward. We took the plea bargain offer of a misdemeanor charge to be a good omen. But we were in the "looking for good omens" business. So everything that happened or didn't happen was viewed as a good omen.

Trip explained that the DA assigned to the case, Mike Foote, was on paternity leave. (I wondered if our founding fathers ever anticipated paternity leave.) The clock for a "speedy" trial started when we entered the plea, so delaying the plea filing gave the investigators (i.e. police detectives) longer to investigate. Operating under the assumption that with more time to investigate the detectives would decide to drop the charges, Trip asked for an extension until the assistant DA, Foote, would be available. The date for the new conference hearing was set for four weeks later, on May 28th.

I was skeptical about justice being blind and/or correct—and I was certain it was not swift. So Steven continued his now random alcohol tests. That meant that every morning he called a certain number that told him what color needed to check in on that day. He was green. After the hearing, he was going to take me out to breakfast—just an ordinary thing that a husband and wife might do. No big deal … just one of the things that made up ordinary life. Only it was 9:45 a.m. and he had to do his breath test before 10:00 a.m. We rushed to the "addiction center" so he could get in under the wire. It only took a few minutes for him to breathe into the tube and return to the car. When he did, I asked him to drop me off at work. I no longer felt like going out for breakfast—something had changed my mood during those few minutes. Stopping at the substance abuse clinic seemed to have that effect on me.

I was going to turn sixty in two days. I wasn't neurotic about the age milestone. In fact, in all honesty, I thought I looked pretty good for sixty. The whole fiasco had allowed me to shed the few pounds I had gained in the prior decade. (I do not recommend this as a diet program. Maybe I should have named this book *The Bogus Allegations Diet Book*.) But it would have been nice to go out for dinner and celebrate the event with a glass of champagne, or even a glass of wine from our cellar. We would celebrate with sparkling water this year. Actually, I had begun to think that when served in a crystal glass it was almost as satisfying as a glass of wine. (Can you tell when I am lying without looking at my face?) Another ordinary event in an otherwise ordinary life that wouldn't happen. Life was now full of non-ordinary things that happened and ordinary things that didn't happen.

Trip told us what Ward was telling the investigator about "the incident." The description of the gun was morphing. In his original statement to the officers at the scene, Ward indicated that the gun was a "flintlock." A flintlock is an old-fashioned black powder gun—not at all common, not modern, not of much use for protection or anything else. It has to be loaded with a wad of gunpowder. Think civil war muskets. It is also not a type of gun we own. In later statements, he described the gun as "like a flintlock," and much later it was a "long, silver barreled gun."

Ward denied ever entering our house to force Steven to follow him. I guess in his version, he calmly came to the door and asked me to have Steven follow him to his folk's house. In his version, I wondered when he suggested, "pulling [Steven's] head off and shitting down his neck"? Or when he threatened to break Steven's legs? In Ward's version, the two walked calmly on the driveway to Ellie and Lee's home.

He said he had one "gimlo" (gimlet to the civilized world) and at most two glasses of wine. This was really absurd. The lies he was telling were actually confusing. I hoped they were confusing to the investigator. Trip hesitated to detail Ward's statements because he thought it would infuriate me—not necessarily Steven, but me. Actually he would normally be correct, but I was past getting infuriated. I was just numb.

Trip, Steven, and I had speculated as to motive. At first we couldn't understand why Ward was doing this. Then Trip said, "Think about this. This guy—a Navy Seal captain—comes into your house and threatens Steven. Really seriously threatens him with bodily harm; forces him to go out into the night despite the fact that Steven doesn't want to go; makes Steven apologize. Everything is good until Steven threatens to tell the navy what he has done. Steven threatens to ruin his career. What's this guy got besides his career? He's scared. Sure, he's white as a ghost. This guy just saw his whole navy career go down the tubes if they find out that he threatened an unarmed civilian and basically kidnapped him. He's brilliant. He turned the tables. He accuses Steven, so now he's not the instigator or the bad guy. Now he's the victim."

The investigator was apparently going to speak to Tom that afternoon. If Tom was truthful, and I had no reason not to think he would be, he would collaborate the events during dinner, including the amount of alcohol Ward drank. One of the officers who spoke to Ward after the 911 call indicated in a written report that Ward appeared intoxicated, that he could smell alcohol on his breath. That raised the question of why the word of a drunk (okay, a Navy Seal drunk ... but still a drunk) was sufficient to tear our world apart.

Think about that. One person, obviously drunk, says something and your world as you know it no longer exists. Your good reputation is trashed in the newspapers. You start hanging out in prison and in court. Your savings start hemorrhaging. Everything you have worked for or fought for is threatened. Because a drunk said you did something you did not do. No one besides Steven and Ward saw this supposedly threatening encounter. Since I was with Steven the whole time before he left for that fateful walk with Ward, I knew he had no opportunity to get a gun much less conceal it on the walk. Yet he was presumed guilty and has to fight (and pay) to exonerate himself.

Yes Steven had guns, so I guess that meant he could have done it. Of course, that also means that any male could be accused of sexual harassment or attempted rape because he has the equipment. It is not as far-fetched as it sounds. It is totally possible.

Chapter 16

May 3

My sixtieth birthday passed quietly—no party, no celebration, nothing to differentiate that day from the ones before it or soon after it.

Let me emphatically say that I was *not* feeling sorry for myself. I had a lot to be grateful for and I had always disliked whiners. As my mother used to say, "As long as you have your health you have everything." Okay, she tended toward exaggeration and platitudes, but there was a lot of truth in that. I might have amended her saying to cover both Steven and me. As long as we were both healthy, we were very fortunate. As far as "the incident," I had moved toward "Let's get this over with." I was disappointed and mad, but I was not feeling sorry for myself. I still feared for our lives—but I was not feeling sorry for myself. There was a big difference.

Having said that, my sixtieth birthday pretty much sucked. My mother had died days before my birthday four years before. I spent that birthday in church at her funeral. That seemed to start a trend. The next year, the gas pedal on my race car stuck while I was driving on the grid at Road Atlanta. Not only had the race not started, but we weren't even on the track yet. I panicked. I should have pulled the key out. I didn't. (What is it they say about hindsight?) Instead, I rammed right into the back of a good friend's meticulously prepared Lotus Élan. Not only was he a friend, but he was on the pole for the race. The trend had started. The next year I was out of town on business by myself in some remote little town on the Rhine River. (In retrospect, not the worst of the streak.) Last year Steven really did have diverticulitis and was sick on my birthday.

This year I spent most of the day on the verge of tears. Since I was not going to feel sorry for myself, I certainly don't expect you to. I knew we had a very nice week in Italy. I had this puppy (that I thought might have had ADD) to keep me busy. Steven took me out for breakfast and for pizza at lunch. He hung some pictures on the wall that had been waiting to be hung for weeks. You have no idea how big a gift this was unless you have a husband like mine who absolutely hates to put a nail in a wall. My co-workers gave me a nice bouquet of flowers. And I really did not want to go out to eat and have a nice glass of wine with dinner. (Do the lies show up in different type here?) Okay, maybe I did. But I didn't say anything. We did go to the dog park and that was fun.

We were going to go to the mountains, but with the random alcohol testing we couldn't really leave Boulder for more than a day without permission from Steven's counselor. The conditions of the bond were not to leave Colorado, but the reality was that you couldn't leave Boulder easily. The reality was that living under this "innocent until proven guilty" regime was very limiting—we felt as if we had already been convicted.

I received a card from Jean that said something insipid like, "Wishing for the old times. Lots of love ..." What exactly was that supposed to mean? We had done nothing wrong. There was no reason to be avoiding us or not to phone with a personal birthday wish. I didn't need friends before nearly as much as I needed them while this was ongoing. I wanted to call her and say, "You were the one who made the decision not to be involved." News flash: The old times were not coming back! Things might be better in the future. Things might be worse in the future. I didn't know. But I was certain they would be different. This was not the kind of event that left anyone untouched.

Jean wasn't even here that night. Maybe if Tom or Jean had said, "We don't know what happened, but we have known you long enough to know that Steven didn't do anything wrong." Or maybe, "We've been told that we aren't supposed to talk to you, but please know that we think of you often and hope you get through this quickly and safely." Or if Jean had said, "Michelle, I wasn't there that awful night but why don't we talk about it. Is there anything I can do?" Anything would have played better with me than the silence and the "wishing for the old days" routine. Hell, if they were yearning for the old days, think about how I felt.

The other absurd thing that happened in the few days following the conference hearing was on the topic of the protection orders that Lee and Ellie filed. Steven asked Trip to request through their lawyer that they agree to remove a provision in the order that Steven not have proximity to any ammunition. Our guns were all gone from the house and Steven had packed away most of the ammunition, but we still had gunpowder (for his reloading) in the house and there could certainly still be ammunition someplace. How dangerous was that without a gun from which to shoot it? Steven was worried that a zealous cop would search the house for some reason and determine that we were in violation of the protection orders because there was ammunition in the house. We remembered what Trip had said: "If they can't convict you, they can find you in violation of your bail and prosecute you for that." Perhaps protection orders offered the same opportunity. Trip made that request.

Ellie and Lee's lawyer sent an e-mail stating (and I quote this time—not just paraphrase) that "they are willing to be reasonable." They were prepared not to require that all ammunition be removed from the premises. But they were still requesting the protection orders. I was amazed that they thought this was being "reasonable"? What exactly would being unreasonable entail? Were these folks on drugs or something? According to their lawyer, in their effort to be "reasonable," they would amend the protection orders to require only that Steven not leave the house armed with a gun. I didn't know how long protection orders lasted, but under that provision we couldn't take a shotgun or rifle with us to go hunting.

I felt more and more frequently like I was operating in some sort of theater of the absurd. These folks called 911, had Steven arrested for something they never saw happen, and then took out civil protection orders against us—neighbors who until then had frequently called Steven to ask for help. Now they thought agreeing to a condition that was simply consistent with Steven's bail was "being reasonable." Alice never felt so confused falling through the hole as I did when considering the situation.

As if this part of the conversation wasn't enough, there was more. Trip went on to say that Ward told the investigator that someone had called him and threatened him—told Ward to "back off" or there would be consequences, that his career would be ruined if he didn't back off. This was totally absurd. The only person who would have even thought about doing that was my Uncle Jack and he's been dead since 1971. I'm Italian, but my family was not in the mob or anything—at least not that I was aware. Neither Steven nor I called Ward. In fact, we were in Italy when the call supposedly happened, and our cell phones didn't work overseas.

No one else—not even Jimmy or Don who knew something about what happened—knew Ward's name. Ward was lying ... again. I wasn't a detective, but I would think this kind of accusation would have been easy to verify. When did he get the phone call? If he really did get a phone call it would seem that phone records should confirm who placed the call, or at least where it came from. There was just no way anyone we knew called him. Was he looking for a way out of this? If so, I wished he would hurry up and find it. I wished the investigators would investigate the accuser and see if his statements could be collaborated. If he was lying about this, why didn't they realize he was lying about the events of that night?

The lies and contradictions kept mounting. Certainly someone's bullshit meter had to be triggered by this tsunami of lies. We could only hope.

I decided that we would celebrate my sixty-and-a-half birthday in November. Hopefully this whole thing would be over (except maybe the defamation and recovery of costs lawsuits), and we could go out and have a nice dinner with a glass of champagne—assuming we could still afford to do that of course!

Chapter 17

May 6

I was beginning to think that everyone was either crazy or seriously over-dosed with Prozac—except of course you and me.

We had agreed with Trip that the "best" way to handle the protection orders was to request extensions for as long as possible and eventually fight them in court. We thought that would increase Ellie and Lee's interaction with their attorney and the resulting cost to them. The uncertainty regarding the orders might also affect them, so Trip had filed a motion to extend the protection orders and delay the related court proceedings.

We found out that we had to make an appearance in court just to extend the period of the protection orders by another month or two. We didn't realize originally that the request for an extension by us required a court appearance. Perhaps seeing us, as well as knowing that the protection order issue wasn't going to be resolved for another month or two, would further increase the stress level for Lee and Ellie. One could only hope. I wanted them to share our pain and our stress. Our stress level was so high that a court appearance for the extension didn't even register on the stress meter.

We always dressed with care when we had a court appearance. That meant I wore clothes that didn't have dog slobber on them (easy in the morning, but a challenge not to have those shiny spots by the afternoon). In my case it wasn't really that different than how I dressed normally—what might have been considered business casual. Steven always wore a sport coat and tie—not typical for him as he was retired, and we lived in Boulder, Colorado, where apparently only accused felons and their lawyers wore sport coats.

So I was relatively calm that morning when I got to work. The puppy was a large part of that, as she was funny and cute and kept me distracted. She had her first puppy class the previous night and had discovered water. The training facility we used had a small pond and Lola thought that the pond was awesome. I had never seen a puppy that excited about being able to go swimming. Thinking about that kept me smiling all the way to work.

Then I get the most absurd e-mail from Jean. Her e-mail said—and I quote:

I hear that things will be pretty much over today. I'm glad there won't be any sort of a bitter trial. Tom and I chose not to talk to your lawyer because we'd be expected to talk to Lee and Ellie's lawyer, and we simply did not want to get in the middle of this. Had the court demanded, well that would have been a different story.

We'll gladly chat more about that if you want. Actually, it's been a bit of a strain hearing only one side of the events ...

Come over for a glass of wine if you're in the mood later today.

Let me get this straight, she felt the last month had "been a bit of a strain"? I hate to sound like I was born and raised on the south side of Chicago (which I was), but what the hell did she think it had been like for us? And where did she get the impression that it "will be pretty much over today"? "Today" was just the restraining orders hearing—it had nothing to do with the criminal charges. And, excuse me for ranting, but was it really possible for her to think that this wasn't going to lead to any sort of bitterness whether or not it went to trial? Of course they were expected to talk to Ellie and Lee's lawyer—that's the Boulder County assistant DA. They didn't have a choice about that. And why would I ever want to have a glass of wine with folks who "simply did not want to get in the middle of this." "This" had become my life in the last month. "This" was what occupied my thoughts and emotions and fears. "This" was what I had become.

How could she possibly think that her decision not to "get in the middle" would not affect our friendship? I had long felt that too many people in our society had lost the understanding that their actions had consequences. Was it possible that Lee and Ellie really didn't understand that their son had accused my husband of a felony? Was it possible that they really did not appreciate or understand the legal ramifications of such a charge? Was it possible that Jean and Tom didn't realize how this had disrupted our lives? Was it possible that any of them thought everything on the mountain (well, at least in our driveway) was just going to be fine and there would be no consequences or repercussions from this? Was it possible for Jean and Tom to think they could avoid getting involved? Was it possible for Jean and Tom to think that we could all just go back to being friends and drinking wine together like we did before the incident? No offense, but how stupid or naive could folks be?

I was thinking about a lot of things like:

Being surrounded by a swat team with drawn rifles and a police dog in my own driveway a month ago

My husband spending the night in jail

Being afraid for our lives

Being in and out of court

My husband having to appear for random breathalyzer tests

Not being able to leave the state without special permission

The reports of the accusations in two newspapers with only Steven's name, not Ward's

Spending our retirement money at who knows what rate (since we have yet to receive the first bill)

And someone else had the audacity to think they have had stress? I was amazed and disappointed in my neighbors. The disappointment was really hard on me. But I kept trying to focus instead on the friends who had been quick to voice their support; on those friends who were quick to say they knew Steven hadn't done anything wrong; that he couldn't have done anything like what the paper said. Those were the folks who gave me hope.

I forwarded the e-mail to Trip and asked him if I could reply the way I wanted. He instructed me to limit my response to a few sentences:

Thank you very much for your e-mail and your concern, however, I think it best that we not talk right now as Steven is still facing serious felony criminal charges of which he is completely innocent.

I sounded so in control. It was a total deception.

Despite the fact that I said I wasn't stressed, the truth was that every time we had to go to court for anything, we both got stressed, but pretended we were not. As we drove to court that afternoon, Steven stopped at a red light. Good. When the light changed, he didn't move. Bad. I said, "It's green." He drove forward. When I suggested that his poor driving was due to stress, he insisted it wasn't stress. "I'm used to court," Steven said. "Remember I spent a lot of time in bankruptcy court in New York. You're the one who gets stressed." Then to make my point, he turned left in front of oncoming traffic that I thought was too close—and I was the one on the passenger side!

"You know it's okay to be stressed. The court in New York was bankruptcy court and you were there for someone else. This court is personal. It's about you, our future, jail. It's not the same."

"Yes it is. I am not stressed. I can deal with it. You're the one who is out of control."

But I wasn't driving. If we got through this whole ordeal without an accident, it was going to be a major accomplishment.

• • •

We had both begun to snap at one another. If I mentioned Jean or Tom, Steven would say, "Enough already. We've been through this." But who else could I talk to? When I talked about Ward, Steven would say, "He's not going to show up and kill us. Trip told you. No one is focused on him." But I was. When Steven suggested going out to eat, I'd snap, "But we can't have a glass of wine. I don't think we should spend the money."

He'd answer, "I'll have a non-alcoholic beer. I'm actually getting to like them. And our life is not over just because I have been accused of something." It wasn't? These exchanges were repeated regularly.

I really needed someone else to talk to, someone to take into my confidence. But I was too afraid of not doing exactly what Trip said to do. And he said not to talk to anyone about that night or about what was happening, so I didn't. Instead I wrote, but no one was reading what I wrote. Although it was therapeutic for me, it didn't give me what I needed. I needed someone to tell me that everything would be okay, that I was responding to what was happening in an acceptable and perhaps even extraordinary manner. I guess I will never know if that was true.

I wished my mom was alive but knew that I wouldn't have talked to her anyway. She could never have kept quiet.

• • •

When we met with Trip before the court session, he cautioned us not to "raise our eyebrows" or otherwise acknowledge our neighbors. The afternoon session went relatively quickly. Steven and I kept our eyes focused directly ahead on the judge during the whole proceeding. The civil protection orders were extended for a little over two months. Not only was the ban on ammunition lifted, but the ban on guns inside the house was lifted—though there weren't any there because of the bail conditions. When the session was over, we were careful not to look left or right and we left the courtroom before Ellie and Lee.

In a brief conversation with Trip after the appearance, Steven once again began talking about what legal action we would be able to take afterward—afterward to him meant when the charges were dropped. I kept telling him to focus on the current issue—getting the charges dropped. He assumed that would happen soon. I didn't assume anything. His focus on afterward and my focus on now was becoming an issue between us.

Trip once again carefully went through the possible results for the path we had elected. Detective Ainsworth might decide:

Steven was guilty. If this is the case, Ainsworth will proceed with prosecution. This was obviously bad for us since Steven was not guilty, and we had already passed on a misdemeanor plea bargain. It would also mean we would proceed to trial, which would be emotionally trying, financially trying, and time consuming—all with no guarantee of what we would consider justice.

He couldn't figure out who was or was not guilty of doing anything. Trip wasn't sure how this would play out.

That Steven most probably didn't do anything and recommend that the charges be dropped. I thought this was the best outcome. Steven agreed this would be good—but in his mind not the best outcome.

That not only was Steven not guilty, but that Ward had lied to the police for whatever reason and, at the extreme, should be charged with a crime. This was Steven's preferred outcome. I thought it unlikely. I just wanted this whole thing to be over.

My mantra had become "let's stay focused." We had one goal and that was to get the charges dropped. But we couldn't do anything more to make that happen. It was all up to Ainsworth. We could only hope he had an open mind and didn't assume that because Steven was accused of something that he was guilty.

Trip must have sensed some despair when we asked the same question we had asked numerous times before. How was it possible that the first police to answer Ward's call smelled alcohol on his breath and they still came to our house with a swat team, in the dark, with weapons drawn—and a police dog?

Trip explained patiently for the umpteenth time that most folks didn't understand the criminal justice system. *Lucky them,* I thought. He told us once again, "This is how it works—you are guilty until proven innocent. You don't have to be proven guilty. You have to be proven innocent. And it takes a lot of work, a lot of time, and unfortunately sometimes a lot of money to prove you are innocent. That's why we talked about the plea bargain option. But I still think Ainsworth is going to take a look at what happened and realize he's being taken. Unfortunately, Foote isn't going to look at anything until we are a lot closer to trial. We'll just have to let it play out."

When I returned to work I had another e-mail from Jean saying she thought everything was over. I suspected she had been getting her information from Lee and Ellie, though I could only speculate. Trip said the DA had called Ward and asked if he was okay with Steven being offered a misdemeanor as a plea bargain. Apparently Ward had to agree before they would do that. Perhaps Ward had told Lee and Ellie that the criminal part was over under the assumption that Steven would accept the plea bargain. If Jean was getting her information from Ellie, she was severely misinformed. I thought it ironic that we, the accused, had been instructed not to speak about the events of that evening or what was happening, but that the individuals bringing the accusation were apparently free to talk to whomever they wanted.

Chapter 18

Mid-May

There really wasn't anything for either of us to do after the conference hearing. Steven called each morning and checked his color. We didn't go out to eat because it just wasn't very enjoyable. We weren't entertaining. We certainly weren't inviting the neighbors over to share a glass of wine. So we were saving money, which was good. Phone calls were few and far between. We were watching a lot of movies at home and spending time unsuccessfully trying to train the new puppy. The good news was that Steven had lost a lot of weight since the incident. The bad news was the reason for the weight loss.

We had canceled our car racing for the next two months, so there were no cars to prepare and no motor home to get ready. I got to work each day and wrote in my journal when I had something to say. Steven had nothing that he could do to move this whole thing toward closing and the dropping of the charges. I kept saying, "Stay focused." He always answered, "On what?" There wasn't really anything for us to do and that was very frustrating. Our lives and our lifestyles hung in the balance and all we could do was wait. I had never had medical issues that were out of my control, but I suspect my feeling of frustration and inadequacy was similar to what I would have felt in that situation.

We were both stressed but refused to acknowledge the stress. My right eye developed a twitch. I had no idea why. This had never happened before but I suspected it was "nerves." I cried whenever I got one of those soppy e-mails about friends, or religion, or what really matters. If my co-workers were aware of the situation or the difference in me, they were smart enough not to say anything. I yearned for the time when I could sit them all down in my office and give them the short version. Instead, I found myself frequently shutting my office door so they wouldn't overhear my conversations with Steven.

It was only at this point that I went online to read the articles that had appeared in the Boulder *Daily Camera* and the *Denver Post*. In hindsight, it was strange that I hadn't looked at them before. I don't know why except that on some level I'm sure I didn't want to actually see a report in print about Steven's arrest. At some level, reading about it in the paper(s) would make it even worse. The article was brief.

> Boulder Daily Camera, April 6, 2009
>
> Headline: Sheriff's deputies: Boulder County man threatened with gun
>
> A Boulder County man was arrested late Sunday after officers said he pointed a handgun at his neighbor, who had asked him to apologize for insulting the neighbor's mother, Sheriff's Office spokesman Cmdr. Rick Brough said.
>
> Mark Steven Gesse, 62, was booked into the Boulder County Jail on suspicion of felony menacing, prohibited use of a weapon and harassment after deputies received a call at 7:55 p.m. Sunday about an altercation involving a handgun outside a home in the … Subdivision west of Boulder.
>
> The caller, whose name hasn't been released, told police that he and his mother were invited over to Gesse's house for dinner, and Gesse made an inappropriate comment to his mother, Brough said. The victim asked Gesse to "come over later and apologize, which he did, Brough said.
>
> "But as he was leaving, he made a threatening remark and pulled a gun," he said.
>
> Sheriff's deputies are continuing to investigate the incident."

I felt physically ill after reading this combination of facts (they were invited over for dinner), omissions (the accuser's name wasn't given), and lies (there was no polite invitation to apologize and there most certainly wasn't a gun!). Reading this short article made me feel dirty and tainted, though I was at a loss to explain why or how. The article seemed to assume that my husband was guilty. The "spin" of the article didn't leave any room for innocence. The article in the *Denver Post* was almost the same, except it said the incident happened at our house (an error if not a lie) and gave the approximate address.

As I reread the articles, I began to laugh almost hysterically. My administrative assistant stepped into my office and asked if everything was all right. "Sure," I replied, still laughing but with no humor evident in my laughter or my facial expression. As I reread the article, it struck me as so absurd I was surprised anyone printed it as news. The sequence of events sounded outlandish. Steven pulled a gun because some guy came over and demanded an apology after Steven insulted his mother while they had been at our house. That sounded absurd. Did someone actually read this and think it was credible and newsworthy? Surely someone besides me could see that this just sounded ridiculous.

As I read farther down the page, I realized that a blog of comments followed the articles in both newspapers. People were commenting on these articles. I read:

> "This is not news. It's a spat between two guys and who knows if there were any witnesses. Or for that matter, who cares."
>
> "So who was the 62 year old victim?"
>
> "Too influential in Boulder to dare utter his name?"
>
> "Gesse is an idiot ... I don't pretend to have the whole story but based on what has been reported he deserves to be prosecuted."
>
> "Isn't it amazing how the gun nuts always try to spin a story..."
>
> "Gesse must not have been wealthy enough to avoid being arrested."
>
> "Only thing I can see here is that someone stated to the police that someone else pointed a gun at him."

There were many more comments. Even though some of the comments suggested that all of the facts were not disclosed and that the whole incident seemed to be based on what one person said, I focused and subsequently remembered only the comments that insisted my husband should be prosecuted, the ones that referred to him as an old man, a gun nut, etc. Reading these comments was worse than reading the newspaper accounts.

I felt invaded; naked in front of a group of strangers. I never thought either of us would be the subject of blogs. People we apparently didn't even know were discussing what was printed. None of them knew the facts—just what the articles in the paper said. Yet they had strong opinions about Steven's guilt or innocence. I couldn't believe it. Didn't these people have anything more important to do than read and comment on small, inaccurate articles that appeared in the newspaper? The reality was that there was no longer any privacy in the world. "Reality" was created on the Internet—not by what had really happened but by what was "posted." Once it was out there how could you ever get it back? I knew instinctively that when (and unfortunately if) the charges were dropped, neither newspaper would print that news. The last written word on the incident would be two short articles saying that Mark Steven Gesse was arrested for felony menacing with a gun.

Years later when someone googled my husband's name, these articles and the comments that followed would be what they found. I was sickened by that thought. Selfishly perhaps, it occurred to me that someone googling my name might come upon these articles. Once this thought materialized in my mind, I felt traitorous and petty. This wasn't about me. It was about my husband. My concern about the taint it might place on me seemed very out of place. I was ashamed.

Chapter 19

Late May

Steven was angry. I was worried. We were both stressed. I believe those were our dominant emotions, but at any time either of us would be cycling through disbelief, anger, worry, stress, loneliness, paranoia, suspicion—a host of emotions. For the first time in my life I wondered if our marriage would survive. That was very scary. I didn't want our marriage to be a casualty of this bizarre event in our lives.

Over two weeks passed after the conference hearing without either of us speaking to Trip. We both fought the urge to call him (and run up our bill). We assumed that no news from Trip meant just that—there was no news. The date of the next conference hearing had been set, and we assumed we would hear from him before then. We thought that Foote, the assistant DA who had been assigned the case, would have returned from paternity leave by then. We also hoped that Ainsworth would have, hopefully, had time to "investigate" further. We also hoped that by then someone would have reviewed the file and noted the discrepancies, the lack of evidence, and the lack of collaboration. Trip thought, perhaps "hoped" was a better word, that they would then decide to drop the charges.

I could tell Steven was angry, though he didn't admit to any emotion. He was distracted. He did things like stop at green lights, leave the freezer door open, use the wrong words in sentences, etc. He was not living in the present. He would get mad at the radio. He would actually raise his voice and begin to rant about current events. He tended to snap at me when I asked a question. He woke up at 4:30 a.m. most mornings. Our sex life was suffering. He would get angry when we discussed the limitations on our life because of his random alcohol testing and the travel restrictions. I couldn't imagine his reaction when we would get our first legal bill. He wanted to sue everyone involved once he was cleared of the charges—Ward, Lee, Ellie, the sheriff's department, the newspapers, etc. I didn't think that was going to be possible—but I wasn't a lawyer. I didn't tell him this because I sensed it was important for him to believe this was possible. I also assumed that when (not if, but when) Steven was cleared, Trip would advise him if this was an option.

I was getting more worried with every passing day. It had been almost two months since the incident. On one level, I understood Steven's absolute desire to get the charges dropped. He had done nothing wrong. Why should he have considered accepting a plea bargain to a lesser offense when he was not guilty of any offense? But I was weary—not tired like I needed a few more hours of sleep, but weary. It was as if my spirit was weaker and heavier. What if Ainsworth and Foote decided to prosecute? How much time and money would we spend dealing with a trial? What emotional toll would that take on each of us and on our marriage? How many more months of random (which might as well be daily) alcohol testing and travel restrictions would we have to endure?

I worried about how the recent events would affect our lifestyle. Both Steven and I were outgoing. We liked all sorts of people, we liked to meet new folks, we enjoyed entertaining, we tried to be friendly. If these things weren't true, we would never have invited Ward and his folks over for dinner. Would we change?

I worried about going to trial. How could I assume a jury would provide justice when my experience so far didn't show any evidence of what I considered justice? I had come to realize that the prosecution didn't have to prove guilt. We had been treated as the guilty parties for the last two months. Trip would have to prove us innocent. What if he wasn't successful? In my darkest moments I wondered how I would cope if Steven was found guilty and sentenced to serve time in prison. Folks who were sentenced to prison for crimes they didn't commit weren't supposed to be PLU's (People Like Us). They were supposed to be criminals or individuals who lived on the edge of society. You know—homeless, unemployed, dependant on welfare, drug addicts, etc.—not people like us! How would he deal with that? How would I? Was it possible? I was worried all the time now because I had come to believe that it was possible.

I worried about our marriage. In the beginning Steven and I spoke to one another candidly and frequently about what was happening and how we felt. There really wasn't anything to add to our original sentiments two months later. Though each of us thought of little else, we didn't talk about it very much anymore. It was just there. It was there all the time. It was like the sound of traffic if you lived in the city or the sound of the water if you lived by the ocean. It was the background of our lives. And because we thought of little else, but didn't talk about what was happening very much, we talked less than we did before.

Our conversations were scripted. If I said, "I can't believe Tom never called to see how I was doing or that Jean never came over," Steven would reply, "We've been over this a hundred times. Stop already." If I said, "Have you talked to Trip? Is there anything new?" He would answer, "No. I'll tell you if I hear anything." If I said, "I know you're worried," he would say, "I'm fine. I'm used to stuff like this. I spent a lot of time in court in New York." If I tried to point out that was a bankruptcy court, not a criminal court, and he was there as a consultant or potential investor, he would reply almost verbatim each time, "Really. It doesn't bother me. I'm fine." If I started crying, Steven would invariably say, "Stop already! I can deal with this, but I can't deal with you crying all the time." We had these same snippets of conversation all day long, every day, and nothing happened or changed. It was all so useless.

Steven was growing restless and tired of the limitations he had. It was awkward for him to go out to dinner with friends and order iced tea. He did, but I could tell it made him chafe. On some days he would talk about not doing a random alcohol test just because he didn't want to make a special trip down the hill and into town for that reason. I would always tell him he had to do what was required, had to play the game their way for a while longer. I was all about abiding by the rules—even if I didn't think the rules should have applied to us. It created tension between us. He wanted to get on with our lives. I was worried and afraid to get on with anything.

We made plans to go fishing in Colorado for a weekend in June. We talked about our annual July race at Road America in Wisconsin. We talked like we were going to go, but we both knew otherwise. We told our best friends that our attendance depended on if we were going forward with a jury trial, then we wouldn't attend. They said they couldn't imagine Road America without the Gesse's. I couldn't imagine my current life.

My stomach was constantly churning. I didn't eat as much as I would normally. I no longer enjoyed a glass of wine with dinner. On the bright side, I could fit into clothes that I hadn't worn in two years, and Steven had lost over twenty pounds. I thought I looked haggard. I thought Steven actually looked better than he had in a long time because of the weight loss. I worried about whether to buy clothes for my new, worried weight or for my heavier, happier, pre-incident weight. No one could worry like an Italian.

I found it harder and harder to get out of bed in the morning. It wasn't just harder, I simply didn't want to get up. Steven was waking up at 3:30 or 4:00 in the morning. He would let the dogs out and then give them their frozen beef patties for their breakfast. When they were done eating, they would come back to the bedroom upstairs. Lola, the puppy, would jump on our bed and lie lengthwise along my side. I would roll over and put my arm around her. She would begin to snore softly while I dozed on and off for another hour or two. She was about sixty pounds then, and her length was almost as long as me so we could actually cuddle spoon fashion. I was just reluctant to get up.

Steven and I used to walk two to three miles every morning, but we weren't anymore. Steven would spend the time before I got out of bed pouring over his computer and his files. I would finally get out of bed and get ready for work. The energy for walking or exercising just wasn't there. I needed all of my energy for pretending during the day that nothing was different. Despite the lack of exercise, I continued to lose weight. This wasn't a diet I would recommend to anyone.

Chapter 20

Late May

Steven called me at work a few days later to say that he did have some news. Unfortunately, it wasn't good news. Steven had spoken to Trip earlier in the day. Trip indicated that Foote was set on going forward. Apparently Tom had told Ainsworth that there had been only two or three glasses of wine consumed that evening. That would imply that Ward wasn't drunk and made his accusation more likely to be true. I didn't know what to think. Tom was supposed to be a friend. He was here that night. All we had expected of him was to tell the truth. Whether by accident or intent, he didn't. He should have remembered that he brought one bottle of white wine and we were already drinking a bottle of red. Even if he thought it was some sort of miraculous, never-empty bottle of red, he should have remembered the bottle of white Sin Quo Non and the bottle of 1991 red Silverado Reserve. That would have been at least four bottles. How did he reconcile the facts that he had multiple glasses of red wine, Ward was drinking red wine, I was drinking red wine, while Steven and Ellie drank white wine with two or three glasses of wine in total? How could he say that? All of a sudden, Ward's allegations and lies had more credibility. My hope that this whole thing would go away by the following Thursday, when we had our next scheduled "conference," was decidedly fading after this news.

Tom and Jean used to volunteer at a winery in Santa Barbara. They considered themselves wine aficionados. In the past, Tom could recount exactly what wines had been drunk at any dinner party, complete with appropriately descriptive adjectives. Why had he suddenly developed wine amnesia? How was it possible that at this, perhaps the most critical dinner party we had ever had, he couldn't remember what we drank?

As I sat in my office trying to absorb what he had told me, I fought back tears. I didn't want anyone to see me crying at work. I so wanted this to be over. I knew I shouldn't have expected it to be over, but I had been hoping it would be in the next few weeks. I felt like we had done our penance—for what I wasn't sure—but once your penance was done, the rules were that the punishment should be over. I wasn't sure exactly what the news meant since Steven had given me just a summary on the phone, but I understood it to mean we were going to trial. And that, if you'll excuse the term, was at best a crapshoot. I had business trips planned for the summer. There were things we were going to do. I didn't want to be gone when Steven was dealing with this. I had to be here. What were we going to do?

The news was even worse when I got home.

"I can't believe this shit," were Steven's first words to me when I walked in. "Trip thought that if Tom had collaborated my account of the night's alcohol consumption, Ward's credibility would have been suspect. The charges might have been dropped. "

"Oh my god. Why do you think he didn't? Tom always knows what wines were drunk."

"Now Trip thinks Foote is digging in his heels. He's going to go forward with prosecuting me."

I was having difficulty processing this conversation. Tom was a wine buff, and I found it hard to believe that he didn't remember not only the number of wine bottles opened, but the actual types of wine we served. What was prompting him to tell the investigating detective that only two or three glasses were consumed instead of the six bottles that were actually consumed?

"Does Tom think this is about him? Doesn't he realize what this means? Is he afraid they'll think he drank too much? Who cares what Tom drank? Do you think he really doesn't remember?" I almost shouted.

Ward had lied about so many things, but unless Ainsworth could confirm he was lying about some fact or statement, Ward's credibility remained intact. Ward lied about Steven having a gun. But that was Steven's word against his. Though I could confirm Steven didn't have a chance to procure a gun before leaving, I wasn't "there." Ward lied about coming into the house … he said he stayed outside. That was Ward's word against Steven and me. If Ward had stayed outside, it was more likely that Steven could have procured a gun … but he didn't. Ward lied about the amount of alcohol he consumed, saying he had maybe two or three glasses of wine. That was the one lie that could be exposed by someone else since Tom had been there and knew that Ward had more than that to drink. That was the one small detail that would have exposed Ward as the liar he was. It was so easy. It was so evident. Why in the hell hadn't it happened?

I went into the bathroom to hide the fact that I was crying. Steven said to the closed door, "Are you okay?"

"Fine. I'll be out in a minute."

"Was there anything else?" I asked when I finally emerged.

"Tom apparently told Ainsworth that he found it hard to believe that I would use a gun to threaten Ward." *That's good,* I thought. Then Steven continued, "But he also said he didn't believe Ward would lie."

Holy shit, I thought. What I said was, "I can't believe that."

"That's what Trip said."

Tom had known us for as long as he had lived in his house—seven or eight or nine years. Tom had met Ward for the first time that evening in April at our house. How in the hell could he even have had an opinion about whether or not Ward was capable of lying? Ward boasted about having the spirit to seriously hurt people, perhaps kill them. Lying didn't seem nearly as bad as killing without remorse. But Tom didn't think Ward could lie?

"And," Steven continued, "Tom refused to meet with Trip." That was the final blow. Someone we considered a really good friend had refused to meet with our lawyer to help us resolve this situation. There really wasn't a lot to be said after that last comment. I didn't even bother to respond.

We talked of little else all night. Steven had asked Trip to request changes in the conditions of his bond. He would have liked to have the random liquor checks removed for a number of reasons. One was that our ability to travel, even within Colorado, was severely limited by that requirement. Another was that there was no real evidence that the incident was alcohol related, though both of us did believe that Ward had been drunk. And finally, it was a royal pain in the ass.

Steven also asked Trip to request the elimination of the travel restriction so that we could go to races outside Colorado. We wanted this even though we doubted if we would travel outside Colorado that summer, unless something good happened soon. It would cost too much. Steven speculated that short trips might have the same effect our trip to Italy had, and allow us to relax for a few days. I was worried that, given our preoccupation with current events, we wouldn't be sufficiently focused on the racing and make a fatal and/or costly mistake on the track. I didn't want to trash the race cars, which were in pristine condition at the start of the season. It was strange that, in the past, the thing I liked most about racing was that when you were doing it you couldn't be focused on anything else. Driving required 100 percent of your concentration. You were absolutely not thinking about anything else when you were on the track. But the current "event" was so overwhelming that I was worried that we wouldn't be able to concentrate 100 percent. Steven actually agreed. That was amazing, as we seemed to agree on less and less as the stress of the situation increased.

Trip told Steven that he might have asked for another continuation of the status conference if he hadn't received copies of the police files and the detective's account of Tom's interview.

"Maybe I should ask Jean to ask Tom to speak to Trip," I suggested. "Maybe if he knows how important it is to us, he'll understand and do it. Maybe they just don't know."

"We'll ask Trip tomorrow," Steven answered.

"Why?" I asked. When Steven looked puzzled, I added, "Why do you think Tom isn't helping us? We're not asking him to lie. Just to talk to Trip and tell him the truth. Why doesn't he understand that Ward has to be lying, because if he's not, then you are?"

"I don't know," Steven said. "I've thought about that a lot. He knows us, he knows me, he doesn't really know Ward. All I could think of is that

Ward and Tom are both ex-military, so maybe Tom has a hard time finding fault with him. I really don't know. I am disappointed though, and hurt, too, though I don't like admitting that.

"But there isn't anything we can do about it. So don't worry about it. Let's focus on what we can do," he said.

I refrained from asking him exactly what should we be doing. Instead I said, "Well, we can't ask him since Trip said not to talk to either Tom or Jean about this. He thought someone could interpret it as trying to influence them."

The decision to proceed to trial was a big one. Steven had not done anything wrong, but the serious financial and emotional tolls associated with proceeding were obvious. Steven still believed we could sue Ward in a civil court for damages after a trial where Steven was found not guilty. Steven thought that if we accepted a plea bargain to a lesser offense, then our chances for a civil trial were less. Nothing in our prior experience had prepared us for what was happening right now. There was no roadmap. There weren't even any good street signs.

Chapter 21

May 28

The conference hearing the following Thursday was held in the same room at the jail where Steven was released on bail. The hearing wasn't formal like any trial you might have seen on TV. The judge was announced, we all stood, and then were instructed to sit. Steven wasn't supposed to answer any questions directly. When asked if he was present, Trip answered by saying he was representing the defendant—i.e. my husband. The judge read the case number and the charges, then reviewed the motions Trip had filed. They were all denied in short order and Foote, Trip, and the judge agreed on a date for the hearing at which Steven would plead not guilty, or prior to which he would enter into a plea bargain with the prosecutor.

The date that was agreed upon was July 10, 2009—the date of our thirty-eighth wedding anniversary. At the very least, I would probably always remember that anniversary and what we did on that date.

The court denied an extension of the conference hearing. Part of the reason for the extension request was the hope that the prosecution would lose momentum or focus. And in our case we were hoping that if they reviewed the facts (or the lack thereof), they would drop the charges. The court also denied a reduction in the random alcohol testing. I was amazed that the DA opposed every one of Trip's motions. Foote said there was a lot of alcohol involved ... but Ainsworth had said there wasn't. Steven was never given a breathalyzer test or a blood test. I thought the focus on alcohol was probably my fault. I had repeatedly told Officer Witte how much wine had been consumed that evening. But Tom had told

Ainsworth that only a moderate amount of wine had been consumed. It was funny that the only thing I had said that Ainsworth seemed to believe was that a lot of wine had been consumed. But he apparently chose to believe that only Steven had been doing the consuming, not Ward.

Foote had told Trip ahead of time that he was going to oppose all of Trip's motions, so his opposition wasn't a surprise to any of us. What was a surprise was the apparent lack of information Foote had. It appeared that he had not yet reviewed the file or the various accounts of the incident. Foote didn't even know that the supposed incident occurred on Ellie and Lee's porch. He thought it had occurred on our porch. We didn't even have a porch.

To the assistant DA, Foote, and, perhaps to a lesser extent, the judge, we were a docket number. We were not Steve (and Michelle) Gesse, a couple in their mid-sixties. We were not successful business people. We weren't individuals. We were not nice people. We weren't even not nice people—we were a docket number, we were guilty, we were treated as being guilty, and the docket number had to be processed.

In reality, the DA had no horse in this race, or any race in which he is involved. He wasn't accountable for how he was spending the taxpayer's money. He wasn't looking at a cost/benefit analysis of a plea bargain versus fighting to be acquitted of all charges. Hell, his salary was going to be the same regardless of whether or not we went to trial and regardless of the outcome. If he pursued a ridiculous case, no one was going to hold him accountable. His retirement funds weren't going to be affected. He had absolutely no incentive to review the facts in the case and determine that it bordered on the ridiculous and should not be pursued. What difference did it make to him if he ruined the reputation of an innocent man? What difference did it make to him if our life was destroyed temporarily—or perhaps for the remainder of our lives?

If the DA was worried about anything at all, it was simply keeping the (supposed) victims satisfied with the progress and prosecution. It is more likely that a prosecutor will try to get the accused to "cop a plea." If that fails his/her philosophy is simple. "Look, if your case is so strong, have the jury decide." The DA doesn't have to consider the financial or emotional toll on the accused. He/she just wants to make sure they themselves don't look bad to the world of potential victims out there. The cards are stacked against anyone accused of a crime. Once you are accused, they stop looking for another perpetrator (if that is a possibility) and they assume you are guilty.

We met with Trip in the lobby after the conference. Steven began that conversation as he had begun many. "Let's talk about civil action." This was absurd to me. The issue wasn't civil action, the issue was criminal charges. I had, however, come to realize that this was what was keeping Steven going—the idea that he would be acquitted and able to pursue legal action against his accuser. I didn't think he really cared about getting any of our costs reimbursed. He just wanted Ward to feel some pressure, some anxiety—to have a glimpse of what we were dealing with daily. Steven wanted Ward to be exposed as a liar. Trip cautioned against even thinking about civil actions at this point. He looked directly at Steven and said, "I am fighting for your life right now." Nothing more, nothing less, just our lives. This phrase stayed with me all day, all night, and into the next day—and for weeks and months to come. I kept thinking Trip is "fighting for (our) lives." And I was a wreck!

Before we left, I asked Trip, "Do you think I should talk to Jean? Should I ask her to talk to Tom and ask him to meet with you? How important is it that you talk to him?"

Trip thought for a moment before responding. "It wouldn't hurt. She might be able to talk him into meeting with me. And I would like to talk to him. Not just to try to get his version of the evening, but to see what kind of witness he will be on the stand. See if we can count on him or if we need to worry. Try it. It won't hurt to have you say something—but not you, Steve."

All the rest of that day and the next I was either crying or on the verge of tears. I was as raw and exposed and emotional as I was at the start of this adventure. My stomach was in knots, and I couldn't sleep that evening. We were fighting for our lives. That was the short and accurate version of what was going on. And the only person fighting for us right now was Trip. God, I hoped he was really good.

We ran into Tom that evening. He asked casually how we were doing, and smiled like everything between us was good. All the while I was thinking that because he failed to confirm our account of how much Ward drank, Steven was going to be prosecuted for a felony. "What a two-faced SOB," was all I said when we drove away. Steven said nothing.

I saw Jean the next morning as I drove by her house on the way out of our driveway. She was watering plants with her garden hose. She was recovering from some fairly serious surgery, so I stopped the car and asked how she was doing.

With a pained look of concern, Jean said, "I'm doing pretty good. How are you doing with all of this?"

"It's serious, Jean," I said. "Steven did not do anything that night. He didn't have a gun. He didn't commit a crime. But it is very serious. Jean, can you please ask Tom to reconsider speaking to our lawyer. We really need for him to do this." I surprised myself by sounding so calm.

"Tom doesn't want to get in the middle of this. He is actually thinking about getting a lawyer. If he talks to your lawyer, then he feels like he will have to talk to Lee and Ellie's lawyer."

I was dumbfounded. Why in the hell did Tom need a lawyer? He was already involved. Lee and Ellie's lawyer for this incident was the Boulder County assistant DA. Tom had already spoken to him.

"Tom did speak to Ellie and Lee, Jean. And he has spoken to the detectives prosecuting Steven. This is really serious. Do you realize that Steven has been accused of a felony? We really need Tom to talk to our lawyer. Trip is very professional. He won't ask Tom to do or say anything other than just talk to him about the truth. He won't ask Tom to do anything illegal or immoral. He just needs to talk to him." By the time I was near the end of this plea, my voice was cracking and I didn't sound either calm or assured.

"I know how you feel," Jean assured me. This was blatantly absurd. How could anyone know how I felt?

"I'll speak to Tom."

"Thanks. We would really appreciate that," I said, and drove away shaking, with tears in my eyes and muttering about "that son-of-a-bitch." I realized I was talking about someone who a mere two months ago I had considered a friend—the only person I had called in desperation after Steven had been taken away.

Chapter 22

Musings

Things were bad. I would often find myself listening to the words of country and western songs and finding truth and wisdom in them. That was scary even to me.

My mind moved between two different issues—neither pleasant. Most of my thoughts concerned Steven's legal issues. I spent a lot of time trying to figure out how this could be happening to us. The other issue, though not as potentially damaging to us as the felony charge, was my disappointment in Jean and Tom.

When I reflected on the previous conversations with Jean and Tom, I realized that not once had either of them said anything to the effect that "We know Steven is innocent. We have known the two of you too long to believe that he would have done anything like that." Was it possible that they doubted his innocence? These were neighbors who we got together with once or twice a week when all of us where in town. It was unbelievable to me that they were not solidly in our camp at this point. I knew I wouldn't have acted that way if the roles had been reversed.

It was around this time that I noticed I seemed to panic whenever Steven was out running errands and I hadn't spoken to him in a few hours. I felt like I had let something terrible happen to him before and worried that something even worse could be happening to him without my knowledge.

I spent a lot of time thinking about what could have been done to prevent this position. If Ward had waited ten more minutes to come back to our house, we would have been in the bathtub and never answered the door. If I had asked him why he wanted to see Steven before letting him in, this may not have happened. If, if, if …

Sometimes I would stand at the stove cooking, look outside and marvel at the fact that everything looked the same. I really liked where we lived, but wondered if we would decide to move. I looked at all my familiar surroundings with new appreciation, wondering how they could still be the same when the entire world had changed for us. I wondered if I would ever be happy again.

I still didn't feel safe—even now two months after the incident. We continued to lock our cars and our front door. We didn't go for walks that involved walking down the driveway we shared with Lee and Ellie and Tom and Jean. Instead we put the dogs in the car, drove up the mountain, parked and then walked them. I still worried about Ward doing physical harm to us. I wanted a restraining order so that I would know if he was in Boulder. I didn't want him anywhere near either of us. Trip said to wait until this was over before pursuing anything like that. I think it was his way of telling me we wouldn't ever be able to do that.

We had almost six weeks before the next court date and I didn't know how I was going to survive that long. I didn't know if my decision not to talk to any of my friends about this was correct. Sometimes I felt a strong desire to talk to someone other than Steven about what was going on and about how I felt. I thought that perhaps during the summer I would talk to one of my friends from out of town when they visited. Talking to someone who didn't live in Colorado didn't seem to be a serious violation of Trip's admonition not to talk to anyone about what was happening. At my suggestion, Steven had confided in his brother. They spoke regularly anyway, and I thought Steven needed someone besides me to talk to about what was happening. Since Gregg, Steven's brother, lived in Tennessee, that was consistent with my conclusion that it would be acceptable if we limited our conversations to one individual who didn't live in the state. I was rationalizing, but I felt we had to do whatever we needed to do to get through the next few months.

Chapter 23

June 10

We were one month away from our next court appearance and nothing was happening. We had, with difficulty, refrained from calling Trip under the apparently correct assumption that he would let us know if he had anything new to report. We were also being careful to avoid incurring costs that were not essential, so avoided using his time unless there was a reason. On TV shows, everything got resolved in less than an hour. In real life, a lot of time was spent waiting for the next move. Criminal justice was more like chess than like TV.

I received an e-mail from Jean a few days after our accidental meeting, saying that Tom would meet with Trip when next asked. I was grateful for that.

Steven still thought I should "cut Jean some slack" (to use his words). He thought I would benefit from "the friendship." He didn't think she had really done anything. I thought he was naive. I had known for a long time that words said can't be taken back. If a loved one says something hurtful to you, you can forgive them, but you never really forget what they said. Because of this, in some small, perhaps immeasurable way, your relationship would be changed. The same can be said about what wasn't said. Jean never said that she knew that Steven wasn't guilty of anything; she never said that she did not believe he had a gun. That's what she needed to say to me and to Steven. And because she didn't say that, I knew our relationship would never again be the same.

We did get an e-mail from Trip confirming that he was still waiting for copies of the investigator's report, as well as copies of the dispatch tape and other documents he had requested under discovery. He reviewed what his "plan" was, and indicated that the first step was to get copies of the requested documents. A month had passed since our last court appearance and nothing seemed to have happened. It was no longer surprising to me that two months after the incident, no one in the "judicial system" had really weighed the facts of the case.

I had come to realize that the criminal justice system (except perhaps for really high visibility crimes) was a "flow business." The DA and everyone involved with prosecution had a lot of cases in the queue at any one time; they were used to dealing with guilty individuals; they were used to dealing with repeat offenders; and they had a prescribed way to handle cases that reduced the risk to them. The risk to them didn't come from prosecuting the innocent, but instead from not placing sufficient constraints on the guilty. So they routinely objected to any motions that made the bail period less onerous; they proceeded assuming guilt. They also assumed that all cases would be resolved through a plea bargain agreement. This allowed them to handle a large number of cases at one time. Maybe focusing was something they did right before a trial in those rare cases that actually did go to trial. I didn't know when they actually looked at the particulars of a case, but knew that at this point in our saga, no one had.

There was a new "normal" now. We acted somewhat normal though both of us were preoccupied and short tempered. We did go out to eat occasionally now. Steven would drink a couple of non-alcoholic beers while I would have one glass of wine with dinner. It was interesting that my tolerance for wine had decreased. It was nothing to be proud of, but I used to be able to drink three or four glasses of wine over the course of a long evening. Now if I had two glasses of wine, I felt the effect of the alcohol and then didn't sleep well.

We had planned some weekend fishing trips in Colorado. Steven met with his substance abuse counselor and discussed how to handle the alcohol testing if we were gone for a few days. We no longer found this bizarre. It was part of the new normal.

The feeling of normalcy (or at least our new normal) was strangely comfortable. When something as innocuous as an e-mail from our lawyer happened, my body physically reacted to the reminder that all was not normal and we were still in the midst of the fight for our lives. I suppose my physical reaction could have been due to either stress or fear or both. My stomach would tighten, my teeth would clench, and I would feel my heartbeat speed up. I would get agitated and focused on the incident and our current situation. I couldn't seem to get anything done when this would happen. If we were home, Steven and I would stop talking. I don't think we ever made a conscious decision not to speak to one another; it was more like we were thinking about the situation, what had happened and what might happen. Because of this preoccupation, we couldn't actually think of anything to say to one another.

We thought the pace of activity might accelerate as we got closer to our hearing date. Heaven knows it could hardly slow down.

Chapter 24

June 26

We were two weeks away from our next criminal hearing and three weeks away from the next protection order hearing. The only recent communication we had from Trip was a copy of the DA's investigator's conversation with Ward. It was full of lies. There was the obvious lie that Steven had a gun. Ward, the Navy Seal, couldn't describe the gun. Of course he couldn't … there was none. But he himself said during the interview that he was "knowledgeable" about firearms. Yet he couldn't describe the gun. He had already described the gun as a "flintlock," "like a flintlock," a gun with a long "silver barrel," and "black." The two guns the police confiscated both had fourteen-inch barrels and scopes on them and weighed three to five pounds or more. Neither could have been concealed easily.

In his interview, Ward said he spoke calmly to me in the entranceway, but didn't threaten me or come upstairs. He said he asked me to have Steven come down and go with him to apologize to his mom. He said Steven must have heard us talking because he walked downstairs with his winter jacket on and walked behind Ward to his folk's house. The reality was that he asked me if he could talk to Steven and when I said yes, followed me upstairs. The reality was that he threatened Steven as Steven stood at the kitchen sink with a towel in his hands. The reality was that Steven followed him downstairs with slippers and no coat on, grabbed a jacket, put on boots and walked outside with Ward behind him. That contrasts with Steven's version of events, which was that Ward pushed him up the hill all the way to Ellie and Lee's house, even when Steven suggested putting off the meeting until the next day.

Ward said he arrived at 4:00 p.m., Ellie arrived at 4:45 and they left at 5:30. My cell phone records showed that Ward called his mom at 5:09—that's a fact. She probably arrived around 5:30, and they didn't leave until 6:30 p.m. He said he came back to our house ten minutes after leaving. But between the time Ward left and returned again, Steven let the dog out, folded a load of clothes, and washed all the knives, glasses, and pots and pans that weren't going into the dishwashers. I started the tub and put all the food away, cleaned up the counters, loaded two dishwashers, dried the dishes Steven had washed, and tidied everything up. We did this without any hurry, talking about the evening as we cleaned up. You don't get all that done in ten minutes. All those chores had to take at least forty-five to sixty minutes, forty-five minutes to an hour between when Ward left and returned.

Ward said he didn't remember what Steven said when Steven threatened him. Steven admits he "threatened" Ward. Would you believe that a Navy Seal couldn't remember what someone said to them as a threat? I thought these guys were supposed to be good under stress. I certainly remembered details of that evening, and suspected that Ward remembered the real details. You just didn't forget the details of an evening like that one—unless perhaps you were drunk. Both of us certainly remembered.

The more I read, the more upset I got. Steven said he wasn't going to read the e-mail because he didn't want to get upset. But he did read it and every time he read a new paragraph, he would come out of the office upset and grumbling. He was once again focused on how we could recoup our expenses and have legal recourse to Ellie and Lee and Ward. The possibility of subsequent legal action was keeping him on track—I thought. I'm sure recouping our expenses was one factor. I was also sure that revenge or whatever you wanted to call it was another factor.

I suspected Lee and Ellie were talking about us and the supposed incident to other folks. The fellow who had washed our windows for the last seventeen years used to live in Jean and Tom's house. He and his wife purchased the house from Lee and Ellie. I had left him two messages asking if he could wash our windows, and hadn't received a return phone call in over a month. That behavior was unusual. I assumed that for some reason, he didn't want to wash our windows. I assumed that was because of something that Lee and Ellie had told him. Maybe after washing our windows two or three times a year for the last seventeen years, he thought we were going to get a gun and threaten him if his bill was too high or if we found streaks. I should have told him that we had no guns on the premises, so it was probably safe to wash our windows.

We had followed all of Trip's advice. Steven was being a well-behaved accused felon—doing his breath tests more frequently than required (he said he paid for the week, so why not?), meeting with his counselor, and not talking to anyone (with the exception of his brother). I wasn't talking to anyone. Of course we did talk to one another, but since we were married that was apparently okay. In the process, I began to believe that we were slowly losing our marbles. The stress on us and our marriage was real, but most of the time I had begun to think we would survive. I believed that if a marriage had been challenged beforehand, there would be little chance of it surviving an ordeal like this.

Trip was still waiting for copies of the police reports, interviews, 911 call, etc. He hadn't received any of those documents more than two months after the incident, after requesting them for the first time the day after the incident. Think about that. Have you ever seen an episode of *Law and Order* where the dates indicated that two and a half months after the incident the defense attorney still hadn't seen copies of the reports and the DA hadn't read them yet? In fact, have you ever seen an episode where an innocent person's life was disrupted for months on end because of a false accusation? When I thought about it, I wondered why the idea of blind justice ever gave anyone comfort.

I liked to read fiction when I was traveling. It seemed now that every book I selected had an innocent person being charged with a crime. One book, *Shadow of Power* by Steve Martini, had some quotes that stayed with me because they rang so true. "But for certain aspects of terminal cancer, there is nothing I can think of in life that will destroy a person faster than the perils of dealing with the American judicial system." The book was good. The quote was so insightful that I wondered how the author knew this. I prayed that we would not be destroyed by the system and the incident. I knew we would be changed (and despite Steven's urge to sue someone, I have no doubt that we would be poorer), but I hoped that we would not be destroyed. They say that what doesn't destroy you makes you stronger. I hoped this was true.

On June 26, almost three months after the incident and barely two weeks before our court date, Trip received copies of the documents he had requested. We heard from him that he was going to review them looking for inconsistencies, and that we should plan on getting together the following week.

Chapter 25

June 29

On a morning a few days later, Steven stormed out of the house angry. In the almost thirty-eight years we had been married, I actually didn't remember him leaving the house angry ever before. His words as he shut the door scared me because they verbalized my greatest fear. "If you keep snapping at me, you'll see, you'll be alone a lot." I am sure he didn't realize that this was exactly what my greatest fear was at that time—that I would be alone. Steven wasn't being mean, he was just tired of my constant bitchiness. Even I realized I had turned into a shrew.

The curious thing was that two days later, when I went to record the event in my journal, I couldn't remember what he had said, what I had said in response, or even what we had been talking about. The topic and the exchange were not significant—it was just the breaking point for civility between us.

I was sixty years old. We had no children. Both of my parents were dead. I had no siblings. I had no family. Because of what Trip had said, I hadn't talked to anyone about what was happening. Could I have snapped both verbally and perhaps emotionally? Certainly, I had no doubt that I did.

Steven had assured me that he wasn't going to jail. The DA had already offered him a misdemeanor plea bargain, which he had refused. Trip had pointed out numerous times that juries could be unpredictable. What would I do if Steven did get sent to jail? Or if the stress of the whole situation was too much on him or our marriage? I would find myself alone for a while, or forever. That was absolutely my greatest fear.

I was getting tired of pretending that everything was fine when I was away from home. I left the house minutes after Steven and went to my scheduled haircut (and, yes, color) appointment. I sat in the parking lot crying and trying to get myself together before going into the salon. Then I pretended my allergies were bothering me. (What allergies?) I didn't know how much longer I could carry on this charade.

When we both returned home that evening, Steven said that I had to learn how to deal with the stress. He was right, but I thought he needed to take his own advice and stop pretending he was fine. If the only thing I did was snap at him, perhaps he should have considered the reason and given me a pass. I wanted to say that I wasn't the one who got us into this mess. But at least for a while that night, I learned to be quiet.

The next two days were busy. We met with Trip on both days. Just the anticipation of meeting with Trip upped the stress level and made the reality of the felony charges real to both of us. The stress continued for days after the actual meeting. I was sure that had been a contributing factor to our blowups.

Tom met with Trip and Phil, the private investigator ("PI") hired by Trip on our behalf, before our meetings for over an hour. The private investigator's presence was necessary since Trip couldn't testify to what Tom said, but the PI could. Phil was formerly with the sheriff's department, and in fact used to be Ainsworth's boss. After their interview, both Trip and Phil drove up to our house. They wanted to see the layout of the house and go over once again the series of events of that evening.

Tom apparently collaborated much of what we had said. He wasn't clear on how many bottles of wine were consumed. Tom indicated that he wouldn't have driven home and would not have gotten into a car with either Steven or Ward. Tom acknowledged that he probably had a bit much to drink and thought both Steven and Ward also had. Tom collaborated what the 911 call recorded and provided additional information. Ellie had called Tom while still on the line to 911. Because Tom had arrived while the 911 call was on-going he could tell Trip what he had heard and what was going on in their house during the call. Tom's recollection of Ward's comments at the house contradicted much of Ward's most recent account of events to the DA's investigator.

Much of the 911 call borders on the absurd. On the recording, Ellie was saying "he" (Steven) could still be out there with a gun" when she suddenly says, "We have to call Tom" and hands the phone to Lee. I assume at this point she or Ward called Tom using a cell phone since the 911 connection was not severed. These were Tom's good friends? They thought there was someone out there with a gun so they called Tom and asked him to walk from his house to theirs through the dark night? Was Tom supposed to draw the fire? These folks really were off the proverbial wall!

Tom told Trip that in all the years he had known us, he has never known Steven to even raise his voice; never known him to get angry; never known him to mishandle a gun or bring one out after a drink. Tom acknowledged having met Ward for the first time at our house that night. Perhaps because Tom was retired military, he could not acknowledge to Trip that Ward was lying—even when Trip pointed out that if Ward wasn't lying, then Steven must be.

Trip apparently asked Tom, "As a former officer, how do you think the navy would view Ward's possible promotion to admiral if they found out he had threatened Steven?"

According to Trip, it was like the proverbial light went on as Tom slowly replied, "His career would be over. He'd never get promoted. He'd never know why, but he'd just never get promoted again."

That's when Trip told Tom, "Steven did threaten Ward that night. On the porch—he told him that if he ever threatened him or came onto his property again, he would ruin his career. He would let the navy know exactly what Ward had done and ruin his career, as well as sue him personally."

According to Trip, Tom looked stricken when Trip summarized our theory of what prompted Ward to make the accusations he did. Steven's threat to his career was what we had come to believe prompted Ward to accuse Steven of threatening him with a gun. It was reasonable. Steven did threaten Ward with something worse than physical harm. He threatened him with the destruction of his career. By accusing Steven of threatening him with a gun, Ward directed the "investigation" toward Steven and assured himself that neither his parents nor his superiors would ever know that he, Ward, was the one who had entered our house and threatened

Steven with physical harm. He deflected the potential spotlight for wrong-doing from himself to my husband. Brilliant actually—wrong, but brilliant.

We spent about an hour and a half with Trip and Phil going over details of the evening. Trip thought Steven's crude comments to Ellie would make the jury mad. Those comments weren't a crime, but they made Steven less sympathetic.

Trip and Phil were in our court. By that, I don't mean they would be on our side in the physical court (which they would), but that they believed in Steven's innocence. As we talked, they both expressed astonishment that Ainsworth didn't or couldn't see that Steven was innocent. The whole chain of events as described by Ward didn't make any sense to either of them. Ward's account kept changing. We speculated that perhaps like Tom, Ainsworth had trouble thinking that someone with a military grade of captain would lie. They assured us that it wasn't personal—though I couldn't really think of anything more personal than what was happening to us.

Over lunch the following day, Trip reviewed the inconsistencies in Ward's testimony. He also went over his "plan." The plan was to prepare for trial. It was July 1, 2009, and I realized that this meant our ordeal wouldn't be over until the end of the year or maybe early next year. This thought just seemed to drain all of my remaining energy. We were nowhere near done.

Here's what was going to happen in the legal system:

We would go to court in ten days, and Trip would plead not guilty on behalf of Steven.

The court would set a date for our motions hearing. Trip will have a motion requesting that certain things be suppressed (or whatever the legal word was). He might have some other motions, but I couldn't focus on more than that.

The court would set a date for the trial. The requirement for a "speedy trial" meant the trial date had to be within six months of the date the plea was filed. Trip already had another trial scheduled for mid-November (we were apparently not his only case) and he needed a few weeks at minimum to prepare after that for our trial. So we were probably going to trial in December.

Christmas has always been my absolute favorite holiday. We put up two or three live trees, entertain a lot, have parties, and just generally celebrate. This incident had ruined Easter, my birthday, and our anniversary. Why should I have expected it to leave Thanksgiving and Christmas untouched?

In the meantime, "our" strategy was to try to put pressure on Ward. Phil was going to try to interview him. We expected he would decline, but at least it would put him on notice that we were preparing for a trial. We had speculated that a trial of any sort would not be good for Ward's military career. We were hoping that this realization would make him reluctant to proceed. It was interesting that the 911 call came from Ellie, not Ward. Ellie gave the phone to Lee after some period of time. And Lee finally gave the phone to Ward. My theory was that Ward wasn't the one who wanted to get the sheriff's department involved. I suspected that once he lied to his folks about Steven having a gun that they called 911 without his full buy-in. At that point there would have been no way for him to stop them or the process without admitting that he had lied. This was just my theory and of course it couldn't be substantiated, but I suspected Ward hadn't intended for his first lie to balloon into a potential trial involving him.

We were going to fight the protection orders requested by Lee and Ellie. There were no grounds for these, as neither of them was threatened by Steven—even in Ward's account.

Trip was going to continue looking for inconsistencies in Ward's various accounts of the incident. Already there was the inconsistency in the description of the supposed gun, which I have already described. There was also the changing distance. Ward initially reported that Steven was three to five feet from him, but in subsequent accounts Steven was at least ten feet away. Ward also said that Steven's arm was fully extended. If that was the case, and if Steven was three to five feet away from Ward, that would have put the barrel of the gun behind Ward's ear. It also made Steven an easy target for a Navy Seal to disarm. Ward initially acknowledged threatening Steven. Then he changed his story to say he politely asked me to have Steven go with him to his folk's house to apologize. There were more inconsistencies and more lies. We were hoping that there would be even more as Ward had the chance to embellish his tale even more. Ward wanted a lawyer before talking to Ainsworth. What did that tell you? Does an innocent man threatened by someone think they need a lawyer? But then an innocent man threatened by someone didn't change his story.

Trip wasn't going to spend any more time trying to convince Ainsworth that Steven was innocent or that the case didn't make any sense. Though initially he thought there was a good chance of that strategy working, it hadn't gone anywhere and might backfire on us if he continued.

The reality was that, in all likelihood, Foote still hadn't read the file. He probably wouldn't read the file until shortly before the trial date. Think about that. The DA wasn't even going to review the facts to decide if the case had merit or if he really wanted to pursue prosecution for another five or six months. The incident had happened three months earlier. An innocent person, my husband, could end up being treated like a guilty person for nine months and possibly longer before anyone on the prosecution side of the American judicial system even looked at the facts. Trip said the plea bargain offer would probably come a week or so before the trial date. Our legal system was a criminal attorney's job security. Obviously we had to prepare for trial and would incur tremendous costs doing that.

• • •

Steven was very conscientious about his random breath tests. The facility he was using was conveniently located near my office. The allocated time for the random breath tests there was between 8:00 and 10:00 a.m. Most mornings that wasn't an issue. But on Sundays or holidays, Steven would go in later in the day and sometimes in the afternoon. It was a half hour trip into town from our house, so he tended to combine his visit to the facility with other errands. His counselor told him that he was fine as long as he went in on the same day his color was called. On Sundays (and only on Sundays) when he went in after 10:00 a.m, the person recording the results "scolded" him and said he was going to have to notify his counselor that he wasn't meeting the conditions of his bail. Steven didn't think that was an issue since his counselor had approved the anytime on Sunday rule. Ironically, Steven was actually paying for the drug and alcohol testing.

When Steven went for his breathalyzer test a few days before the court hearing, he was told that he could no longer use that facility because he had violated their terms. This was bizarre. His counselor had said not to worry about what time he did the test, but the facility was banning him from using their resources.

His counselor suggested another facility and switched Steven from four tests a week to three. We learned that each facility had its own set of rules. The new facility was closed from 11:00 a.m. to 1:00 p.m. and after 9:00 p.m. Steven had to pay each time he went, instead of weekly. And in this particular facility, the three tests a week were actually twelve per month. Theoretically he could be called twelve times in the last twelve days of any month. (I doubted if the tests would all come at the beginning of the month since that would leave you free to have a drink later in the month.)

I didn't like this facility. It was busier than the other one and there seemed to be even fewer PLU's in evidence. The facility included a halfway house and I didn't even like waiting in the car for Steven. His counselor suggested he look for another facility. This made me wonder exactly how many facilities like this there were in Boulder and how many people did they employ? Drug and alcohol monitoring must be a much bigger business than I ever realized.

Each facility collected some very privileged information. They had personal information including address, phone number, birthday, social security number, and fingerprints. They also had Steven's DNA collected from urine specimens. We had no right to ask about their privacy policies and precautions to secure this information since Steven was now an accused felon, so we felt violated and at risk.

Steven was bitter. That shouldn't be a surprise to anyone. Steven wanted revenge on Ward, Ellie, and Lee. He didn't want any type of physical revenge; he wanted to recoup some of our legal expenses; he wanted his reputation reinstated; he wanted them to deal with the legal system as defendants in a civil case; he wanted them to hurt as badly both financially and emotionally as we were; he wanted to see Ward's promotion thwarted by his actions. My husband had never been a bitter person. Maybe he hadn't had a lot of reason to be bitter. But I was worried that this bitterness would change him. It was a real understatement to say that this experience would change both of us.

Chapter 26

July 9

A lot seemed to have happened during the nine days before our next court hearing. A lot had happened but nothing had changed.

Tom actually called us up. This was the first time since the incident that he had done that. His cover story was that he saw Steven towing one of our cars up the driveway and wondered what had happened. (The fuel pump went out right in front of our driveway.) I didn't know if he was trying to make nice, but I answered his questions succinctly. I also told him that we were still under "orders from our lawyer" not to socialize with him or Jean to avoid the appearance of trying to influence witnesses. I had the distinct impression that since his conversation with Trip, he realized that: a) Steven was innocent and unjustly charged; and b) his waffling had enabled the current situation. I didn't tell him that the reason we were probably going to trial was because of his original conversation with Ainsworth and because of his reluctance to believe that a navy captain would lie. Let him read about it here.

If I were a skeptical person, I would suspect that one of our mutual friends who had been invited to our house for the Fourth of July had called to see what Jean was bringing to dinner. That would have alerted them to the fact that we were having a party on the fourth and they weren't included. Actually it was a very nice party and I think everyone enjoyed themselves. We now advise everyone that when they leave, we will absolutely not answer the door if they show up a second time! You can't be too careful.

We had noticed a car with California plates in Ellie and Lee's driveway the last few days. The possibility that Ward was visiting and was once again in close proximity to us was extremely disturbing and scary. When I told Trip about it, he once again advised me not to worry (*Easy for him to say*, I thought). But he also suggested that might be an opportunity for Phil, "our PI," to confront Ward directly.

Phil and his assistant drove up to Ellie and Lee's house on the Fourth of July to try to interview Ward. Ellie told them that he was in California. (So whose California car was parked in their driveway the prior week?) Phil and his assistant stopped to see us before leaving. Steven thought Phil wanted to see what his assistant thought of Steven—kind of like getting a second opinion. I thought Phil was being honest when he said he wanted a second witness to any conversation he might have had with Ward. Steven thought our "team" (Trip, Phil, etc.) all felt better when professionals they trusted agreed with their conclusion that the charges were ridiculous (or to quote Harry Potter "RID-DIK-U-LUS") and that Steven was not guilty.

Trip forwarded copies of Phil's interview with one of the officers who arrived at Ellie and Lee's house after the 911 call, as well as copies of Tom's interview. As usual these had the effect of getting me (us?) riled up. Ward continued to insist that the gun he saw was a flintlock. Ward had seen many of our guns including the Thompson Contender at our house years before. And he knew from Steven's comments when he (Ward) first arrived on the night of the incident that the Thompson was in the downstairs family room. But he insisted during all of his interviews that the gun was a flintlock. Yet by the end of the same evening Ainsworth was saying that the Thompson Contender fit the description of the gun Ward described.

The officer also said Ward smelled of wine and spoke slowly. The report ended by saying that the officer was "surprised that Captain Ward didn't take the weapon away from Mr. Gesse and wrap it around his neck like a pretzel." You know, that's what I had wondered a number of times. If this hot-shit Navy Seal captain was being threatened, why didn't he just use some of his skills to disarm Steven and subdue him? No offense to my husband, but if you saw the two of them and had to decide where to place a bet about the outcome of a fight, even I would have put my money on Ward.

I had a short two-day business trip scheduled in New York. My Aussie friend and her husband were flying to Colorado from New York around the same time. We were both able to change our return flights so we would be together on the flight back to Colorado. That was great. For the first time since this whole thing happened, I actually talked to someone about what was happening. (Don't tell Trip!) It somehow seemed to make me feel lighter. We even laughed about some of my experiences, like sitting in the waiting room of the jail waiting for Steven to be "processed." We laughed about Steven coming out of booking with the fellow to whom he had offered a ride. As Glenda said, "That's Steven."

Glenda said that if it was her, she would want to run away or at least move away. I told her we had nowhere to run and no resources with which to have a life anywhere else. I had absolutely no intention of letting anyone force me out of my house or change my life. Neither of us had done anything to be ashamed of. I genuinely liked where we lived and liked our house. I confessed that having Lee and Ellie move would be satisfying, but I doubted they could do that. I didn't think their home or the adjacent building with two rental units could pass inspections in a sale. No one was going to set my agenda. They might be trying to ruin our lives, but damn it, I was going to try my hardest to prevent that. And yes, in case you are wondering, I wouldn't mind them suffering the same emotional and financial stress that we were. That would be justice, not what was happening right now. But that wasn't my current agenda. My current agenda was to get the legal system to review the facts and confirm that they did not support the charges. I was trying to be patient.

We met with Trip the day before the hearing to discuss some options. We all agreed that we were turning down the DA's plea bargain. This apparently surprised Foote when Trip had spoken to him earlier that day. Trip thought that the search warrant could be suppressed, as the gun that was specified in the search warrant was never detailed by Ward prior to the search warrant. Trip clearly presented both sides of the argument for suppressing the warrant. One advantage of suppressing the warrant would be that the gun could not be discussed or admitted into evidence. On the other hand, not suppressing the warrant meant the gun would be entered into evidence at the trial. The gun was so large and heavy and had such a long barrel that we didn't think any reasonable person could view it and agree that it could be easily hidden under a short coat. We decided to allow the gun to be entered into evidence.

Ward was adamant in his early versions of the incident that the gun was a flintlock. The gun that would be entered as evidence was not a flintlock. You had to wonder why he focused on a flintlock, an almost archaic type of gun. The only connection I could make was that the Navy Seal insignia includes a flintlock. The gun that would be entered into evidence also has a cumbersome scope on it. Ward never mentioned the gun having a scope.

The police theory was that Steven had the strap of the gun under his jacket since he could not have concealed the weapon in his pants (which were belted) at his then two hundred and thirty pound weight. But that theory is flawed because if he had a gun with the sling on his shoulder under his carhart jacket, there was no way he could have drawn the gun without taking his jacket off.

The inconsistencies that should have been apparent upon viewing the gun seemed to be to our advantage. Trip warned of a possible counter argument. An expert brought in by the prosecution could argue that Ward had "weapon focus"—meaning that as a victim he saw nothing except the barrel. It didn't seem reasonable to me that an experienced Navy Seal would react like an untrained individual like me, or possibly you.

Phil did speak to Ward on the phone. Ward was being careful to reiterate his most recent version of events. When Phil said something about the trial, Ward commented, "It's not me bringing the charges, it's the government." Phil thought Ward sounded reluctant or hesitant about the whole bloody mess (my words, not his). This could have been the situation, but there would be no case without Ward's testimony.

The next day was the hearing. We would plead not guilty, set a date for our trial, and set a date for our motions hearing. You may think it strange that I continued to use the words "we" or "our" or "us" instead of "he" or "him" or "Steven" or "my husband," but I never thought that way. To me everything that happened had happened to "us." That was just the way it was.

Our protection hearing, or more accurately the hearing to decide Lee and Ellie's request for protection, was the following Wednesday. We were going to fight the continuation of the protection order on principle, as we believed there was really no basis for it. We thought that perhaps fighting the order would put some pressure on Ellie and Lee, as they would have to attend additional hearings and continue to pay their own lawyer. It wasn't as if we were going to go over there or wanted to see them … we didn't. But we had never threatened them and found the order insulting.

The next day, the day of our plea hearing, was also going to commemorate our thirty-eighth wedding anniversary. As someone said to me, "You will always remember this anniversary!" Unfortunately I am pretty sure they are right! I'm not usually sentimental, but even with the events of the three months leading up to that day, it had been a great adventure and I would have gladly done it again. But needless to say, I wouldn't have invited Ward to our house for dinner. This chapter in our relationship wasn't one I relished.

Chapter 27

July 10, 2009:
Our Thirty-eighth Wedding Anniversary
and the Date of Our Plea Hearing

Court wasn't at all like the TV versions—at least the plea hearing wasn't. The hearing was held in a courtroom at the Justice Center, as opposed to in the jail. The judge was different. We thought this was the same judge that would hear the case. There were three DA's, five or six prisoners in cuffs and prison garb (I guess those who couldn't post bail), multiple public defenders, and lots of accused felons and their lawyers in the courtroom. And yes, there was also a judge and court personnel.

I could best describe it as controlled chaos. There was constant movement of people and constant chatter from the benches. Lawyers and their clients would walk up to the podium and explain that they had accepted a plea bargain, or needed some more time to make a decision or follow up on some action. As long as the assistant DA had no objections, the judge would reschedule for another hearing. One charge was dropped because the accuser had moved to Sweden and would not be available for trial. (Would it have been wrong for me to begin praying that Ward would be deployed to Afghanistan or Iraq?) But while a defendant and his lawyer were at the bench, everyone else kept talking—the folks in the seats, the other DA's, defense attorneys, etc. No one hit a gavel. No one said to be quiet. We did all rise when the judge entered the courtroom, but that was about the only parallel to court TV dramas. During the whole time we were in the court, we were the only ones to enter a plea and set a trial date. In my mind that confirmed what Trip had told us—the system was geared toward getting rid of cases by offering plea bargain deals, which were most often accepted by the accused.

This was the first time I saw Foote, the assistant DA who was prosecuting us. He was very young, early thirties I would guess, light brown hair, medium build, short. That didn't speak to his competence or his energy. Trip didn't know much about him and had never worked with him or defended a case against him. This lack of information and experience with him was a definite disadvantage. Trip had indicated that some of the other assistant DA's would have been more reasonable. Of course, to us "being more reasonable" meant they would have dropped the charges.

There were a number of court-appointed defense attorneys. All the ones I saw were young. They were also all carrying stacks of files for a number of cases; they were all female; and they were all noticeably pregnant (I kid you not). I know none of these factors should have affected my opinion of their effectiveness or their commitment to their clients, but I was glad we weren't depending on any of them for Steven's defense. I wanted experience, commitment, and professionalism, and I was willing to pay for it.

The court date was set for October 26 through 28. The motions hearing was scheduled for September 10. Everything was going to be over, for better or worse, before the holidays.

The schedule for the next week included a meeting with Trip the following Tuesday to discuss the protection hearing and then the actual hearing on Wednesday. After the protection hearing, we planned to go fishing for a week. This was the weekend we were supposed to be at Road America in Elkhart Lake, Wisconsin, at a race. Friends and even acquaintances kept saying they were going to miss us. Believe me, I wished we could have been there. So, instead, we were going fishing where we thought neither of our computers or our cell phones would work. Hopefully that would keep us from focusing on what we would rather have been doing. The short vacation had been approved by Steven's counselor with the usual condition that he submit to a urine test upon returning. We no longer thought this was strange. It was just the usual condition for any short absence from Boulder.

Trip kept repeating that he felt good about our case. He told us this often and assured me that he didn't say this to everyone. He said his usual advice to clients was to take the plea bargain. I hoped his instincts were right. I hoped he wasn't trying to convince himself as well as us. He said he thought about our case all the time. (I found myself hoping this was free thinking and not metered thinking.) We often received e-mails from him sent on Saturday nights and Sundays. I comforted myself that lawyer time was a flat rate. I didn't think they charged overtime, so weekend e-mails didn't concern me too much. His silences were more disturbing.

Chapter 28

July 14

Lee and Ellie's lawyer contacted Trip the day before the protection hearing and told him that Lee and Ellie had decided to "vacate" the protection order against us. They had decided "that the benefits of continued litigation [did] not justify the time and expense. You should also inform your client that my clients do not desire to have any contact with him and, to avoid future incidents, it is best if the parties stay away from each other." We rarely saw Ellie or Lee before any of this happened. We never went to their home unless it was to drop off food. Did they think that after the trouble they had caused we were suddenly going to start dropping by for coffee?

This was good news. We weren't sure what it meant, but we all agreed that it was good news. They knew we were going to fight the protection order and were going to fight the charges. I suspected their decision was motivated more by concern about the possible cost of trying to defend the extension of the protection order than it was by a sudden realization that it was unfounded. Whatever the reason, the result was the same. They had given up on this issue.

It seemed to me that Lee and Ellie were becoming paranoid. We noticed that they had moved one of the mailboxes associated with their rental units. Perhaps they were worried that someone would be notified that they had a rental property on their lot. We were far too busy with our own issues (thanks to them) to focus on anything like that.

Even though we did not have to meet with Trip because of the protection hearing and didn't have to go to court for that issue, we had already incurred significant legal costs preparing for the protection order hearing. Trip had always thought (and apparently their lawyer agreed) that there were no grounds for the protection order and that we would win in court. But we had to be prepared. And in all things legal, preparedness costs money.

I was beginning to think that legal proceedings were like a big game of chicken. Who was going to swerve first? Well not us, I can assure you.

Chapter 29

July 23

We went away for a week in our motor home to a wilderness area in northwest Colorado—Trapper's Lake in the Flattops. The trip didn't start off very auspiciously. Though Lee and Ellie had decided to drop the protection order request, we had to wait for the judge to sign the necessary forms before taking off. The hearing had been scheduled for 3:00 p.m. and at 2:00 p.m. I was still sitting in my office worrying that we would have to show up in court in our jeans and t-shirts. That would not have been my choice. But we got confirmation about 2:15 p.m. that the judge had signed the necessary forms and we could take off on our trip.

If you have a motor home, you probably have had an experience like ours on the trip to Trapper's Lake. There is something in the genetic makeup of men that makes them ask you to get them a soda, sandwich, or something from the fridge when you are on the twistiest, curviest part of your journey. That's what happened when we were about half an hour out of Boulder. My husband asked for a bottle of water on a very winding two-lane road going up into the mountains. I hesitated, but then my desire to keep him happy and hydrated won out and I walked with difficulty to the fridge and opened the door. That was exactly when the road took a sharp right. A large plastic container of salsa flew out, hit the floor, broke, and splattered salsa all over the white floor tiles in the kitchen section and on the cabinet doors. As I tried to catch the container of salsa, a plastic container of blueberries flew out, opened, and spilled blueberries all over the floor and into every opening under the cabinets. As I slammed the door of the fridge shut before anything else could fly out, the puppy walked over to see what was happening.

I was mad—really, really pissed—at Steven for asking for anything, and at myself for actually attempting to fill an order from the fridge while on this road. I spent the next half hour cleaning salsa off the floor and trying to scoop up as many blueberries as I could, while trying to convince the now eighty-eight pound puppy that it wasn't a great idea to try to help me. When we finally got to our campground that evening and put the slides out in the motor home, there were more blueberries to be cleaned up. At that point I was thinking that maybe we should have stayed home.

But the week was good. It was the total opposite of Italy—jeans, t-shirts, and sweatshirts; long hikes on trails; reading in the screened-in tent that we put up; cooking on the grill; letting the dogs swim and hike and get dirty; campfires at night; fishing; and just relaxing. No e-mails or conversations with Trip. It was almost possible to think everything was normal.

I came to the conclusion that these short getaways were critical during this ordeal. They allowed me/us to realize that we were still the same two individuals, the same couple we were before the incident. These short trips helped us keep our sanity.

As the time to return home got closer, you could almost feel the anxiety increase. We began once again to argue about useless, silly things— whether or not to take the puppy to the vet because she was limping occasionally, the puppy's training (or lack thereof), investments, etc. None of these issues were important. None were the real issue, but they were an easy substitute for the real issue.

I used to have a fantasy about Steven walking up to me in a country/western bar and saying, "Hello Darling" with a newly developed southern drawl. By this point, my fantasy had turned into a phone call from Trip telling us the DA had decided to drop the charges; or getting to Trip's office for a meeting only to have him open a bottle of champagne and say, "It's all over. They dropped the charges!" When I thought about these possibilities, then I would worry that by thinking about these things they would never happen. I thought Steven's fantasy world probably consisted of thinking about bringing civil actions against anyone involved in this debacle—Lee, Ellie, Ward, the Boulder sheriff's department—anyone. I knew, despite the fact that he denied it, that he felt humiliated. He wanted to recoup the money we were spending ... he wanted some revenge ... he wanted some sort of public vindication. You could hardly blame the man. It would have taken a saint not to want revenge.

On the way home from our camping trip, we stopped at the alcohol monitoring facility so Steven could pee in a cup and breathe into a tube. It seemed redundant to have to do both, but rules were rules. A rational person would think it was enough to pee in a cup since that measured alcohol consumption for the past seventy-two hours. But if you peed and breathed, they charged you for both tests, so I guess that's why they wanted both. The people loitering outside the facility did not look like PLU's. There were some college kids, there were kids being dropped off by their mom's for their breath tests. (I just couldn't imagine my dad doing that.) There were the residents of the halfway house located on the premises. We were back to reality.

When we got home, we had phone messages from friends who had been at the race at Road America. They all said that they missed us ... that it wasn't the same without us there. But the weather had been much colder than normal and some of the racing got rained out. For some perverse reason, the bad weather during the race made us feel better about missing the event.

While we were gone we had made an effort not to discuss the case. As soon as we got home, however, we began talking about it again. It consumed a lot of our conversation. And it consumed our thoughts. On the first day back at work, I got a phone call from a friend telling me that the forty-three–year-old son of another good friend died in his sleep a week ago, on his birthday. That news was so awful that it put everything else into perspective. As long as we were alive, we were blessed. We still had a chance for happiness.

Chapter 30

August 10

Time moved forward slowly. It had been one month since the date of our hearing that set the trial date, and four months since the incident. But it was still almost three full months to the trial date.

By this time, the incident, the emotion, the worry had become background noise—not interfering with work or chores, but always there and making anything enjoyable less so. Trip had filed one motion to keep anything Steven said from being used in trial. Nothing Steven said actually seemed to harm our case, but I guess it was because, on principle, anything he said after requesting legal counsel and before being read his rights should not be allowed. Though Trip believed the search warrant was illegal, we had agreed not to file a motion to suppress either the warrant or the gun since we thought seeing the gun made the possibility of concealing that weapon so ridiculous it would strengthen our defense.

In my mind, there were many unanswered questions around the search warrant and the gun conversation. I had been surprised that when Ainsworth arrived at our home in the early hours of the morning with the warrant, no one actually seemed to do any "searching." Though he had me open all of our vaults, no one actually looked at anything in them. No one removed any guns or boxes or any objects from the vaults. They never opened any drawers, looked under the beds, or really looked anyplace. It wasn't like on TV. On TV, police with a search warrant actually search. They look in drawers, in your closet, in the garage—they look for something that you may have hidden. If Steven had a gun that fateful evening, and unless he was really dumb, he would not have left it on the floor, in a case, in plain sight of the entranceway. They never seemed to really be looking for anything. It was more like they found what they were looking for immediately.

They focused on the gun in the case sitting on the floor of the family room and never looked for any other gun. It made me wonder why the police focused on that one gun immediately. In fact, Ainsworth's words when he opened the gun case and saw the Thompson Contender were, "This is the gun." How did he know it was "the gun"? It wasn't a flintlock like Ward had described.

After the police took Steven away that night and walked me back into the house, one of the officers asked me, "Are there any guns here?" My answer was "Yes. There are lots of guns. There's one right there." As I spoke, I pointed to the gun case standing upright against the entrance to the downstairs family room. In the police report filed by Ainsworth, he said the gun case was lying on its side near the entrance to the family room. I hadn't touched it. How did it get from an upright position to lying on its side? Did one of the officers look in the case while the others inspected the upstairs with me? There were a number of officers who remained downstairs while I was walking other officers through the upstairs, so this was a possibility.

Was a sneak preview of the contents of the gun case what prompted the description of the gun in the warrant? The gun described in the warrant wasn't based on Ward's description of a flintlock. It was a description of the Thompson Contender that was in the silver case—except it failed to mention the very large scope that was on the gun. Is that why the case wasn't upright against the wine cellar as it had been earlier that night, but was instead flat on the floor? In the same spot, but positioned differently. That is one explanation of why their search was so limited. They had already decided what they were looking for.

Perhaps it makes sense to someone that an individual who used a gun to threaten another individual came home and put the gun in a case on the floor of the family room near the front door in plain sight. What else would they do? Put it back in a discreet place in a gun vault? Put it under a bed? Hide it in a drawer? In the freezer? In the garbage? Bury it in the yard? In the dog food? In the outside shed? Throw it over the hill? We weren't dumb. We had seen at least a few TV shows. We had lots of time between when Steven got home and the police arrived. What did we do instead of spending two full minutes hiding a weapon? We took a bath and went to sleep. I mean, really, does this sound reasonable?

I didn't know if this was going to be an issue at the trial. And I didn't know how it could be proven, as it was another one of those issues that comes down to "she says … he says …" And I was learning that when the "he" in "he says …" was a police officer or a military officer, the weight of "she says …" seemed to be of little value. But it was an issue in my mind, an issue that helped explain some of what happened that evening. So I focused on it a lot during the weeks after the plea hearing. I felt like someone who had been given a test for color blindness and saw the word in the dots. I felt like I was trying to tell everyone else to look at the word but no one else could see it. They must be color-blind because to me it was obviously a damning fact.

Our PI had made a number of phone calls to Ward—the Colombo approach as he called it. His calls seemed to be irritating Ward. When Ward finally returned his seventh unanswered phone call, he told our PI that Ellie and Lee's lawyer had advised Ellie that Ward did not need to speak to anyone working for us. Ward also told the PI that he didn't think the case could be proven and that he advised the DA that he would not appear to testify. Foote told him he would be subpoenaed and required to testify at the trial.

Perhaps you are as confused as I was. The supposed victim didn't want to pursue the charges, but the DA who probably hadn't read the file yet was insisting that he would pursue the charges. If it was personal, perhaps I could have understood. If there was a real victim, especially one who couldn't speak for him or herself, I could have understood. But we were talking about a Navy Seal who could both speak for himself and defend himself, and Foote was going to force him to appear in court. Foote wasn't making a financial decision; he wasn't spending his money; he was actually spending money provided by the taxpayers of Boulder County—including me and Steven.

Meanwhile we were spending our money preparing for a trial. Our legal bills were already in the high five figures. Steven was still doing random breathalyzer tests. We could not leave the state. In fact, we could not travel within the state for more than a week without getting the court's approval (because of the random breathalyzer tests). My stomach was in constant turmoil. I had become an Academy Award–winning actress when out in public, appearing unchanged by current events. My husband was becoming bitter and focused on getting some financial revenge. And I was probably not far behind. And the puppy has OCD in her front left leg. (Even I knew I couldn't blame that on Ward, Lee, or Ellie, but it just compounded the stress.)

Tom had agreed to be a friendly witness. He was going to be paid $12 for that—it was required by law. We wouldn't have to serve him. We were planning on serving Lee and Ellie shortly. Steven had spoken to Jean and Tom while I was out of town. He ran into them on the driveway. They said Lee wasn't doing well … his back, his heart, this whole thing. I suppose it comes as no surprise to you that I was not really concerned about him, though I did want him to live through the trial just because I thought it would cause him more stress. (See what I meant about becoming bitter? I didn't used to be like that.)

I saw a bumper sticker that sort of summed it up. "You can't make up shit like this."

Chapter 31

September 4

Another month passed with no news, no changes, nothing. During that month we took the opportunity to take a five-day trip to the western slope. I enjoyed the short camping trips in Colorado. We hadn't done these types of trips in years and I found I really enjoyed these somewhat aimless getaways.

Trip's strategy at this point was simply to wait. Though we intended to subpoena Lee and Ellie as witnesses, he wanted to wait until closer to the trial to do that. He was trying to balance the pressure on them and Ward with a hope that the DA would lose focus. Since Ward was at home in California and appeared (based on what he had said to our PI) reluctant to be involved, perhaps the DA would not issue an out of town subpoena in sufficient time to force Ward to show up at trial. We had given up hope that the charges would be dropped, and instead were now hoping for carelessness or incompetence on the part of the Boulder County district attorney's office. It sounded weak to me, but one could only hope.

Our friends sometimes failed to realize the reality of the situation. They would invite us to go with them someplace—fishing or racing—and I would have to remind them that we couldn't leave the state without court approval. They didn't know how to respond. I don't think they realized that there was the possibility that Steven might be found guilty. I'm sure the possibility of a jail sentence never occurred to them. I never verbalized that concern to anyone ... not even Steven. But it scared me. It shouldn't happen—but a lot of things that shouldn't happen did happen.

I kept track of time, not by the actual date, but by measuring the time to important things that were supposed to happen. I would count off: the motions hearing was ten days away; the trial was in two months. That would trigger time from the incident. It would be seven months between the incident and the trial date. You could measure it in time. I could measure it in legal bills paid to a certain date. Other metrics defied measurement. By the point two months prior to the trial, I had decided that we would survive. I was no longer worried about our marriage. We were going to survive. I suspect Steven would have been surprised to know that I had been worried about that. (Men can be so oblivious sometimes!)

Chapter 32

September 10

The motions hearing was held in mid September. Trip filed a number of motions including one to have Steven's statements given while he was in custody excluded from the trial. Trip didn't think Steven's statements were in anyway damaging, but thought they should not be allowed into testimony on principle. The judge's refusal to allow the motion would also provide grounds for an appeal—our parachute if things went wrong.

As I write this, it sounds very matter-of-fact and cold. And in all honesty a motions hearing isn't a trial or really any big deal. But it was a god-awful week anyway. I could feel the tension building all week as we approached the Thursday afternoon time of the hearing.

The motions hearing was held in the Justice Center and was presided over by the Honorable Gwyneth Whalen, Judge of the District Court. Judge Whalen would also preside over the criminal trial in October. According to Trip, Judge Whalen was relatively new to this position. That meant that Trip didn't have any experience with her as a judge. Her reputation, however, was as a fair and sound judge.

Trip thought it would be a good experience for Steven and me to see the courtroom setting. Steven sat at the defense table with Trip, while I sat in a wooden pew in the spectators' gallery. There was no crowd here—I was alone in the spectator benches behind Trip and Steven. There was no one in the benches behind the prosecuting table. This was a private session. Nothing else was going on in the courtroom that morning.

A few minutes before the hearing was scheduled to begin, Foote approached Trip and asked to speak to him. I assumed this was when he would offer us a deal … I was right. It turned out to not be much of a deal, as it seemed to involve some jail time, monitored probation, community service, and who knows what else. After conveying the terms of the plea bargain, we agreed immediately with Trip that he should simply tell Foote that we couldn't respond that quickly, but would reply within two weeks or less. We had no intention of accepting this deal. But Foote didn't need to know that right away.

Once the judge was on the bench, Foote asked that I be sequestered. Trip argued that since the motions had nothing to do with anything to which I could testify that I be allowed to stay in the courtroom. The judge agreed with Trip and I was allowed to stay. That was the only agreement we got on anything that afternoon.

During the hearing I found myself staring at Foote, wondering exactly what type of man this was who seemed opposed to anything Trip requested. What was motivating him? Was it a sense of justice? At least in my opinion, that didn't seem to fit. Was it a desire to achieve a certain conviction rate or to best Trip by convicting his client? I would never know. All I really knew was that I didn't like this person—he made me feel uneasy, and he seemed to want to make this personal. Why? That's what I didn't know.

The first motion involved not allowing Steven's statements while in custody to be used in the trial. Two officers were called as witnesses—one who drove Steven to the booking center (sounds better than "the jail") and another who processed the arrest. Trip had told us beforehand that he didn't think the judge would allow the motion, but he wanted to get both officers' statements documented so there would be no surprises at trial.

The hearing took almost two hours. As I sat behind Steven and Trip in the hard pew, I was reminded of footage that you see of women rocking back and forth in grief. That was what I found myself wanting to do as I sat there—just rock back and forth. That's what I had done that evening with Officer Witte as I waited for the search warrant. The motion could be comforting for some reason. Maybe it brought back early memories of being rocked as a child. But I couldn't or wouldn't give in to that desire in the courtroom. So instead, I folded Kleenex into small tight packages and squeezed my hands tightly.

Trip took each officer through every line in their report. There was only one surprise. The officer who drove Steven to the booking station said that Steven told him that he had showed Ward some guns during our dinner party. That wasn't in his written report, which was supposed to include any statements made by the accused that were relevant to the charges. And I don't know why Steven would have said that (he says he didn't), since no guns were ever out of their cases or the vault at any time during the evening. The same officer said Steven was intoxicated. I wanted to ask why, if they thought that and thought that alcohol had played a part in the evening's events, why didn't they put him on a breathalyzer or take a blood test?

It was very frustrating to be sitting in the courtroom even in a hearing like this one. There were many questions I wanted to ask and things I wanted to say to the officers. But I couldn't say anything. So I sat quietly and thought that things were not going well. The momentum seemed to be tilting toward the prosecution.

The second officer said that Steven asked if he could press charges against Ward, since Ward had threatened him. The officer told him he couldn't.

I found it both strange and troublesome that the officer immediately dismissed Steven's request to press charges. The only explanation is that once you are taken into custody you are guilty and no one is willing to consider whether you were possibly the victim. As I sat there, I thought that if a person intended to threaten another person, they should do exactly what Ward did. Threaten them and then call the police and tell them that they were the one who had been threatened. The focus would move off them, they would get a pass, and the person that was actually threatened would be powerless and enmeshed in the legal system trying to prove they didn't commit the crime. It seemed to be a great way to deflect blame and prosecution. Was this what is meant when they talk about "gaming the system"?

I was touched when the second officer said that Steven asked him to check on his wife. He was worried about me even though he was the one sitting in the booking area of the Boulder County sheriff's office.

Trip made two verbal requests. One was for permission for us to participate in a charity car rally that would involve one night out of Colorado (in Taos, New Mexico). The conditions of Steven's bail did not allow us to travel out of state. The other was permission for Steven to take our godson camping for a week in October, just before the trial. Though the trip was in Colorado, Steven would not be available for his random alcohol monitoring. The DA did not oppose these motions and the judge agreed as long as Steven's counselor was agreeable. His counselor had been agreeable to absences of up to a week (as long as Steven did a urine test when he returned), so both short trips should be allowed.

I didn't get much of a sense of Judge Whalen during the proceeding. Trip and Steven thought she acted like we were wasting her time and resources. Why weren't we accepting a plea bargain and moving on? Perhaps because we weren't guilty? Apparently that concept was fairly novel in the judicial system.

We met with Trip afterwards as had become our custom. "I know we've talked about this before, but you have to think about it. A trial doesn't guarantee you will be found innocent. The cost of going to trial isn't insignificant. It will probably be at least what you've spent so far. If you take a plea bargain, the legal bills stop, the court appearances stop. It will be over. I can try to negotiate a plea with no jail time."

"But I'm innocent," Steven said feebly.

"Yes, I know that and you know that and Ward probably knows that. But will the jury? Despite what you hear, the jury assumes you are guilty. Why else would the Boulder DA prosecute you? Sometimes they let someone off for a technicality, but they still think he or she is guilty. The problem here is they may decide there isn't enough evidence to find you guilty on the felony charge, but find you guilty on the misdemeanor. That's the jury's way out. They find you not guilty on the big charge but wink at the DA by finding you guilty on the lesser charge. That's why the DA will typically bring a felony charge and a misdemeanor charge against someone. If there's not enough evidence to find guilt on the felony, the jury may still find the defendant guilty on the second charge. Going to trial isn't a sure bet and it's an expensive bet. Just think about it."

"Okay," whispered Steven. And then with a bit louder voice he asked, "What would your counter offer be?"

"I don't know. Maybe a deferred sentence—probably twelve months. If you don't get in any trouble during that period, except a traffic violation or fish and game, the charges go away after a year. But during that year, it's like you are on probation. And you would probably have to do community service."

"Would the deferred sentence continue to have travel restrictions and alcohol monitoring?"

As Trip nodded, he added, "Probably counseling and a requirement not to contact Ellie or Lee, too. But at the end of the year it is erased from your record. The DA won't offer a plea bargain unless Ward and Ellie and Lee agree to it, too, so they may not accept the counter offer of a deferred sentence anyway."

Steven continued, "I'm not accepting a deferred sentence to a felony. I'm not going to say I did anything wrong. I didn't do anything wrong."

I remained quiet during this whole exchange. I wanted this nightmare to be over. I was tired and scared. Finding an end to the ordeal was very attractive to me at this point, but I knew this was not my decision. It was our ordeal, but this had to be Steven's decision.

"I don't think any of them want to appear in court. Not Ward or Lee or Ellie. Maybe if we delay on responding to the plea bargain offer, Foote won't get Ward served with an out-of-state subpoena in sufficient time. If he doesn't show up in court, there's no trial," Trip said.

For the first time, I said something. "Ellie and Lee look so pitiful. The jury is going to feel sorry for them just because they are old and look so awful. We don't look that awful yet. How do we deal with that?"

"We just deal with the facts. That's all we can do," Trip said.

• • •

When we got home, as I was preparing dinner and Steven was sitting at the kitchen counter he said, "We need to talk."

I stopped what I was doing, walked over to the counter and nodded. Steven continued, "If I take the plea bargain, I know it is going to shorten my life. I can't live with myself if I agree to having done something wrong when I know I didn't. I'll think about that every day and every night and it will eat away at me. I know this."

"But what if they find you guilty?" I whispered.

"That will be different. I would not have agreed to having done anything wrong. I will have gone down fighting and telling everyone I was innocent." After a short pause during which I hadn't said anything but had begun to cry, he continued, "But here's the thing that worries me. I won't do this if continuing is going to affect your life. I can't do this unless you are in agreement. I feel like I am dealing with the stress, but I can't take you crying all the time. Every time we talk about it, every time we meet with Trip, every time we get another e-mail or you read something, you start crying. I don't want to shorten your life. If you can't deal with this, tell me and I'll call Trip and ask him to negotiate a plea bargain."

I didn't know what to say. I wanted to tell him, "Fight the good fight"—that's what Katherine Hepburn would have said to Spencer Tracey. But I only said, "We've got some time to think about it. You want an honest answer?" When Steven nodded, I said, "Let's talk in the morning." And we said nothing else about it that night.

In the morning, Steven got up first as had become our pattern. He let the dogs out, gave them breakfast, and made coffee. Then he returned to the bedroom and sat on the edge of the bed while petting Bella. Lola was lying lengthwise next to me on the bed. I turned to Steven and without making a conscious decision said, "We're not accepting a plea bargain. We're going to trial."

Chapter 33

September 14

In our next meeting, Trip explained that the courtroom at the motions hearing would be the same courtroom where the trial would be held. During the trial, however, I would be sequestered outside and not allowed in the courtroom until after I had testified. I asked, "What about Ainsworth?"

"No. The detective can be in the courtroom the whole time." Two different sets of rules. I guess the defense witnesses might be affected by what they hear, but the detective would be above being swayed by what he heard.

We had not discussed details of the case with almost anyone so far, but I did ask Trip, "Do you think we should ask some friends to be there in support of Steven?" My voice cracked as I added, "If I can't be in the courtroom, I don't want Steven sitting there in the defendant's chair all alone. I want them to know we have friends who have supported us and know Steven didn't do anything wrong."

Trip was quiet for a few long seconds and then answered, "I think that's a good idea. Don't have crowds, but a few good friends is a good idea. And you might want to make sure there is someone with you outside. You probably don't want to be alone out there."

After talking about it that evening, Steven and I decided to invite his brother, Gregg, to come up from Tennessee and to ask Don, Jimmy, Roger and Diane, our old friend from Chicago, John, and maybe Tony or Cathe if they could be there. We realized that we had not actually discussed any of this with John or Tony or Cathe, and didn't know if they knew anything about it. Steven hesitated and worried out loud, "We haven't talked to them about any of this. Don't you think it's funny now to go back to them and ask for their support?"

"No," I answered quickly and decisively, and we divided up the phone calls to be made.

The next night we went out with our friends, Betsey and Art. They lived in Mancos, Colorado, which was either a short flight or an eight-hour drive away. Steven had three non-alcoholic beers. When we mentioned the trial dates to them, they immediately said they would be there. I wasn't even going to ask them because of where they lived—it was too long of a drive for us to ask them to come. Their insistence on coming made me begin to cry. We still had good friends.

By then it was six weeks to the trial and two weeks till our puppy's elbow surgery. We were very good at picking lovable dogs, but not very good at picking ones that had good bones.

I was trying to take a lesson from our dogs and live in the present. I didn't want future possibilities to keep me from enjoying what was going on right now. This was hard, but I felt I owed it to my husband. For the next six weeks I was going to try to focus on what was happening now and on enjoying that experience—not focusing on what might happen. That was my goal. Well, at least for the next four weeks. I decided to take it one day at a time.

Chapter 34

September 17

The names of all possible witnesses needed to be provided to the court weeks before the trial. Trip had asked for the names of individuals who had seen Steven under stress and could testify that he did not at that time become violent or belligerent or threaten anyone. Actually this was pretty easy, as I couldn't think of a situation where my husband lost his cool, yelled, or even raised his voice to anyone. (I guess we were lucky I wasn't on trial, as the same could not be said about me—or probably any Italian.) We gave Trip numerous names—Steven's brother, as well as three or four friends of ours who have been on the volunteer fire department with Steven or involved in racing with us. All of them were eager to testify, they wanted to do something. These individuals would be what I would have called "character witnesses." More specifically, they were going to be asked to confirm that Steven was a "peaceful man."

One of the more upsetting disclosures in the weeks prior to the trial was learning what Ellie had said in an interview with Ainsworth prior to the trial. She was no longer just repeating lies, she had begun to lie out-right. According to Trip, Ellie "prattled" (Trip's term) on about how Steven was a drunkard and how he was abusive to others. Ellie had *never* seen my husband intoxicated. We had rarely been at any social gatherings together. After hearing Trip's comments on Ellie's testimony, I began typing and recording all of the interactions I could remember that involved Lee and Ellie over the years. I ended up with four pages of typed comments. They did not read to me like the kind of interactions anyone would have had with a neighbor who was an abusive drunk.

I could actually sympathize with Lee and Ellie supporting their son's accusation of being threatened with a gun by Steven. Once their son said this happened, what choice did they have but to assume it was true? What I couldn't understand was their attempts to reshape history by saying that we were drunkards, that we were abusive. Where did they get this? What was the point of these lies? If it was true (which it wasn't), why the hell did they send their son over to our house and why the hell did Ellie come over? If we were the type of people they said we were, then they were really stupid (or should I say STUPID) for having anything to do with us. When I tried to remind myself to live in the present and that I shouldn't get mad, the results were ineffective. It was a futile experiment at best.

We had set up our safety net. Gregg was coming up from Tennessee for the trial whether or not he was going to be asked to testify. Our "character" witnesses (Don, Jimmy, and Roger) were all on board and would come to the trial whether or not they were going to be called to testify. Diane, Don and Patricia, and Art and Tony all said they'd be there. The dogs were booked into doggie camp for the duration of the trial so we didn't have to worry about them being home long days by themselves. We each had an appointment with Trip for our pre-trial preparations in the days before the trial.

Ann, Trip's secretary, called me at work to confirm the time for my pre-trial meeting a week before the meeting. She stressed that Trip would be very tough on me during that interview. Ann said he would be preoccupied with the trial and wouldn't be focused on making me feel good. She encouraged me to keep a list of my questions and to call her to talk about them if I didn't get them answered by the end of that meeting. Questions that I had already considered were how to dress, what the trial protocol would be, etc. Ann was very nice and assured me they (her and Trip) would get us through this. By the end of the conversation when I thanked her, I was in tears. Our administrative assistant stopped at my open office door and asked if everything was all right. Such a simple question. I assured her everything was fine, but in reality nothing was fine— even if you were trying to live in the present. I often wondered what my employees thought was going on. Surely they realized something very bad was happening.

It was only going to get worse.

The following week we would be gone on our charity car rally. I was actually glad Steven was going camping with our godson the week before the trial. I thought it was going to be such a difficult time that it was better if he was busy and elsewhere. I would be home to stress out in my own way. Actually, my godson's mom, who also happened to be my oldest and best friend, was coming out with him and would be with me the weekend before the trial while Steven and Nick were camping. And if Steven wasn't here, I wouldn't feel bad about having a glass of wine. It would, however, be the first time since the night Steven was arrested that I would have to spend a night in our home alone. I assured myself that it would be only five days. And I really wouldn't be alone. I'd have the two dogs.

There were still five weeks to the trial.

Chapter 35

Mid-September

We had begun liquidating certain assets that could be sold relatively easily. It was a non-taxable option for raising some cash against our mounting legal bills. Steven sold our 2000 Mazda Miata to Trip. I hoped he really wanted a sports car and didn't just buy it to help out. Our sixteen-foot fishing boat got sold next. That left our motorcycle in the "for sale" department. I sold some gold jewelry that I hadn't worn in a long time, but that didn't bring much. I'd taken out the maximum loan possible from my 401(k). I'm the plan administrator, so I didn't have to justify the reason for the loan, but I think it definitely fit under the "hardship" category.

And speaking of hardships, I developed TMJ. I began to clench my jaw and grind my teeth at some point during the ordeal. It got so bad that I couldn't open my mouth for a bite of yogurt without my jaw popping. Steven kept turning to me during dinner and saying, "Stop that." He didn't understand that it was not something I could control. I started wearing a tooth guard at night and that helped a little, but it was still serious enough to be painful. It was physical evidence of my stress level.

About this same time, I began to worry that we were underestimating Foote. He had gotten subpoenas out to everyone on his list in a timely manner. He got his way at the motions' hearing. Trip was a former assistant DA with a good reputation—highly regarded, very competent, and, because of the Jon Benet Ramsey case, well known. I was worried that Foote saw winning this case as a way to prove his metal ... besting Trip. I hoped and I prayed a lot that at some point the decision to proceed and the verdict if we did go to trial would be based on the facts of the case and not on other issues.

• • •

Our five-day charity car rally in New Mexico was a very pleasant diversion. We had a good time and for the five days didn't focus on the upcoming trial. But before the dinner on the last day, Steven spoke to Trip to check on the status of the subpoenas and witness lists for the trial, which needed to be submitted on the final day of the rally.

During the rally I marveled at how my husband and his sense of humor were so well received by the many people we met for the first time. No one took offense to anything he said. Folks joked about all sorts of things—many of which had some sexual undertones. Women took compliments for exactly what they were … compliments. It made me think again that Ellie had no sense of humor, or maybe perhaps she protested too loudly. Did Steven's comment about her male students strike too close to home? I was still trying, unsuccessfully, to find some logical reason for her reaction to his comments. I had to keep reminding myself that Steven was not on trial for making comments to Ellie. He was on trial for supposedly pointing a gun and threatening Ward many hours later—nothing more, nothing less.

We contributed an "Italian dinner for four" to the charity auction at the rally. It was so popular that I added a second dinner. Two different couples paid $600 to come to our home for dinner. Think about the irony there. Folks were paying to have dinner with someone accused of insulting a dinner guest at our house and then threatening a man with a gun. Hardly makes sense, does it? But, as I've mentioned, there were two parallel universes running simultaneously in my life at this time.

• • •

The witnesses were now named by both "the People" (what a joke) and by "the defense." Interestingly, I am actually named by "the People." (What "People"? Most people I knew thought this was a farce!) So I did not have to be named as a witness by the defense. I didn't have to be subpoenaed and neither did our friendly character witnesses, since there was no risk of any of us not showing up at the trial.

My mother used to say, "It doesn't take strength to die. Dying is nothing. It's living that's hard." I think she was right. Just giving up would be easy. Finding the strength to go on when things are difficult is the challenge. And at a run rate of over $500 a day, defending ourselves was also expensive. In case you are into numbers, that bill was through the first five months and didn't include trial prep, which was going on at this point.

Perhaps cleaning is a female strategy for coping with stress. Perhaps it's my strategy based on how I was raised. In any event, it was something to do—something that had results—something that kept your hands occupied but didn't take a lot of concentration. So I cleaned. And I made arrangements to have things cleaned. The carpeting and the windows were scheduled to be cleaned before the trial. I cleaned out drawers and arranged my socks, I cleaned wall light switches with an old toothbrush, I cleaned light fixtures. I groomed the dogs to within an inch of being bitten. I kept busy. The house would be spotless before the trial.

I had absolutely no idea why this was important to me, but it was. The incident and the trial were the kind of events from which time would be measured. In the future we would say, "That was before Steven was arrested," or "That happened after the trial," or "We didn't do that in 2009 because of the trial." If an event was going to be that memorable, I guess it was important to have a clean house beforehand. At least cleaning the house was something I could control. In an environment when so much was out of my control, I wanted to control something.

Chapter 36

Early October

Trip sent us copies of e-mails between him and the assistant DA. Foote assured him that his client (my husband) would serve jail time for what he did if we go to trial … and incur the cost of travel for the witness (i.e. Ward). He wanted Steven to "cop a plea" and said he would withdraw the plea bargain offer the following Monday. Foote said he assumed we were preparing for trial since we had subpoenaed "his witnesses." But there were no witnesses except Ward to the alleged threat with a lethal weapon. Was it really possible that Steven might go to jail because one person said he did something? I couldn't even try to explain how that thought made me feel. It was more than unhappy and scared. It was a feeling of despair. I would lay awake at night holding onto Steven and think, *What if things go wrong? What if he is found guilty?* It could happen. Trip assured us Steven wouldn't get jail time, but … no one knew what was going to happen. The "what if's" were keeping me awake at night. "What if's" kept my stomach churning. "What if's" were very scary.

I know I was impatient at work and with friends. I used more expletives in my speech. My emotions were going through stages similar to those brought on by a fatal illness: anger, bargaining, isolation. I just hadn't gotten to the acceptance stage.

I tried not to be noticeably upset in front of Steven, but I didn't always succeed. I kept my crying to times when I was alone. Trip assured us that the more bluster the DA showed, the weaker his case. It was his way of scaring us. On that count, Foote was very successful—at least in regard to me. I guess, if I could be rational, it made sense. If the case was strong,

Foote wouldn't have to threaten us with jail time since he would have confidence that that would be the outcome. But sometimes folks make good on their threats. At times I felt the only solution for me seemed to be to pour myself a glass of wine and sit down and have a good cry. But guilt made me think I should vacuum first so I could do both with a clean conscience.

We met with Trip on a Friday afternoon shortly before Steven's camping trip. He said he felt good about the case. I thought this meant he thought we could win. We should win. If justice was going to be done, Steven should be acquitted. Trip went over the strategy for the trial, our roles in it, the importance of Steven's demeanor in the courtroom, our dress, the demeanor of our witnesses and spectators, etc. He said he would be working on nothing else for the next two weeks and we should call him with any questions at any time or if we simply needed to talk.

Full Time? Forty hours a week times two weeks times his billing rate plus his assistant's billing rate? I didn't really care about money at that point, but that calculation was sobering when I thought about it. I just wanted Steven to be acquitted as he should be, and for us to get on with our life—whatever it took.

Steven seemed to have gone to a quiet place within himself. He said we made our choice about what to do and things just needed to play out. Me? I was a wreck. I could feel the tension building within me literally day by day. Steven said I was being negative. I tried to explain that I was scared. He said I needed to be positive. I couldn't tell him I was afraid to be positive.

Trip e-mailed us copies of motions he intended to file. One pre-trial motion was to keep Ellie from running off at the mouth about us—our personalities, drinking habits, etc. It still amazed me. When she needed neighbors because her kids weren't around or when Lee was in the hospital, I guess we were okay. Now she wanted to demonize us. The motion was not based on how I felt, but on a legal precedent and law that conversations about the past have no bearing on the charges and should not be allowed.

I thought all the motions had two purposes. First, in this case, was the intent to keep Ellie's testimony (based on her recorded conversations with the DA and investigator) from prejudicing the jury, since no matter what Ellie said about Steven's comments or conduct in the past or about his/our drinking habits, it had nothing to do with "felony menacing." If the motion was granted and Ellie did begin to talk about things that she had been instructed not to discuss, it was grounds for a mistrial (and hopefully an acquittal). The other purpose of all the motions was that if Steven was found guilty (God forbid!), denying any of the motions might be grounds for an appeal.

There were other motions that Trip had prepared and was ready to file at the trial. One was to have the 911 recordings played. I believe the intent of playing the tape was to allow the jurors to pick up the verbal cues from voices during the recording. Reading the words alone wouldn't convey the same meaning that hearing them would. Another motion was to drop the misdemeanor charge and present the jury with instructions to consider only the felony charge. If Steven did not have a gun, his threat to Ward, which was basically, "If you ever come onto my property and threaten me again, I'll shoot you," was not an "emanate" threat. It required Ward to do something in the future, i.e. to come onto our property and threaten us. The final motion was to allow statements that Ward made to be read into testimony. These statements show that he had been inconsistent at best, or perhaps perjured himself, about a number of different "facts." If this motion was allowed, we wouldn't have to rely on his rehearsed testimony at trial, but would be able to show the jurors how his testimony about facts had changed over time.

We had friends asking if they could come to the trial, and friends who felt bad not to have been asked to be witnesses. But even the "character" witnesses might not be called. All they could be asked was, "Do you think Steven is a peaceful man?" I didn't think that answering yes to this question was much of a testimony or very enlightening. References are always favorable. If you couldn't supply character witnesses who would be positive, why would you call them?

It was my assigned task to "organize" our spectators. I didn't want to hurt anyone's feelings by not making them welcome to attend, but I didn't want to make anyone think they had to attend. Steven noted that after months of refusing to discuss details with anyone, it was really strange to suddenly be asking them to come to the trial. We wanted the "appropriate number" of spectators—enough to show that Steven had friends, but not too many to make it a spectacle.

We each had separate meetings scheduled with Trip in the week prior to the trial. Trip told me that my testimony would be critical. I already felt responsible for enabling the events of that evening, and now felt that the outcome would also depend on me. Was it any wonder that I was a wreck?

Chapter 37

Late October

Steven left on his camping trip on Thursday, a week and a half before the trial was scheduled to begin. Judy came out the day before Steven and Nick left and stayed for an extended weekend. It was good to have someone with me who knew what was going on and could lend support. Judy offered to come back the following week and be here during the trial, but I didn't think that was necessary. She taught kindergarten and it wasn't that easy for her to get time off. Steven's brother, Gregg, was going to arrive the following Saturday and I hoped our friends would be rallying around us.

With nothing to do, I focused on what to wear. Should I dress business casual? Did I want to look good? Haggard? Poorly dressed? I couldn't find any information on line about appropriate dress for court, other than those suggesting that men wear a suit or sport coat. Didn't women ever have to go to court? I bought some new clothes when Judy and I went shopping the weekend she was here, but I didn't know if I was supposed to wear new clothes. Would last year's more worn and less stylish outfits be better?

I kept detailed lists of things to do to keep busy. The dogs were beginning to think I intended to remove their skin with combs and brushes. I made soup, crock pot meals, cakes, and cookies while Steven was gone. He thought I was trying to undermine his weight loss. I wasn't, I just didn't know what else to do after a while—so I cooked and baked.

I planned to talk to my management staff the Wednesday before the trial was scheduled to begin. I thought they needed to know. No one at work had said anything to me, so I wasn't sure if they already knew or not. Based on how many people apparently read at least one of the newspaper articles, it seemed likely that they did know. There was a lot going on at work, and I needed to make decisions about the company's health insurance renewal and credit facility renewal this month.

In the weeks prior to the trial, I applied for an SBA loan for my company. The terms and the rates would be really advantageous compared to the company's existing loans. I assumed that since I owned 100 percent of the company stock, my name on the forms and the guarantee would be sufficient. The bank indicated that they wanted Steven to sign the financial statements also, as many of our assets (like our house) are owned jointly. This didn't sound like a big deal … except for the question at the bottom of the form. "Are you a defendant in any lawsuits?" I could truthfully answer "no," but obviously Steven couldn't prior to the trial. How was I supposed to explain this to a business banker? Would it kill the deal and mean that my company would have to pay significantly more interest and fees than otherwise? The resolution turned out to be fairly simple. We would wait until after the trial to have Steven sign, since then he would no longer be a defendant in a lawsuit. He would either be a free man or a convicted felon, but he would not be a defendant.

I don't think I had ever been as scared as I was in the days before the trial. I could no longer remember life without the charges and the trial hanging over us. I was like a person living in a war who no longer remembers what peace was like. Steven and Nick arrived home two days earlier than anticipated and I was grateful.

That was the day I told my management staff what was happening. None of them had apparently read either of the newspaper articles or had any conversations with anyone who knew what was happening. This was actually hard to believe since so many people seemed to know what was happening, but my staff appeared truly stunned by the news. Naturally I couldn't explain the situation without reverting to tears, but we got through the telling.

They knew something was out of the ordinary because of my personal calendar. I kept a copy of it on my desk so they would know when I was traveling and could plan accordingly. The calendar showed that I planned to be gone the first three days of the following week, but with no indication of a place or a reason. It also showed that the dogs were being boarded Sunday through Thursday, which meant it wasn't a car or motor home trip since they would accompany us on such trips. The calendar also showed that Gregg was arriving on Saturday and staying until the following Thursday.

My staff thought it was unusual that I would take time off while our group health insurance was up for renewal and our credit facilities were being refinanced. Typically these priorities would not allow me to be gone. They had speculated about the reason, but hadn't been anywhere near the truth. They thought that perhaps Steven had health issues, but that wasn't consistent with his week-long camping trip. Then they speculated that Gregg was donating part of his liver to Steven, but that didn't reconcile with Steven's apparent good physical health or his camping trip.

None of them knew anything, yet they admitted that I was acting strange. The reason they gave was that I seemed to be baking and bringing a lot of cookies to work. I didn't know that my baking was an indication of stress, but they recognized it. Coincidentally, I had brought cookies and containers of homemade sauce for all of them the morning we had our conversation. Perhaps they knew me better than I knew myself.

It was a difficult and tearful conversation, but necessary. I don't think they would have been more surprised if I had told them we were going to adopt children from a dozen foreign countries. The good news was that I thought I had a few more folks praying for us.

The following day, the Thursday before the trail, I met for four and a quarter hours with Trip to prepare for the witness stand. Trip went over questions he would ask and questions he thought Foote might ask. He cautioned me to limit my answers to the specific question, and he tried to prepare me for direct examination and cross-examination. I actually expected the experience to be much worse. I expected to be in tears. It was draining and tiring, but not emotionally exhausting—even when I had to listen to the recorded conversation between the Comm center and Steven.

Trip asked me to read some of the police reports. When I was done reading one written by an officer discussing what had happened outside our house that evening, he asked, "Why didn't you do what the officers told you to do that night?" At my look of non-comprehension, he continued, "When they told you to get behind the cars with them. When Steven was still in the house, why didn't you do what they said?"

"Because I was afraid of them, not Steven. I didn't really think about it at the time, but Steven was in the house. They had guns, a dog, too, and they were pointing the guns at me and at the front door. I wasn't going to let Steven walk out and get shot. I wasn't afraid of Steven. I was afraid of the guys with the guns. I didn't want to leave the front door and go with them. I had no idea what was going on and I didn't know them."

"You could have been arrested for that," Trip said simply.

"I wasn't thinking about that. In fact, I had no idea, but it doesn't matter. I'd do the same thing today if I had to choose again."

"Why did you tell them they couldn't search the house without a search warrant?"

"Was that wrong?" I responded.

"No. No. It was absolutely the right thing to do. I'm just curious about why you did that. Sometimes folks don't think about that and let the officers search."

"That's what they do on TV. They always say 'Not without a search warrant.' So that's what I said. Again, I didn't really think about it. It just seemed to be what I should say."

"Ward is in town. Foote subpoenaed him for the trial."

"Shit." Though that single word was my only response, I felt a new wave of paranoia and fear. When I drove home, I watched in my rear view mirror for someone trying to force me off the road. When I arrived home, I carefully locked the car doors and house doors. When the dogs barked in the afternoon, I was sure someone was trespassing on our property— probably preparing to shoot me or Steven with a high powered rifle. I was apparently wrong, as I survived the day and to the best of my knowledge, no one took a shot at me.

"I bought a new black suit," I told Trip. When he looked at me inquisitively, I added, "For the trial."

"No power suits or business suits ... more casual ... no fur, nothing too expensive. Dress like you are right now." I was wearing an old pair of brown slacks and an old leather jacket. This was how I was supposed to look at trial? I didn't think I looked good enough for such a momentous occasion, but I answered, "Okay." I wasn't about to start second guessing Trip at this point.

Trip's disappointment in Foote and Ainsworth for pursuing this case was obvious. "I just don't understand why they're doing this. It's almost like there is something else motivating them. I've reviewed the charges, the evidence, everything with a lot of other lawyers and folks whose opinions I value and trust. None of them think Steven can be found guilty. None of them understand why the case is being prosecuted."

"But that doesn't mean things can't go wrong," I responded.

"No. It doesn't."

"Why do you think they are going forward?"

"Maybe because Ward is a Seal. Lots of cops are retired military. Maybe they think you and Steve are wealthy and need to be taken down a notch. I don't really understand it."

"We're not wealthy," I responded quickly. "We have wealthy friends with houses twice as big as ours or maybe more, and better decorated ... and they have nicer cars."

"Maybe," replied Trip. "But to a detective or a cop, your house is pretty nice. So you look wealthy."

"Even with the dog hair and Newf drool?" I asked.

Trip smiled and said, "Even with the Newf hair and dog drool."

• • •

When I arrived at work Friday morning, three days before the trial was to begin, I found milk chocolate bars and a nice card on my desk. My staff was now worried that I wasn't eating. Of course I was eating, although my stomach did feel like it was tied in knots. I did, however, weigh less than I had at any time since recovering from bacterial pneumonia three years earlier. For one of the few times in my life, eating wasn't the pleasure it usually was.

Gregg arrived the Saturday before the trial was to begin. Steven kept insisting that he wasn't nervous and was "looking forward to the trial."

Perhaps—though the evidence suggested otherwise. On the Sunday morning prior to the trial, Steven and Gregg left to deliver the dogs to "doggie camp." Steven backed up and put the two tires on the driver's side over the edge of our driveway. He had never done that in the seventeen years we had lived there. They had to get the other car, put a tow strap on the car hanging over the edge of the driveway, and pull it out onto solid gravel. But he wasn't nervous. No sir. That was just a coincidence that he literally drove off a cliff.

I at least admitted to nerves. I had baked so many cookies that the only excuse I could think of for the batch I made Sunday morning was to give it to the friends coming to the trial. So I prepared boxes of cookies for everyone who would join us the next day. Prosecution is no reason not to be gracious. I found myself whispering little prayers all morning as I went about my chores. My domestic chores were a godsend as they kept me busy.

It was good that Gregg was at the house. It gave us both someone to talk to who was supportive. Plus Steven and his brother always seemed to have a lot to talk about and they laughed together. Laughter was important—and scarce.

We spoke to Trip on Saturday. He was working on trial preparation all day, but assured us he wouldn't charge for his time on Saturday or Sunday. That was not one of my concerns. Trip met with Jean and Tom on Saturday. Ellie had told Foote that Steven had said "bad and offensive" things to Jean. Steven and Jean used to banter and joke as friends do, but neither of them ever seemed to take offense at anything. Ellie's comments were lies and they were very nasty lies. She recounted some social event after Jean's mastectomies, where Steven told Jean that her blouse would look better "if she had boobs." My husband would never have said something like that. What kind of person would say that? I can't even remember any social event at which all of us were present. It was a nasty, hurtful lie, and I had absolutely no idea what any of this had to do with the events of April 5th.

Trip wanted to talk to Jean to see what her reaction to Ellie's comments would be. According to Trip, Jean was surprised to read Ellie's comments and said she had no idea what had prompted them. Jean told Trip that she had never said anything to Ellie relating any incident similar to the one Ellie described. She also told him that what Ellie said had never happened. In fact, she said it could not have happened because her reconstruction occurred at the same time as her surgery. I wondered how reading Ellie's "story" made Jean feel? She had to know with certainty that Ellie was lying—intentionally or not. Perhaps Jean justified it by deciding that Ellie had lost her hold on reality. Did Jean think it was worth giving up our friendship for people who would lie to this extent? If she could lie about something like this, why would anyone think she was telling the truth about anything?

Trip advised Jean that she might be called as a witness if Ellie was allowed to testify about this supposed "event." According to Trip, Jean was reluctant, but said she would testify if asked. I suspected that she and Tom both better understood the seriousness of the situation after meeting with Trip. And I suspected that Ellie's comments may have made them realize that their attempt to continue to be friends with both families wasn't going to work. Maybe it even caused them to suspect that Ellie was neither truthful nor sane.

I really did feel like we were on the eve of a battle. I was certain this was the correct feeling to have the day before the trial began. To paraphrase: "There may be a day when innocent people give up without a fight, there may come a day when innocent people plead guilty just to avoid cost and stress, but that day is not today or tomorrow!"

Sunday afternoon I was more nervous than a fart in a skillet, to use a midwestern phrase. I had eaten all of the chocolate in the house—malted milk balls in the candy dish, peanut butter/chocolate cookies, and white chocolate macadamia nut cookies. I had never felt like this—not before my wedding day, not on the first day of a new school or a new job, not even before my first colonoscopy. And I missed the dogs. The house was empty without them. It was also quiet ... too quiet.

Steven spent a few hours going over his notes from his meeting with Trip. This caused me a sense of panic ... I didn't take any notes! Did I need notes? I was just truthfully answering questions about what happened. I knew the answers, didn't I? What if I did something wrong, or wore the wrong outfit? Everything was going to be my fault.

We had nothing else to do. We watched a movie. We worked on our computers. We read. We didn't even talk that much. We didn't have anything to prepare or anything else to do. I cleaned the stove and started the self-cleaning oven. It was the only dirty thing I could find in the house.

Hang in there, Michelle, I thought. *Just a few more days, and then everything will be over. One way or another, it will be over.* And I started my litany of prayers again.

Chapter 38

Monday October 26, 2009: Day One of the Trial

Both Steven and I viewed the trial as a battle. We agreed on that. Each of our approach to battle, however, was apparently different. On the night before the first day of the trial, Steven turned to me in bed and was amorous. I was amazed. I was wound tighter than a top and not able or willing to even consider sex. He on the other hand, thought that would be an excellent way to prepare for the first day of the trial. Not surprisingly, his advances were not successful.

I had no control over anything that was happening. The only thing I could control was how I dressed. I decided on a plum colored sweater with a matching scoop neck top and grey pants. I wore a pair of small gold earrings and wrapped a plum and grey scarf around my neck. Then I found an old navy pea coat that I don't think I'd worn in twenty years (in fact, it might have been Steven's) to wear as a coat. Steven predictably wore a navy sport coat, pink shirt, multi-colored but tasteful tie, and a pair of grey pants. No coat. These details don't sound important, but believe me, we both spent a lot of time on them.

We arrived at the courthouse early. Trip and his assistant Ann arrived shortly after us. They had four large boxes filled with files, notes, transcripts, and other papers. There was also a poster board–size display of our property and the adjacent properties, and another with a schematic of the entranceway to our house. Steven, Gregg, and I helped carry them up to the courtroom.

Steven and Trip went into a small conference room that they would use during the trial as a private place to meet. I waited with Gregg outside the courtroom. While Steven and Trip were in the conference room, our friends began to arrive. Don and Patricia arrived first; then Barry, their son; John arrived next; then Diane; then Tony; then Art who flew in all the way from Durango. Shortly after the trial had begun, Chris Hazlitt, our corporate attorney and the head of the Boulder Law office, arrived. Chris's presence there for the full length of the trial offered additional visible support for us. (We were especially grateful once we found out that his time wasn't being billed!)

When Steven and Trip emerged from the conference room, Trip stopped to speak to the gathering. "Your demeanor out here and in the courtroom is important. The jurors will be walking by you when you are out here during their breaks. You won't know who they are, but they will definitely know who you are. I don't want them to see you joking or laughing or cutting up. They need to realize that you understand how serious this is. So just keep that in mind. If you are in the courtroom, try to avoid making faces or comments. This is serious business and you need to maintain a serious and respectful demeanor."

"Where do you think Don and I should sit while everyone is in the courtroom?" I asked. Don was the only potential witness there and, like me, he wouldn't be allowed in the courtroom until after he had testified. Roger and Jimmy, our other two possible character witnesses, were not retired like Don so were at work that day. They would be there on Tuesday and Wednesday, if necessary, to testify and support Steven.

Trip thought about it for a while, then said, "For today at least, don't sit right outside the courtroom. Maybe in this area here," he said, pointing to where we were—outside the small conference room that he and Steven had been using and outside family court.

"The first order of business will be motions in limini, then jury selection," Trip said. At the confused looks of our friends, Trip explained. "Those are motions before the trial. The trial won't begin until after that, so it may not be until this afternoon." After a moment's pause, he added, "Oh, by the way, the judge had a murder trial that went to jury on Friday. If they reach a verdict, she is going to recess our trial to finish the murder trial. That may happen sometime today."

As 8:30 approached, we saw Foote and Ainsworth enter the court-room. Steven and Trip went in and were followed by all of our friends except for Don, who sat with me on the bench outside family court. It is challenging to describe the day because there were two stages running concurrently. Don and I were sitting outside pretending to read our Kindles, but neither of us actually read anything. We were speculating about what was going on inside the courtroom, commenting on the individuals going in and out of family court, and visiting about a variety of things over the course of the day—but our minds and hearts were in the court-room. During the day our only information about what did or did not happen in the courtroom came at breaks when our friends came outside.

I will try to recount what was happening in the courtroom, as well as what was happening outside the courtroom. I can recount what was going on outside the courtroom from direct knowledge, as that was where I was most of the time. I will use the transcripts of the trial to recount much of what was going on inside the courtroom. Since I wasn't actually inside the courtroom until I was called to testify, I won't be able to tell you first-hand what the jury's reaction was or how they looked, or make any comments about the non-verbal activities in the courtroom. I will try to keep my comments and notes about the testimony to a minimum.

If you are like I was before this experience, you may be "disappointed" in some of the questions and answers and perhaps in some of the language in opening and closing arguments. We are used to lawyers on television and in movies delivering well rehearsed, smooth speeches. They don't look at notes, they don't pause or use the wrong word on occasion. They don't repeat themselves. They're actors—their dialogue, their speeches are part of a script. The following transcripts are from the actual trial and are the words of the lawyers and the witnesses—not professional actors with scripts. I have not modified the quotes from the transcript to make the dialogue smoother. What you read is what was said.

Chapter 39

Monday, October 26: In the Courtroom

The judge's first order of business was the first motion in limini filed by Trip on behalf of his client. Basically the motion was intended to prevent Ellie from "volunteering information" about Steven's prior behavior (or her perception of it) that was not prompted by their interviews. In support of the motion in addressing the Court, Trip said, "... they want to bring in the discussion about other episodes of comments as late as ... as long ago as 2007. ... So once I found out that the prosecution intended to introduce that, I called Jean into my office this weekend to talk to her about whether or not this comment was made. She said it was not.

"Ellie told Detective Ainsworth ... she says that Steve Gesse is constantly making inappropriate remarks, even though by her own interview she hasn't really seen him since she docsn't socialize with him since 1992. ... She [Ellie] gave an example one time when Jean had just had a double mastectomy and she had not had reconstruction yet. She said that Gesse had said to her, Jean, you would look great in that blouse if you had some boobs. I brought Jean in. She said absolutely did Mr. Gesse never make that comment. In fact, Your Honor, she said he couldn't have made that comment because she had her reconstruction in the same surgery as her mastectomy. So it was factually impossible for him to have made the statement ... for Mr. Gesse to have made the statement."

In reading the court transcript, the judge ruled in our favor when she said, "What is relevant is what occurred that evening. And so that's what the victim can talk about. I'm not going to permit generalities about it because ... that's too unfairly prejudicial to the defendant."

Foote received permission for Ainsworth to be an "advisory witness," meaning he could stay in the courtroom even prior to his testimony. Trip received the same approval for Phil, our PI.

After reviewing the jury selection process, the Court (meaning the judge) said, "I'm not minimizing this case, but it seems to me that it's pretty straightforward in terms of picking a jury for three days."

After a short recess, jury selection began.

Judge Whalen instructed the potential jurors about the process; the requirements for selected jurors; the fact that jurors may be required for as long as four days; that there would be no sequestering of jurors for this trial; and other details of the process. She then read the "complaints" against my husband.

"The complaint simply describes the charge made by the prosecution against the defendant. It is not evidence of anything. The complaint in this case reads as follows: Count 1, Menacing, and Count 2, Prohibited Use of a Weapon.

"As I said, the charge against the defendant is not evidence. By pleading not guilty to the complaint, the defendant says that he did not commit the crime. The defendant is presumed to be innocent. Therefore, the prosecution has the burden of proving the counts beyond a reasonable doubt.

"Reasonable doubt means a doubt based upon reason and common sense which arises from a fair and rational consideration of all of the evidence, or the lack of evidence, in the case. It is a doubt which is not a vague, speculative, or imaginary doubt, but such a doubt as would cause reasonable people to hesitate to act in matters of importance to themselves.

"The jury will decide whether the prosecution has proven beyond a reasonable doubt that the defendant has done the things that were contained in the complaint."

All of the potential jurors then took their oaths prior to being called individually into the "box" to be seated. Then questioning by the judge, Foote, and Trip began. Jury selection took all of the first morning and some of the early afternoon. The transcript includes 156 pages that cover jury selection. It was a longer process than I envisioned. I assume that both the prosecution and the defense were trying to identify jurors that would be sympathetic to their cases. Many of the prosecution's questions seemed focused on a potential juror's willingness to convict someone of a crime with no evidence other than a "he said, she said."

Chapter 40

Monday October 26: Outside the Courtroom

Many of the candidates in the jury pool were given nicknames by our support group. There was the "rancher," the "priest" (that one was easy), the "bridal consultant," etc. There were lots of engineers—most candidates had either advanced degrees or PhD's. Gregg said he'd never seen such an educated jury pool. But you have to remember, this was Boulder, Colorado, and he lived in rural Tennessee. There probably was going to be a difference. We speculated whether an educated jury was good. Were we better off with the orderly mind of an engineer rather than a graduate school student? Was former military good or bad? Interestingly, the DA used one of his preemptive challenges to disqualify a potential juror who was former military when his response to the question, "Would you have any problem believing a military officer would lie?" was (and I do not paraphrase) "No. They all lie."

The judge's murder trial jury had reached a verdict mid-morning, so the jury selection process had stopped for the resolution of that trial. Every time there was a recess, Steven and Trip would emerge from the courtroom with hardly a look left or right and walk into the conference room we had commandeered. These meetings were always private and neither I nor anyone else was allowed in. This set the pattern for the whole time of the trial. I would look at their faces to see if I could tell how things were going, and all I could see was very serious people—one of whom I loved.

During breaks, our friends would gather around me and assure me that everything was going well or tell me anecdotes about some of the potential jurors' responses. They kept saying encouraging things, but I kept thinking that they were my friends, what else were they going to say?

At lunch, Steven and Trip left together to eat sandwiches in a conference room at Trip's nearby office. I encouraged our friends to get outside and have lunch at one of the local restaurants. Gregg and I ate lunch in the small lunchroom in the Justice Center. As we waited in line to order, Gregg would whisper to me when he thought he identified one of the potential jurors. Needless to say, it wasn't a very enjoyable lunch.

Despite their words of encouragement, none of our friends thought the judge was initially sympathetic to our not guilty plea. In fact, the consensus opinion (and you have to realize that none of us except our lawyer and his staff had ever been to a criminal trial) was that she thought we were wasting her time by not accepting a plea bargain. But this was just the impression from our supporters.

The "Peoples" witnesses had an escort, so they didn't have to wait outside like Don and I and our other witnesses would when they arrived. They were sequestered in a safe, perhaps nicer place. The only prosecution witness I saw that day was Ward when he was called as a witness in the afternoon. This was a very different looking gentleman than the one who had shown up at our house buffed, in a tight t-shirt and full of bravado. This gentleman was wearing a poorly cut grey suit, seemed slightly out of shape, and looked middle-aged. He didn't look like the cocky, cheeky Navy Seal who had bragged about his mental and physical toughness and his combat missions at our house six months before. I wouldn't have recognized him.

Chapter 41

Monday Afternoon, October 26: In the Courtroom

The trial began with directions to the jurors. This was followed by opening comments, with the prosecution going first. Here are some excerpts from Foote's opening comments:

" … Ms. Gesse answered the door. He [Ward] speaks to her. He says I need to see your husband, he's got to come down and apologize.

"After a couple of minutes of this conversation, Mr. Gesse appears out of nowhere, at least Ward didn't see where he came from. And he already had a trench coat on. …

"… Ward won't be able to tell you exactly what type of gun it was. He'll tell you that it had a long silver barrel somewhat like a flintlock type gun. He knows this because he knows what a flintlock type gun looks like.

"… [This] is a story of a man [Steven] who wanted to have, in fact demanded to have the last word …"

Excerpts from Trip's opening comments:

"Good afternoon. Mr. Gesse never had a gun. No matter what else, the evidence is going to show he didn't have a gun.

"… the evidence is going to show that not only was there no gun, there was no reason to have a gun.

"When my client said that he was corrected, Ellie corrected him. Steve you can't talk to women like that and that was it. It was over. There was nothing further.

"... the Navy Seal decided to come back to the house and he came up to the door and knocked on the door, and Michelle answered the door. And he said is Steve here. And Michelle said yes, and he asked can I talk to him. And Michelle said sure, and she took the Navy Seal into her house and walked him up to the kitchen where Steve was doing the dishes ...

"He was cleaning. He was bent over the sink. He had no opportunity... He's standing over the sink when the Navy Seal comes up behind him. ... He's not ... he's not armed doing the dishes. ...

"... from that moment forward the captain, who is a captain in the special warfare unit of the Navy Seals was in constant contact with Mr. Gesse from every moment forward from that time.

"... I thank you for listening to both sides of the story for the first time. Thank you."

The People called their first witness, Ward. Here are some excerpts of his testimony as taken from the trial transcript.

Foote: And what are your current duties in your current job there in your station?

Ward: Commanding officer of the training there for the basic SEAL course and the basic special warfare combat course and advance training schools.

Foote: Now, being a special officer in the navy or a Navy Seal, does that mean that you're out in the field all the time doing these special operations?

Ward: No. I haven't been out in the field as an active member of a team since 1989.

Foote: So since then if you haven't been out in the field what have you been doing?

Ward: A lot of staff work and Power Point.

(Note: this is very different from what Ward was telling us over drinks and dinner that night!)

. . .

Foote: And could you talk about that [your family] a little bit?

Ward: ... And then we had my daughter who is six in 2001.

(Note: this is verbatim from the transcript in Ward's testimony on October 26, 2009)

...

Foote: Did anything happen when your mom first arrived?

Ward: Everything was fine. And I think within five minutes Mr. Gesse made an inappropriate comment.

Foote: What was that comment?

Ward: I think the first comment was that she was a hottie or Ellie, you look like a hottie.

Foote: What did you think about that particular comment?

Ward: Didn't—just kind of didn't—kind of a surreal experience, couldn't believe he said that, kind of looked at the Tom guy and then we just kind of went on our business and talked about something else for a few minutes.

...

Foote: ... Now once you were in this discussion with your stepfather and your mom, was there—what was your stepfather's demeanor during the course of that discussion [after Ellie and Ward returned home].

Ward: Extremely upset, extremely angry and very—he's a very non-confrontational person. And I don't think I've ever in my time of knowing him seen him that upset and angry.

Foote: So take us through what your thought process was at this time that this discussion was going on.

Ward: I didn't want him going up there. I was a 100 percent convinced he was going to go up there. And I knew I only had one day of leave left before I had to go back to San Diego. And rather than wait until the next day to deal with it, you know, because I wanted to spend my last day of leave with my dad I decided to go up and confront Mr. Gesse that night.

. . .

Foote: So what happened once you got up to the residence?

Ward: Rang the doorbell one time, and there was no answer. I rang it a second time. Michelle came to the door. I said hey, is Steve there? He needs to come down and apologize to my mom, very calm. And then when I saw Mr. Gesse I told him, you know, you need to come down, apologize to my mom and that if he ever talked to my mom that way again I made an inappropriate comment which I regret.

Foote: What was that comment?

Ward: I told him if he ever talked that way again to my mom I'd rip his head off and shit down his neck.

(Note: Now I ask you, does that sound like the kind of comment made by someone who was "very calm"?)

. . .

Ward: I didn't plan on making that comment at all until I—until I saw him. Then I became—seeing him again made me angry.

Foote: Okay. Do you think you were conveying that anger? Do you think that someone could tell that you were angry?

Ward: Yes.

. . .

Foote: Where were you specifically when you started talking to Ms. Gesse?

Ward: In the entrance of the doorway.

Foote: Okay. And like inside or outside?

Ward: Outside.

(Note: This is called perjury.)

Foote: And did you see when you were talking to Ms. Gesse at the beginning Mr. Gesse anywhere?

Ward: No.

Foote: Okay. Did you see what direction he came from when you …

Ward: No.

Foote: … saw him?

Ward: No.

Foote: He just kind of appeared?

Ward: Yes.

Foote: When you saw him was he—what was he wearing when you first saw him?

Ward: He had pants on. And I'm not sure if he had a jacket on at the time or not. I don't remember.

. . .

Foote: So talk about how things transpired to that point?

Ward: He came in, he apologized to my mom and he asked me to step outside with him.

. . .

Foote: … let's pick it up from Mr. … Mr. Gesse asked you to come outside, you said okay. Then what happened?

Ward: … He walked about eight to ten feet away. He pulled out a large handgun with a very long barrel, a silver barrel. He pointed it at me and cocked it and he told me that if I ever came on his property again he'd kill me, did I understand.

. . .

Foote: Okay. Now, when Mr. Gesse pulled out the gun did you see where it came from?

Ward: No.

Foote: The general area where it came from or just didn't see it at all?

Ward: If as a guess I would guess that he had it in the back of his pants.

. . .

Foote: You mentioned that you were terrified as a result of this?

Ward: Yes.

Foote: Now, I guess the first question on people's minds is you're a Navy Seal, so why would you be terrified of something like this if you've been trained to deal with these things?

Ward: Well, I was home on leave. I wasn't in the combat zone. I wasn't, you know jumping out of an airplane, you know. Wasn't prepared at all for this situation.

. . .

Foote: Now, you mentioned that the—your description of the weapon, what you saw was a silver barrel?
Ward: Long silver barrel.
Foote: Did it remind you of any other type of weapon?
Ward: Flintlock.
Foote: Was it a flintlock?
Ward: No.
Foote: Okay. It just reminded you of a flintlock?
Ward: Because of the length of the barrel.

. . .

Foote: And do you remember how they [his parents] reacted?
Ward: I—I was terrified. And my mom, I think that her first action was to go call the—I told her to go call the police.
Foot: Was that something that you asked her to—told her to do?
Ward: Pretty confident that I told her to call the police.

. . .

Foote: So you mentioned that there was no weapons in the house to protect yourselves. But eventually did you find something that you thought you could use?
Ward: I went downstairs to the log pile outside the back door, got a log about five feet long, and then stood by the door jam and waited for the neighbor Tom to come down who had a pistol. I think he brought a .22 down with him. And he stayed with us until the police arrived.

. . .

Foote: Did you call Tom to come down?
Ward: My mom called him.

Foote: Was that something that was your direction, or do you know whether or not she did that on her own?

Ward: I'm pretty—pretty confident I remember telling her to do that, and if he had any kind of side arm if hc could bring that with him.

. . .

Foote: Do you remember how he [Mr. Gesse] was holding it at the time? I mean, was he holding it close to his body or out?

Ward: It was extended out.

. . .

Here are excerpts from the cross examination by Trip that began on the first day. As with all excerpts, these are taken directly from the trial transcript.

Trip: And on the night of this offense two officers came to your house; is that right, or your mother's house?

Ward: Yes sir.

Trip: And you told that officer—one officer talked to you, and the other one was kind of standing back, is that right?

Ward: Yes sir.

Trip: And do you recall the name of the officer that spoke to you?

Ward: Steve Ainsworth.

Trip: Steve Ainsworth spoke to you at the house?

Ward: Yes sir.

Trip: Okay. Is that this gentleman here? [pointing to Ainsworth seated at the prosecution table next to Foote]

Ward: No sir.

Trip: This is not Steve Ainsworth, Detective Ainsworth?

Ward: No sir.

(Note: Trip was pointing to Steve Ainsworth. Ainsworth had not been one of the officers to arrive at the scene. His first appearance at either home came when he arrived much later at our house with the search warrant. Ainsworth's appearance, with his very large handlebar mustache, is not like that of any other officer I saw that night or any other night.)

Trip: Okay. This is not—are you sure it wasn't Deputy Smith that spoke to you at the house?

(Note: Police reports show that it was Deputy Smith and not Ainsworth that spoke to Ward at the house on the evening of the incident.)

Ward: I—the guy gave me his card. He had a uniform on and he had a weapon.

Trip: And it's true that you told that officer that the gun appeared to be a flintlock?

Ward: Told him that it had a long silver barrel which reminded me of a flintlock because the flintlock also had a long barrel.

Trip: So you never used the words that it appeared to be a flintlock?

Ward: I said it looked—it had a long silver barrel and it appeared—it looked like a flintlock because it had a long barrel.

Trip: So at some point you did say the gun looked like a flintlock?

Ward: Because of the length of the barrel.

Trip: That was all part of it? You didn't just say it looked like a flintlock at one point with nothing else added to it?

Ward: It was a handgun with a long silver barrel that reminded me of a flintlock because of the length of the barrel.

Trip: No, I understand. I understand, Captain. What I'm asking is when you were talking to Deputy Smith, to the officer in the uniform, did you use the words by themselves it appeared to be a flintlock, or did you also say it had a long barrel like a flintlock?

Ward: I don't remember exactly, sir.

Trip: Is it possible you said it appeared to be a flintlock?

Ward; I don't remember, sir. I don't think so.

Trip: Okay. It's not—you don't think it's possible that just by itself you used the words it appeared to be a flintlock?

Ward: No, sir. I used the word flintlock in reference to the length of the barrel.

Trip: Okay. So likewise, it's your recollection that you would have never said it looked like a flintlock without reference to the barrel, just it looked like a flintlock?

Ward: It reminded me of a flintlock due to the length of the barrel.

Trip: I understand. I'm just asking you if you used the words that night while Tom was there and Deputy Smith were there it looked like a flintlock period?

Ward: I don't remember, sir.

Trip: You think you did not use those words?

. . .

This is followed by four more questions from Trip regarding the gun, Ward's statements to the officer answering the first call, and subsequent statements made by Ward regarding the type of gun. Ward is very consistent in his answers. They are always the same. He answers, "I don't remember, sir."

Trip: Okay. Isn't it true that the officer suggested to you that it could be a Thompson Contender? Do you remember that?

Ward: No, sir, I do not.

Trip: Okay. Isn't it true that he suggested it could be a Thompson Contender? You don't remember the officer talking to you about is this a Thompson Contender?

Ward: No, sir.

Trip: You don't remember replying I know what a gun looks like. Do you remember that?

Ward: No, sir.

Trip: Is it possible that you said that, or you just don't know?

Ward: Sir, I don't remember exactly what I told the officer. I don't think— the only thing I know for sure is what I wrote in my written statement and what I told Mr. Foote thus far.

Trip: You don't recall that despite the fact that the officer in the uniform

suggested that it could be a Thompson Contender you would not get
off the flintlock description and you stuck with it? That's not an accurate statement, is it?

Ward: As I stated previously, sir I—the length of the barrel reminded me
of a flintlock due to the length of the barrel.

(Note: This is most interesting for a number of reasons. A Thompson
Contender is not a common gun. Why would the officer suggest that that
was the gun Ward saw? Could it be because he saw that gun in the case
at our home? I suppose I will never know. All of the officer's notes and
Tom's testimony confirm that Ward used the term "flintlock" without reference to the length of the barrel.)

. . .

Trip: How much of it [the gun] did you see initially?

Ward: When it—the weapon first came out I saw about that much of the
length of the barrel [indicating]

Trip: Okay. So how far is that? Can you estimate how far that is?

Ward: I don't know. Is that a foot, maybe twelve inches. I'm not sure, sir.

Trip: In fact, you told the officer who was interviewing you at the house
that the gun was fourteen to eighteen inches long, correct?

Ward: I don't remember saying that, sir.

. . .

Trip: And you also demonstrated for the prosecutor the gun being fully
extended. And it looked to me like you were sighting down the barrel
as you demonstrated it. Is that an accurate statement?

Ward: Sir, I know it was pointed at me and he cocked it. That's all I can
tell you.

Trip: Okay. But I'm just trying to get back to your demonstration. Did
he have it up high by his head?

Ward: I can't tell you exactly where he had it, sir.

Trip: Did he have it extended down low or did he have …

Ward: Sir, I can't tell you the exact position.

. . .

Trip: And is it also true that you described it as an older flintlock pistol. You described it as older, did you not?

Ward: I don't—I don't remember saying that, sir.

Trip: Is it true or not?

Ward: I don't remember saying that, sir.

(Note: The same phrase, "I don't remember saying that, sir" is used by Ward to answer the next three questions.)

. . .

Ward: Sir, I never said the weapon was a flintlock. I said the barrel had the length of—reminded me of a flintlock … it was a pistol that had the length of a flintlock.

(Note: Ward's first statement as documented by the officers was that the gun was "a flintlock"; subsequently it was "like a flintlock"; only much later did it morph into a "long silver barrel" gun.)

. . .

Trip: Do you remember telling Detective Ainsworth you didn't feel comfortable in giving further information without legal counsel?

Ward: Yes, sir.

Trip: Do you remember that you didn't give any more—any further information until he told you that he was just trying to anticipate defenses by the defendant?

Ward: No sir. He just said he—we're doing an investigation here. We'd appreciate if you'd cooperate. And I checked with my lawyer at work, and they said you know, you're—you—you comply with the DA's office and just be—and tell the truth. And that's what I did.

Trip: Okay. So he didn't tell you that he was just anticipating the defenses?

Ward: No sir.

. . .

Trip: And on June 1, 2009, do you remember talking to a woman from the DA's office, Donna Teague?

Ward: I think she sent me an e-mail, yes, sir.

Trip: And you also talked to her on the phone, too?

Ward: Don't remember talking on the phone.

Trip: Do you remember telling her you did not think the gun was a flintlock?

Ward: No sir.

. . .

Trip introduced into exhibit a photo of a flintlock that Ms. Teague had e-mailed to Ward.

. . .

Trip: She asked you if this was similar to the gun you saw?

Ward: Yes sir.

Trip: And you told her that it meets the descriptions that you gave?

Ward: I said it was similar to the weapon I saw, yes, sir.

Trip: That gun has a black sight on the end of the barrel, does it not?

Ward: Yes sir.

Trip: It has no scope, does it?

Ward: No sir.

Trip: And you never described a gun that you saw as having a scope, did you?

Ward: Sir, once the weapon was pulled, I didn't look at the weapon at all. I just looked at Mr. Gesse.

Trip: You saw the full length of the barrel, but you didn't see whether or not it had a scope?

. . .

Trip: And in seeing a barrel long like that, one thing you knew for sure is it was not a semi-automatic?

Ward: I don't know, sir.

Trip: You don't know if it was a semi-automatic?

Ward: Well, I just assumed it—I mean, I assumed it was not because it was a pistol.

. . .

Trip: Okay. No one was mad or upset at the dinner party?
Ward: Well, I wasn't eating dinner, sir. They served dinner at a bar. I was standing to the side. So to call it a—it wasn't a classic sit around the table dinner party. It was more of a, you know, kitchen oriented bar kind of eating scenario.

(Note: You already know that I think I served a very nice dinner with pasta, salmon, and a salad. I don't know what kind of bars he goes to, but it was "dinner party" food if you ask me!)

. . .

Trip: And the next level of promotion for you was what?
Ward: Be one star.
Trip: Admiral?
Ward: Yes sir.
Trip: Takes congressional approval?
Ward: Takes senate approval to make captain.
Trip: Okay. So admiral takes congressional approval?
Ward: Yes, sir. All promotions do.
Trip: You talked about that at the party?
Ward: Don't remember talking about that.

. . .

Trip: ... when you were leaving. Did they walk you out, the Gesse's walk you out?
Ward: No sir. I think best of my recollection they stayed upstairs with— Tom and me and my mom walked out together.
Trip: So only you, your mom, and Tom walked out?
Ward: I don't know if Tom walked out with us or not, sir. I don't remember that. I just remember me and my mom leaving.

Trip: But your testimony is that the Gesse's did not walk out with you?

Ward: I don't remember if they did or they didn't.

Trip: You don't remember if they did?

Ward: I don't remember.

Trip: Do you remember that Michelle Gesse gave your mother some food to take home to Lee?

Ward: I don't remember her giving him food. But I do remember when I was home—that there was some food from the food that she [Michelle] prepared, in our kitchen. And I don't remember—I don't remember her giving that to my mom.

. . .

Trip: Okay. So you were very calm. You walked up, right, rang the doorbell, correct?

Ward: I wasn't—well, I wasn't—I was—I was upset at walking up the hill. Calm is not an accurate description.

. . .

Trip: … was he [Steven] standing beside her?

Ward: Don't remember.

Trip: You don't remember if they were side by side?

Ward: Could have been behind her. Could have been side by side. I don't remember.

Trip: Okay.

Ward: I think he was to the left of her.

Trip: And after you saw him did you ever lose sight of him again?

Ward: I—I think he went away for a short time, then he came back and he came down the hill with me. But I'm not—I don't remember exactly. He—he could have come right then, or he could have been gone for another thirty seconds, then came back. But I don't remember for sure.

Trip: Did you ever tell anybody else that he came to the door and then left?

Ward: No.

. . .

Trip: Okay. Did he walk away after you said I'll rip your head off?

Ward: Don't remember.

Trip: Okay. Isn't it true that you—he said to you after you said I want you to come apologize to my mom, okay, I'm good to go, let's go?

Ward: I just remember him saying okay. I don't remember him saying— exactly what he said.

Trip: Didn't you say he was eager to go?

Ward: I don't remember. I don't remember what I said, sir.

. . .

Trip: Instantly walked out the door, isn't that what you told Donna Teague, the investigator?

Ward: As soon as he had his coat on ...

Trip: Sorry?

Ward: As soon as he had his coat on he came down the hill with me.

Trip: Didn't you tell Donna Teague he instantly walked ...

Ward: As soon as he had his coat on he came instantly with me, yes.

Trip: Okay. So it wasn't instant, he had to get his coat?

Ward: Sir, I can't tell you the exact sequence at the door. I just know he didn't leave the house until he had his coat on.

Trip: Didn't you tell Detective Ainsworth he already had his coat on when he came to the door?

Ward: I don't remember, sir.

Trip: You don't remember if you told Detective Ainsworth he said okay, I'm going to go, let's go?

Ward: No, sir.

Trip: You don't remember that?

Ward: No, sir.

. . .

Trip: And you deny that Michelle let you in the house?

Ward: I did not come in the house.

Trip: You deny that what you said to her, you asked her if Steve was there, you deny that?

Ward: I said—I told her that Steve needed to come down and apologize to my mom.

Trip: You deny asking Michelle if you could talk to Steve and that you ...

Ward: I don't remember the exact words I said to her. All I remember for sure is he needed to come down, apologize to my mom.

Trip: You don't remember and you deny the fact that she let you in and you walked up the stairs to the kitchen door.

Ward: Did not walk in the house, no, sir.

Trip: And you deny the fact that you walked up behind Steve Gesse who was doing his dishes at the sink?

Ward: Yes, sir, I did not come into the house.

(Note: Ward repeated this statement in answer to at least five subsequent questions posed by Trip. It was probably a good thing that I wasn't in the courtroom to hear Ward's testimony. His lies were so blatant that I might not have been able to be silent throughout his testimony.)

. . .

Trip: Do you remember Steve telling you that he only meant to compliment your mom?

Ward: I don't remember exactly what he said, sir.

Trip: Do you remember that he said that he didn't want to come right now, that you had all been drinking, tomorrow would be better?

Ward: No, sir, I don't remember any of that.

Trip: You don't?

Ward: No sir.

Trip: Did that happen or you don't remember?

Ward: I don't remember.

Trip: Isn't it true that you said no, now. I'm not asking you, I'm telling you?

Ward: I don't remember, sir.

Trip: You don't remember whether you said that or it didn't happen?

Ward: I don't know, sir.

. . .

Trip: [Discussing the walk from our house to Ward's mother's home] It's
    your testimony to this jury that you never touched Mr. Gesse, correct?

Ward: Yes, sir.

Trip: It's your testimony that he walked in total silence to your parents'
    house?

Ward: Yes, sir.

Trip: Okay. Isn't it true that as you got to your parents' house, he walked
    in the front door, you said now apologize to my mother, and you said
    it definitively?

Ward: Don't remember saying that, sir.

Trip: Do you remember then saying now apologize to my father?

Ward: No, sir, I don't remember saying that.

Trip: You do remember that your mother—both your mother and father
    said to Steve Gesse that we love you, but you can't talk to Ellie that way.

Ward: I don't remember exactly what he said.

Trip: Do you remember anything like that?

Ward: I don't remember. I stood off to the side.

Trip: You don't remember your parents saying that they loved Mr. Gesse?

Ward: I don't know exactly what they said, sir.

Trip: So you don't recall that? I need to establish that.

Ward: I don't know exactly what they said.

. . .

Trip: Now with regard to the verbal threat that was made to you outside,
    I think you testified something about if you ever come to my property
    again I'll shoot you.

Ward: Yes, sir.

Trip: Well, you were asked about that before, you couldn't remember ex-
    actly what he said, right?

Ward: It was words to those effect, yes, sir.

Trip: Okay. So actually in fact, whenever anybody has asked you what
    words were used you said refer to my original police report, right?

Ward: Yes, sir.

Trip: Okay. And doesn't the original police report actually say if you come to my house and threaten me—it's both come to my house and threaten me—I will shoot you?

Ward: I don't have my statement. But if that's what I wrote, yes, sir, that's true. If that's what I wrote at that time, that's—if that's what I wrote, that's the best of my memory.

Trip: Well, let me show you the original police report.

(Note: The original police report does show that Ward's original statement indicated that Steven had said, "If you ever come to my home again and threaten me, I will shoot you.")

. . .

It was after 5:00 p.m. during Trip's cross examination that Judge Whalen decided to adjourn for the evening. When the jurors had been dismissed with the warning about not discussing the case, the judge said: "It's my impression that this case is not moving as efficiently as it should, frankly on both sides. The examinations need to be picked up."

Chapter 42

Monday October 26: Outside the Courtroom

When the trial was over for the day, Trip and Steven walked quickly to their conference room without a word. Our friends gathered around me with their summaries of the day's trial.

"Either Ward was really drunk or he has a bad case of 'can't remember shit'," Diane said. Patricia and the others agreed.

"Or he's changed his story so many times, he can't remember what he said to who or when he said it anymore," added Gregg.

Their impression was that Ward's credibility was being seriously impacted by his failure to remember any of the details of that evening, the details of his statements to investigators, and by his inability to identify Ainsworth, who did not show up initially at Ellie's home. They even suspected that the judge was losing patience with the prosecution and with Ward's "I don't remembers." I wasn't in the courtroom, so I wouldn't know. It was difficult for a civilian like me to believe that anyone involved in that evening couldn't remember every detail of their involvement.

"The guy doesn't even know how old his daughter is," laughed Diane.

When everyone else nodded and I looked confused, Barry added, "Yeah. He said she was born in 2001 and was six years old now. I'm no rocket scientist, but I know when Jeremy [Barry's son] was born and how old he is. What do you suppose that was about?"

"Who knows? It's tough to keep your lies straight," Art said. "Although the age of your kid shouldn't be too hard."

Jean had been there that afternoon, as she had agreed to testify, if necessary, to show that Ellie's statements about Steven were lies. I appreciated that. And I felt bad when she approached me and my circle of friends during a recess. She knew all of them and probably considered them friends of hers at one time, too. When she walked up to me, I raised my hand to shake hers. She looked surprised, but recovered and said, "I think a hug is more appropriate." I participated unenthusiastically. In the past, she would have been part of the group. Instead, most of my friends said "Hi" and turned their backs on her. I felt sorry for her a bit, but didn't have time to dwell on it. My feelings for Jean were not the primary focus of the day.

When someone asked, "Does Steven have a trench coat?" I didn't understand, but said, "No, of course not."

Patricia said, "You know, I've had some pretty great meals at your kitchen counter?"

Diane responded, "Ain't that the truth."

I had no idea what they were talking about. We do typically sit at the kitchen counter for dinner unless there are more than five folks eating. It's easier and I can keep talking to everyone while I cook.

John said, "You know he denies coming into the house that night."

I replied, "We knew he did. Think about what that says about his mindset and perhaps his sobriety that night. He came into our home and threatened us. That would not be good for his career or his case. In fact, if Steven had had a gun and had shot him there in our kitchen it would probably have been a good 'Make my Day defense.'"

Gregg said, "What a crock of shit—that the man doesn't know guns. For god's sake, he's a Navy Seal. He can probably put a gun together with his eyes closed."

"Under water," added Art.

My friends and their presence, and yes, even their comments, made me smile. As we said our goodbyes, Diane did temper her enthusiasm for the first day of the trial by adding, "I'm not exactly impartial." That was the truth. As they left, Gregg and I settled in the chairs to wait for Steven.

The wait for Steven and Trip to finish their private conference took about an hour. Gregg, Steven, and I drove home without actually talking very much in the car. It was a strange evening. I had spoken little to Steven all day, as every time he walked out of the courtroom, he walked with Trip directly to their meeting room. Even that evening, we spoke little about what had happened during the day. When I asked Steven what his impression of Ward's testimony and the trial was, his reply was curt. "He's a damn liar. I don't think a very good one, but what do I know. I don't have a clue how the jury is interpreting all this. And I have even less of an idea how what I might have said to Ellie hours before has to do with the whole thing. I feel like I'm on trial for having said something to a sad, old lady with no sense of humor, when all I was trying to do was compliment her. I have no idea how things are going and I'd really rather not talk about it all night. It's a damn farce."

I respected his wishes and didn't ask any more questions. We soaked in the tub and went to bed early, though neither of us fell asleep quickly.

Chapter 43

Tuesday Morning, October 27

On Tuesday, Steven's apparel was much the same as the previous day, but the sport coat was brown, the shirt yellow, and the pants dark brown. I didn't think I would testify on Tuesday, which affected my decision of what to wear. I wore a soft, short leather jacket in a brown/green color, brown turtleneck accented with a brown and beige scarf, brown pants, and small gold earrings. I think the scarves gave me a sense of warmth and protection, as I found them comforting.

The group from the previous day had expanded on Tuesday to include Jimmy and Roger, who along with Don, were going to be Steven's character witnesses. They, like Don and me, were going to wait outside while everyone else was allowed inside the courtroom. Trip suggested we take seats on the benches immediately outside the courtroom that morning, and once again cautioned us about decorum. From our new vantage point, we could see who was entering and exiting the courtroom.

As we waited outside, we talked and worried about the weather. Despite the mild weather on Tuesday, there was snow expected later that day and there were snow advisories. Trip didn't know if the character witnesses or I would be testifying on Tuesday or Wednesday. If we didn't testify on Tuesday, I was worried whether Jimmy, Roger, and Don could get to the justice center the next day. Jimmy and Roger lived south of Denver, and the drive to Boulder was over an hour for each of them in good weather.

Chapter 44

Tuesday, October 27: In the Courtroom

The judge called the jury into the courtroom. The judge's first comments were about the weather. She said, "So we do have a forecast for a winter storm, which is exciting, but can also result in hardship and inconvenience for everyone. We'll just see how the day goes and we'll deal with it as it comes along, but for now we are proceeding according to plan."

Ward was called to the stand and reminded that he was still under oath as Trip continued his cross-examination. Trip began by showing Ward the deputy's report of Ward's statements on the night in question.

Trip: And then it's true that what Mr. Gesse told you is, quote—and it's highlighted there for you, right— quote, if you ever come to my house again and threaten me, I will shoot you, got that?

Ward: Sure.

Trip: And that's an accurate accounting of what he said?

Ward: Yes, sir.

(Note: But yesterday Ward couldn't remember.)

. . .

Trip then showed Ward a transcript of the 911 call, and asked him to begin reading from it.

Ward: [Reading from the transcript of the 911 call] Okay. Okay. So you're telling me it was a service revolver type of gun being clicked back or was it an auto—semiautomatic? No, I don't know. It was—it was a handgun, he cocked it and pointed it at me and told me if I ever went to his house again, he would kill me.

. . .

Trip then provided Ward with a copy of Ward's conversation with Donna Teague, the investigator for the prosecution.

Trip: And does that refresh your recollection that you told Investigator Teague that once Mr. Gesse arrived at the door, you thought that Mr. Gesse already had a jacket on because he remembered letting Mr. Gesse—you remember telling Mr. Gesse that he should go to his mother's house—to your mother's house and apologize, and Mr. Gesse instantly agrees and instantly walked out the front door. Do you see where it says that?

Ward: Yes, sir.

Trip: Does that refresh your recollection that that's what you told Donna Teague happened at Mr. Gesse's door?

Ward: Yes, sir.

. . .

Trip: Does that refresh your recollection that when specifically talking to Investigator Teague about the gun that you saw, um, you told Investigator Teague that you remembered that Mr. Gesse pulled the gun out of the back of his pants. Does that refresh your recollection that that's what you told Donna Teague?

Ward: What I told her, sir, was that my—my guess is if he—where he took it from—that would be where I guess he took it from.

Trip: Okay. And you see there it doesn't say "guess," it says you remember, do you see that on the ...

Ward: Yes sir.

. . .

Trip then showed Ward the transcript of his interview with Detective
Ainsworth.

Trip: Does that refresh your recollection that after telling Detective
   Ainsworth that you did not feel comfortable giving further information without legal counsel, he then responded to you telling you that
   he had specific reasons for asking the question, that they had not been
   answered completely and he was trying to anticipate defenses by the
   defendant. And then you gave a response?
Ward: He—he wrote specifically I understand—I understand—given the
   questions I'm asking. I understand being uncomfortable, believe me.
   I'm not trying to put you uncomfortable. What I am doing is trying
   to anticipate what Gesse's defenses are going to be. That's in an e-mail,
   yes, sir.
Trip: Okay. So that's what—that's what he wrote you and then you responded after that.
Ward: Yes, sir. And I wrote back, Roger, I'll answer all his questions.

. . .

Trip: Now is it true that you told your father also that you've confronted
   the Taliban lots of times and you have walked into a room with a man
   that had a Kalashnikov and that this was the most frightened you have
   ever been?
Ward: No, sir, I never said that.

(Note: The comments referenced by Trip were documented as having
been said by Lee during his interview with officers the night of the incident. Lee also subsequently testified in the trial that Ward made those
comments.)

. . .

Trip: And you say that he [Steven] was slurring his speech?
Ward: I didn't speak with him on the way down to my parents' house. In
   my parents' house he—his speech was a little bit slurred, sir.

Trip: Was he slurring his speech while you were at his house during the—
what I'm going to refer to as party?

Ward: Um, I—I don't remember that, sir.

Trip: Okay. Was he walking like someone who was drinking when he was
at the party?

Ward: I don't remember, sir.

. . .

Trip: And it is your testimony that after calling [your neighbor] Tom, he
brought a .22 pistol to your house?

Ward: Yes, sir.

(Note: Tom subsequently testified that he did *not* bring a gun with him
to Ellie's house.)

. . .

Trip pointed out to Ward that he had initially told dispatch that Steven
was three feet away from him when he raised the gun. Ward subsequently
told Investigator Teague that Steven was eight feet away. In his earlier testimony, he said he paced the distance off and it was closer to eight feet.

Trip: If you could hold the end of that tape measure, that's eight feet. So
is that how—about how far apart you remember?

Ward: About—you—actually my pacing was a little further back.

Trip: So tell me when?

Ward: Keep going. About there, sir.

Trip: Right here?

Ward: Yes, sir.

Trip: Okay. I'm going to show that to you, okay?

Ward: Yes, sir, twelve feet.

Trip: Twelve and a half, actually.

Ward: Yes, sir.

Trip: This is three feet right? Let's look at three feet. This is three feet.

Ward: Yes, sir.

Trip: Can you fully extend your arm for me, please? … Do you recall, um, when they [dispatch]—when he pointed the gun at you, didn't you tell dispatch you were three feet apart when he pointed the gun at you?

Ward: I don't remember saying that to dispatch, sir.

Trip: If I showed you the dispatch tape, would that help refresh your recollection?

(Note: The transcript of the dispatch conversation confirmed that Ward had said three feet and when asked to confirm the distance, once again answered three feet. Trip also asked Ward when he had talked to his father about the incident, and Ward acknowledged after the police left. The transcript of Lee describing that conversation to officers afterwards says that Ward indicated Steven was three feet away. Surprisingly, Ward had no recollection of that conversation either.)

. . .

Trip: Didn't you also tell your father that you thought that you could take him [Steven] down and dive underneath him because you were pretty close together?

Ward: Pretty close, um, but unsure of distances at that time.

(Note: So you can decide for yourself how credible you found this witness.)

Chapter 45

Tuesday Morning, October 27: Outside the Courtroom

The Peoples' next witness was Ellie. I knew this because I was sitting directly outside the entrance to the courtroom and saw Ward exit and Ellie, accompanied by a witness advocate, walk into the courtroom. I was surprised that Ward didn't stay in the courtroom to support his mother and father, as he could now that he had been excused. I remember thinking that if this was all so traumatic for them, why wasn't their son staying close to support them? Why wasn't one or more of their other children with them for support? I was sitting outside with Don, Roger, and Jimmy for support … and I still felt weak.

Chapter 46

Tuesday Morning October 27: Inside the Courtroom

Ellie is sworn in and Foote begins his direct examination.

. . .

Foote: Do you know how long he [Steven] has been a neighbor?
Ellie: I'm guessing about fifteen years.
Foote: And if you saw him today, would you recognize him?
Ellie: Yes.
Foote: Is he in the courtroom today?
Ellie: No, I believe that he is outside.

(Note: I'm no legal expert and we don't watch a lot of TV, but doesn't everyone know the defendant is in the courtroom sitting next to his lawyer? That's where Steven was throughout the trial.)

. . .

Foote: Once you got to the Gesse's house what happened?
Ellie: I came in and, um, Mr. Gesse immediately—I was dressed, you know, and—to go to an opening, he said, um, Ward, your mom sure looks like a hotty today, and I said, Steven, that's an inappropriate re-mark. If you want to compliment me, you can say something else. And he—you know, said something else, oh you look nice, or you look like Susan Sarandon and that was that.

(Note: Sorry, Ms. Sarandon, I don't personally think being told someone looks like you is an insult, but there is no telling how anyone else feels.)

Foote: Did you take any of those comments as compliments?

Ellie: No.

Foote: Why not?

Ellie: I took them as insults because they were sexist remarks.

Foote: Was there anything that you remember specifically besides you look like somebody or what else?

Ellie: That the second remark that I remember was he said you look so good that you should leave your—you should get a younger boyfriend and leave—leave Lee and, you know, go for younger boyfriend.

. . .

Foote: So you said that then his wife gave you some wine, is that right?

Ellie: Yes, and a little hors d'oeuvre of some kind.

(Note: There was grilled salmon, pasta with olive oil and Brussels sprouts, and salad—that is not hors d'oeuvres—that is dinner! I am really getting tired of these folks saying they did not eat dinner at my house that night!)

. . .

When asked to describe further comments that offended her, Ellie responded (in part)

Ellie: … As I walked out the door, Mr. Gesse said to me—or said, Ward, your mom would look great in a thong.

Foote: Okay.

Ellie: And that, you know, was kind of—I couldn't wait to get to the front door so …

Foote: How were you feeling at that time?

Ellie: I was really un—very uncomfortable and—and I couldn't wait to get home.

. . .

When asked to describe Steven's actions when he arrived at their home:

Ellie: He made a—what I would consider to be a feeble apology and, um, I said—and my husband said, it's okay, Steve, you know you can't talk to women that way. We love you, you're our neighbor. And that was that.

. . .

When asked to describe the situation and the 911 call after Ward returned to the house:
Ellie: ... we were all scared for the rest of the evening. That—the nice people at the end of the 911 stayed on the phone until Steven Ainsworth got there and another man whose name I can't member, but they were great. And then a victim's advocate came up about midnight.

(Note: As I indicated previously, Steve Ainsworth did not come to their home that evening.)

. . .

Trip's cross-examination.

When asked to describe Steven's coat:
Ellie: Well, you know, like a big, heavy, um, maybe down coat or something. But it was a big coat ... brown or black.

(Note: In his opening statements, Foote described Steven as wearing a trench coat. Ward described Steven's jacket as light colored. It was a tan carhart jacket, what I would describe as a short rancher's jacket.)

. . .

Trip: And you didn't see a gun at any time when he was talking to you?
Ellie: No.
Trip: And you at no time saw what happened outside?
Ellie: No.

. . .

Trip: Okay. Do you remember the officer who arrived that night?

Ellie: Yes, that was Steve Ainsworth.

Trip: You think it was this—this is Detective Ainsworth right here.

Ellie: Yes, sir, I know it is.

Trip: You're certain of that?

Ellie: Yes, I am.

Trip: As certain of that as you were about the other details of this case?

Ellie: Yes.

Trip: Now—and did you talk to the officer when he arrived at your house that night?

Ellie: Yes.

(Note: As stated previously, Ainsworth did not come to their house that evening. Ainsworth's physical appearance because of his large handlebar mustache is not at all similar to that of any of the other officers from the Boulder sheriff's office who were there that evening.)

. . .

Trip: There wasn't like a gap of five to ten minutes? [when discussing the time between when Ward returned to the house and Ellie called 911]

Ellie: I don't think so.

Trip: Didn't you call Tom first?

Ellie: No.

Trip: You didn't call Tom first?

Ellie: I called him after I had called 911.

Trip: Okay. Didn't dispatch keep you and your family on the phone until officers arrived?

Ellie: Yes, sir.

Trip: And didn't Tom show up while you were on the phone with dispatch?

Ellie: I don't remember.

Trip: You didn't use a cell phone or something like that to call Tom?

Ellie: No, because it doesn't work very well in the mountains.

Trip: If Tom arrived during the—while you were still on the phone with dispatch, I mean, you would have had to have called him before the call to dispatch, would you not?

Ellie: No, he arrived after that because I would have had to have called him on our regular phone and we only have one line.

Trip: And did Tom—when Tom arrived, did he have a—did he bring a pistol with him?

Ellie: Yes, he brought the pistol he uses to scare the bears away, which has rubber pellets in it.

(Note: The transcript of the dispatch tape shows that Tom arrived shortly after the call was initiated. As previously stated, Tom did not bring a gun with him. The gun that shot rubber pellets was a shotgun—not a pistol—and Tom testified that he did not bring either with him.)

Chapter 47

Tuesday October 27: Outside the Courtroom

The end of Ellie's testimony signaled the morning break. We knew this because Ellie exited the courtroom accompanied by the victim's advocate or witness advocate or whoever the escort was. At about the same time, Steven and Trip exited and headed for their conference room and then our friends exited.

"Has she always been a space cadet?" one of them asked.

"Space cadet? I think she's on drugs," another one said.

"There is absolutely no consistency between any of their testimonies. No offense, but you'd think that after all these months they would at least have some things straight," Barry said.

"She couldn't identify Steven—she thought he was out here with you. Everyone knows the defendant is in the courtroom next to his attorney. Even if she didn't know who he was, you'd think she'd pick up on that," Diane said. "And since when is being told you looked like Susan Sarandon a felony? I hope when I'm seventy-two, someone says that to me."

"But you don't look like her at all," I couldn't resist adding.

"Thanks," she replied.

"This whole thing is such a crock of shit," Art said. "I can't believe the whole thing hasn't been thrown out before this. Steven isn't on trial for offending Ellie, so I really don't understand what any of this has to do with the charges. No one besides Ward has even suggested seeing anything criminal."

"And we're paying for it," Don said (our fiscal conservative).

"What a waste of money," agreed Barry.

"Especially ours," I added.

Tom had showed up in the lobby waiting to be called by the prosecution as a witness. He must not have needed the security of the escort as he waited in the lobby where I waited with Don, Roger, and Jimmy. Ellie and Ward sat in the next set of benches about ten feet away. Tom made small talk about things not related to the trial—weather mostly, if I remember correctly. But when he walked over to talk to Ward and Ellie, the four of us knew we didn't want to visit with him anymore.

Chapter 48

Tuesday October 27: Inside the Courtroom

Lee was the next prosecution witness. He was accompanied into the courtroom by an escort and sworn in. Below are excerpts from his testimony
as taken from the transcript.

Lee recounted his version of the comments that supposedly upset Ellie
and Ward, and discussed how terrible he felt.

Foote: … did you start to make decisions about how it should be handled?

Lee: Yes, I did.

Foote: Talk about that.

Lee: Well, you can't hear something like this without it really upsetting
you, and especially someone that you really love and you have loved
so long, and your son was there and your wife was being put through
this. And I became very agitated and upset … I thought, oh my god,
this is like you have—Mr. Gesse, you have imaginatively first, and
then verbally, like, raped my wife.

(Note: Descriptions of the testimony from our friends said Lee was crying
when he said this, although that is not something that was indicated in
the transcript.)

. . .

When asked to describe Steven's apology:

Lee: And then our son said to Mr. Gesse, you need to apologize to my father, too. And just before he did, I—I hate for things like this to hap-

pen, I'm a very gentle person and I very carefully reached out my hand and—so it wouldn't be intimidating—slowly and just touched him on the forearm and I said to Mr. Gesse, Steve, I love you. I want the very best for you, but you can't talk to a woman this way.

(If you remember, Ward "couldn't remember" these comments by Lee.)

. . .

Foote: and why were you so upset? I mean, you hadn't seen a gun or anything like that?

Lee: Well, our son is an honest person, he's a man of great integrity. I felt that any man who could think that these things Mr. Gesse did, and say the things that he did to my wife was like a verbal rape, and I was—I was just—this was horrible. ...

Foote: do you need a couple of moments?

(Lee is apparently crying now.)

. . .

Foote: Do you remember also talking to 911 at some point?

Lee: I don't—I don't think—I don't think I did.

(Note: the 911 transcript shows that Ellie made the call, then passed the phone to Lee, who then passed the phone to Ward. All three of them were on the phone with the 911 dispatch operator at different times.)

. . .

Excerpts from the cross-examination by Trip, again from the trial transcripts.

Trip: And you did not see any of the events that transpired as they walked—as your son walked back from the Gesse home with Mr. Gesse. You couldn't see that, could you?

Lee: I didn't see that.

. . .

Lee: I remember our son coming in saying he pulled a gun on me, cocked it, and I'll kill you if ... and I don't remember anything beyond that, maybe he didn't say anything beyond that. I—I don't know.

. . .

Trip: And Tom came over while she [Ellie] was still on the phone with 911, right?

Lee: I'm almost certain of that. I—there's a little bit of blank there, but we've gone over it since then, and I wondered—I was told that she had called Tom.

Trip: Who told you that?

Lee: I don't know. I was—I think my wife, could have been our son. We have a cell phone, so as I pulled it together I figured that she had the line to the—the detectives and then, um, apparently by using our cell phone, I don't know. I know that—I had been told that—I really blanked out as to when in the sequence of things Tom came down, but I know that he was there shortly after we had placed the 911 call. And the—I'm quite certain it was—almost certain it was my wife who did the calling.

. . .

Trip: And he [Ward] also told you that he thought that he had a 90 percent chance of taking Mr. Gesse down, didn't he, but he decided not to do that. Do you recall that?

Lee: Yes.

Trip: And he said that he thought that he could take him down because they were pretty close together, do you recall that?

Lee: Yes.

. . .

Trip: When did he [Ward] tell you that he had caused all the trouble?

Lee: That he had caused all the trouble? Well, he's used different words over the last seven months, and our son is ... is ... is very sensitive. He's very responsible, and he—it kills—it really bothers him when he's put other people in trouble. And many times since then he's, oh my goodness, you know, I've caused you all this trouble, and every time—almost every time he says that, I say you saved my life. I don't know what I would have done if I had gone up and confronted Mr. Gesse about these terrible things. I don't know if they would have taken revenge on my wife and on you. And I don't want you bearing this awful burden. You did a wonderful, courageous thing by saying, no, you're not going to go up.

(Note: I can't help but point out that Ward came to our home and threatened the life of my husband and gave him no choice but to follow him to Lee's home. If he hadn't come to our home none of this would have happened, and we would have gone to bed thinking that everyone had a nice time at our home that evening—not planning an attack on Lee, Ellie, or Ward.)

. . .

Once Lee was finished with cross-examination, the two lawyers approached the bench. Foote wants to introduce a discussion of what happened in the past with perceived (or as we know—fictional) insults to women. At this point even the judge is beginning to lose patience and says:

Judge: Well, let me tell you, there's a lot of irrelevant information that's being elicited from this witness and others, and I … I am getting somewhat frustrated at the pace of this trial. This case is a simple case. The evidence should have been closed today. I mean, it's basically the people who were there for … and so I'm just flabbergasted when I look at the list of potential witnesses and I look at what time it is and where we are in this case.

So having said that, I will not permit you to go into the more specifics about prior comments that he made. I don't think that it's warranted. It's not relevant. And if you start making relevance objectives in terms of cross-examination I'm going to be sustaining them because there's a whole lot of time wasting going on here.

After a very short re-direct and a discussion about jury instructions, the court took its lunch recess.

Chapter 49

Tuesday October 27: Outside the Courtroom

My friends and I watched Lee emerge from the courtroom with a smile on his face. Don said, "He's laughing. I can't believe it. He looks like he's laughing."

No one else in our little band said anything. We simply watched Lee walk over and join Ward and Ellie. There were smiles all around. We had previously heard Ward speaking on his cell phone to his wife, telling her she had more time to shop on the Pearl Street Mall with their daughter. They had agreed on what time to meet to get to the airport for their flight. Ward had a small, wheeled travel bag with him. He was flying out later that day. Apparently he wasn't interested enough in the outcome of the trial to stay in town—or even to stay in the courtroom when his mother or his stepfather testified. His wife and daughter were enjoying a nice day of shopping on the mall. I had to admit that the difference in mood between "their camp" and "our camp" was palpable. They could have been waiting outside traffic court for a minor violation instead of being the prosecution's witnesses for a criminal felony trial.

Shortly after Lee exited, everyone else began to file out of the courtroom. Diane's first comment was, "I don't know about the rest of you, but Lee seemed able to cry on demand when he wanted to look pitiful."

"Cry?" Don said. "He was smiling and laughing when he came out of the courtroom."

"I knew it," Barry said. "It didn't look sincere to me, though he did look pretty pitiful at times."

"How do you think the jury felt?" I asked. "Do you think they thought it was an act?"

"Hard to tell," Patricia said. "But I wouldn't mind someone saying I should have a younger husband. I'd take it as a compliment." She directed this last comment to her husband, Don.

"Oh, brother," was his only response.

"I don't know," Gregg said. "Do you think Steven's comments struck too close to home? Maybe she did have a younger boyfriend at one time."

"We'll never know, will we?" Art said.

"I still think it's strange how none of them stayed in the courtroom after they testified," Diane said.

"Ward is leaving town this afternoon. His wife and kid are shopping on the mall this morning. It's been a great holiday for them," I said bitterly.

"It's funny," Diane commented. "Lee talked about how trying emotionally this whole thing has been on them, but none of his kids or his wife's kids or Ward's family was here to support them during the trial. His other kids or Ellie's kids could have been here. Hell, they could have been in the courtroom the whole time and could still be there. But they testify and leave. They sure don't act traumatized if you ask me."

No one said anything, but we all nodded in agreement.

Despite all the concerns about the weather, it was still a nice day outside. I encouraged our friends to walk to one of the local Boulder restaurants and have a nice lunch instead of eating in the Justice Center coffee shop. They took off in different directions, leaving Gregg and me with Steven and Trip.

"Why don't you walk with us to our law office," said Trip. "Ann ordered lunch and I'm sure there is plenty for all four of us."

"Do you need to speak to Steven alone?" I asked.

"Don't worry. We'll throw you out after you eat your sandwich and still have enough time to talk. The fresh air will be good for all of us. Let's go."

So Gregg and I followed Trip and Steven and walked the few blocks to his law office where we had sandwiches, chips, and sodas. Gregg and I left Trip and Steven alone after eating and walked back to the Justice Center.

Chapter 50

Tuesday Afternoon, October 27: Inside the Courtroom

Tom was the next witness for the prosecution. The following are excerpts from the trial transcript of Tom's testimony.

Foote: Do you remember anything happening about the time that she [Ellie] came in?

Tom: Yeah. She came in, we made greetings, and she sat down to eat and, you know, continued to make chit chat.

Foote: Do you remember any kind of comments made by Mr. Gesse towards Ellie at that time?

Tom: There was a couple of comments that Steve made towards Ellie having to do with her appearance and, you know, what she'd look like in a thong. And I can't remember all—there was another comment about how she was too young for her husband, you know, those kind of things.

Foote: Okay. So after those comments were made, do you remember about how long you all stayed at the Gesse's residence?

Tom: Yeah. I think we broke up shortly before 7:30. So it was on the order of an hour in total that Ellie was there.

. . .

Foote: Do you remember if she [Ellie] asked you about any kind of weapons or anything?

Tom: Yeah. I think she said something like we don't have any weapons in the house, we're scared, do you have any weapons. And I said yes, I just got an old .22 pistol. But you know, I didn't do anything with it.

Foote: … you didn't take it down with you?
Tom: Correct.

Excerpts from Trip's cross-examination:

Trip: Now you did not take your .22 to the house, did you?
Tom: That's right, I did not.
Trip: Never had it in your possession, right?
Tom: No.
Trip: Didn't show it anybody?
Tom: No.
Trip: The statement about the thong, was that made in the early part of
    the evening?
Tom: It was after Ellie arrived, so approximately 6:15, 6:30.
Trip: The front end of the dinner party or as they were leaving?
Tom: It was on the front end.
Trip: And afterwards Ward gave Mr. Gesse a bear hug?
Tom: Yes.
Trip: It was a friendly bear hug?
Tom: Yes.
Trip: And there were no raised voices?
Tom: Right. Correct.
Trip: Nobody got confrontational?
Tom: Right.
Trip: Nobody's tempers raised?
Tom: Yes.
Trip: And after the bear hug everything was fine?
Tom: Apparently it was fine, yes.
Trip: As far as you could see?
Tom: As far as I could see everybody was calm and, as you say, there was
    no raised voices, harsh words or those kind of things.
Trip: Um-hum. In fact, everybody continued to carry on discussions in
    their normal way?
Tom: Yes.

. . .

Trip: And this carried on until it was time to go?

Tom: Right.

Trip: And as people got up to leave there were no hard feelings that you could detect, were there?

Tom: That's right.

Trip: And in fact, everybody left together?

Tom: Yes.

Trip: And Steve and Michelle walked you out to the front door?

Tom: Right.

Trip: And people said their goodbyes in friendly fashions, right?

Tom: Right.

Trip: In fact, Ward and Ellie said friendly goodbyes to the Gesse's?

Tom: Yes.

Trip: In fact, Michelle Gesse had prepared some of the dinner for Ellie to take home to Lee?

Tom: Right.

Trip: And Ellie was grateful for the dinner?

Tom: Yes.

Trip: And that's as far as—I mean a witness who is standing there at that dinner and as they leave, that's all you see is people getting along?

Tom: That's accurate, yes.

Trip: Also everybody had been drinking?

Tom: Right.

Trip: You didn't see him—Mr. Gesse slurring his words?

Tom: No.

Trip: He wasn't walking like a drunk?

Tom: No.

. . .

Trip: And isn't it true that he [Ward] told you the gun looked like a flintlock?

Tom: That's my recollection, right.

Trip: So it was big and it looked like a flintlock, correct?

Tom: Those were almost his exact words, yeah.

Trip: And when you heard this, in fact, Tom, this confused you because you did not believe that Mr. Gesse had a flintlock?

Tom: That's correct.

. . .

Trip: And you know what a flintlock looks like because your brother has flintlocks?

Tom: Yeah, my brother's into black powder.

Trip: And that's what a flintlock is, it's a—it's a—it's a black powder gun. It's the kind of old like Revolutionary War gun where you have to feed the powder down the barrel and then put the ball down the barrel and tap it down solid, right?

Tom: Correct.

Trip: And then the flintlock itself, what a flintlock is, is that big hammer on the side of the gun that strikes the flint?

Tom: Right.

Trip: That's the flintlock?

Tom: That's—I think that's why they call it a flintlock, yeah.

Trip: And when you —and so if you saw a big hammer on the side of a gun that looks like a flintlock in his gun collection you would have recognized that as a flintlock?

Tom: I would have, yes.

Trip: How long ago did you look at his guns? What was the most recent time?

Tom: I think the most recent time was, I don't know, last summer about a year ago.

Trip: About a year ago?

Tom: Yeah.

Trip: You never saw a flintlock in his gun collection?

Tom: I never did.

Trip: And that's why you were confused when Ward said that?

Tom: Yes.

Trip: And in addition to not seeing a flintlock, you saw no implements of flintlocks?

Tom: That's right.

Trip: Like your brother, people who have flintlocks, they have implements like the balls and the pads and gunpowder, and there's a whole host of implements that go along with having a flintlock, correct?

Tom: Yes. Right.

Trip: And you didn't see any evidence of that?

Tom: Saw none of it.

Trip: How often do you go over to the Gesse's?

Tom: Frequently. It's not unusual to, you know, have them call me up on the spur of the moment. And especially when one of us is out of town, we're offered food.

Trip: And you've never seen any implements of flintlocks at his house?

Tom: Correct.

Trip: And do you have an opinion as to his character for peacefulness?

Tom: Yes, I do.

Trip: And what is it?

Tom: I think Steve is a peaceful man.

Trip: No further questions your honor.

Foote's re-direct:

Foote: Tom, do you have any opinion of the truthfulness of Ward?

Tom: No.

Foote: Do you have an opinion of the parent's truthfulness?

Tom: Yes.

Foote: What was that?

Trip: Your Honor, I'm going to object.

Judge: Approach please.

What followed at the bench:

Foote: Your Honor, Trip has put character into question here. So I think that I can cross-examine regarding character.

Judge: How has he done that?

Foot: He asked about Mr. Gesse's character for peacefulness.

Judge: He—he put the defendant's character for peacefulness at issue, but he didn't attach the character of the alleged victims for untruthfulness through this witness. So do you have anything else to say?

Foote: No.

Judge: The objection is sustained.

At that point, Tom was excused from the stand.

The next prosecution witness to be called was Deputy Bonafede, who drove Steven to the jail. As there was nothing new in his transcript, I will not go into it.

The next prosecution witness was Detective Ainsworth.

. . .

Foote: … and then matching the description of the long silver barrel that you indicated, how many guns matched that description?

(Note: the description that Ainsworth had given moments before was "a silver long barrel handgun with a flintlock—flintlock like appearance.")

Ainsworth: One.

Foote: Where did you find it?

Ainsworth: I found it in a silver zero Weatherby case on I don't know if it was a living room, looked more like a library type sitting room area inside the front door and just down the hallway.

(Note: In the testimony that followed, Ainsworth said he examined the contents of the gun safes and found no other guns that matched the description. You may remember that I thought that there was no real search for any other possible weapon. The gun case and the Thompson Contender were submitted into evidence.)

Trip's cross-examination:

Ainsworth: [reading the description of the gun as described in the search warrant] A silver handgun—yeah, I remember now. Silver handgun fourteen to eighteen inches long capable of being cocked externally.

Trip: A silver handgun, not a silver barrel, right?

Ainsworth: Um-hum.

Trip: Fourteen to eighteen inches long, right?

Ainsworth: Correct.

Trip: And you put that description on there because you wrote in your affidavit that Deputy Smith told you that Ward described the gun as a silver handgun about fourteen to eighteen inches long?

Ainsworth: Correct.

Trip: You didn't come up with that description out of nowhere?

Ainsworth: No.

Trip: In fact, nowhere in your affidavit do you say any other description than that description?

Ainsworth: That's correct.

Trip: You don't say anything about flintlock, right?

Ainsworth: No.

Trip: You don't say anything about long silver barrel?

Ainsworth: No.

Trip: And yet, you knew to look for a flintlock?

Ainsworth: I did.

Trip: And that was the closest thing you found, the gun with the scope on it?

Ainsworth: It was.

Trip: In fact, I think you said for the prosecutor that that was the only gun in the house that matched the description of what you were looking for?

Ainsworth: That was the only gun that I found that matched the description.

Once Ainsworth was done testifying, the prosecution rested their case. At this point, Trip asked for some time to check on the location of his witnesses since the prosecution had rested earlier than expected. He also wanted time to confer with his client. Trip also asked to make a motion. The judge agreed with his requests for a break and asked for his motion.

Trip: Your Honor, the People have rested, and they have not identified Steve Gesse as the person who made the threat. Nobody identified him as the person who went over to that house. The only person who identified him was Deputy Bonafede. He identified the person he arrested.

Deputy Bonafede was clear that he didn't say anything about having earlier contact with anyone. So there's no evidentiary link between—other than, you know, this person, the person that he arrested had Steve Gesse's name, and the people—and the person that was in the doorway was referred to as Steve Gesse. But the person in the doorway was not identified, Your Honor. And they've not met their burden of proof. And I move for judgment of acquittal.

It was a good try but it didn't work. In the words of the Court:

Judge: In ruling on a defendant's motion for judgment of acquittal, the Court must determine whether the relevant evidence, including identification evidence, both direct and circumstantial when viewed as a whole in the light most favorable to the prosecution, not to the defendant, is substantial and sufficient to support a conclusion by a reasonable mind that the defendant is guilty beyond a reasonable doubt as to each element of the charge. And the Court does find that the relevant evidence here meets that standard.

In other words, the trial would continue.

Chapter 51

Tuesday Afternoon, October 27: Outside the Courtroom

Trip walked immediately up to us when he came out of the courtroom. He knew Jimmy, Don, and Roger from his previous meetings with them.

"Good, you're here," he said. "I didn't think you were going to testify today, but it looks like you're going to be called as soon as the courtroom is called back in session. This is good—especially since we don't know what the weather is going to be like tomorrow and the two of you (pointing to Jimmy and Roger) live a long way from here. Just stay here till you're called. And remember, just answer the questions. Don't volunteer anything else."

"And we can stay in the courtroom once we've testified, right?" asked Jimmy

"Correct. And you will probably get called this afternoon, too," Trip added, facing me.

Had I dressed correctly? I wondered. It was amazing that this was the first thought that went through my mind as Trip and Steven went off to their conference room.

"Well, Trip tried to get everything dropped since no one had been able to actually identify Steven," Diane said. Everyone nodded in response.

"What's with the mustache?" wondered Art.

"You mean Wyatt Earp?" asked Diane. Everyone chuckled, but the mood was somber as we moved into the second phase of the trial.

"Why was Tom a witness for the prosecution?" asked Diane. "He was really a witness for us, I think."

As the others nodded, I replied, "He was actually subpoenaed by both sides, so I guess he got called by the prosecution since they go first. Tom had initially refused to speak to Trip, but after I asked Jean to please have him reconsider, he did meet with Trip. And they both met with Trip Saturday to refute Ellie's statements about Steven's comments to Jean. Jean was prepared to testify on Monday if necessary. They did step up to the plate at the end."

"In the end," someone muttered.

"I'll stay out here with you while the others go in to testify," Patricia said. Up until then Don had been by my side, and today so had Roger and Jimmy.

"You don't have to," I responded.

"I know," she said, "but I want to." And that was the end of that conversation.

Chapter 52

Tuesday Afternoon, October 27: Inside the Courtroom

The first order of business was for the Court to review Steven's rights and his option not to testify. Steven had already decided to testify. He felt that this would be the first time anyone had actually listened to him since that fateful night. Of course Ward, Ellie, Lee, and Tom would not be in the courtroom to listen to his testimony.

Judge: Do you understand that you have the right to testify?
Steven: Yes.
Judge: And do you understand that if you want to testify, then no one can prevent you from doing so?
Steven: Yes.
Judge: Do you understand that if you do testify, the prosecution will be allowed to cross-examine you?
Steven: Yes.

Then followed a series of questions where the Court advised Steven that if he chose to testify, any prior felony conviction could be discussed and that the decision to testify or not to testify could be only his.

Judge: What is your decision about whether or not to testify?
Steven: I will testify.

. . .

Thereafter followed a discussion of which witnesses would be called today.

Trip: Your Honor, I have three really short, fast witnesses. And then Michelle Gesse will be testifying. We should be able to get all of that in this afternoon.

The prosecution knew that Trip intended to call Jimmy, Roger, and Don to testify as to Steven's "peacefulness." In fact, an investigator from the DA's office had called all three of these individuals and spoke to them prior to the start of the trial. Trip indicating that he was going to call these three gentlemen should not have been a surprise to the prosecution. Despite this, Foote objected.

Foote: And Judge, based on that I would object. Character for peacefulness I don't think is a pertinent trait in this case. And I don't think that they should be called up to the stand and then asked questions and then me having to object to it, and then if they're sustained they leave. So I'm asking for the Court to exclude those witnesses based on the fact that it seems that they're going to be character for peacefulness witnesses.

Trip: Your Honor, and I have a—I have a bench brief on that.

Basically, Trip presented the judge with a Colorado case in which "Peacefulness is a pertinent character trait when the suspect is charged with a violent crime." After giving Foote time to review the case and raise his ongoing objection, and reviewing the case herself, the judge ruled in favor of allowing the three character witnesses.

Judge: Nevertheless, I do think that it is permissible for the defendant here to present reputation evidence that he is a moral—or maybe not moral, but a law abiding person with propensity for peacefulness. And obviously, the reason for introducing that would be to show that he would probably—he's not someone who would probably commit the crime charged here ... and so I will permit that testimony to be presented.

Each of the character witnesses was called in turn. Each was sworn in, asked to spell their name, state their occupation, and explain how and how long they knew Steven. The gist of each testimony was the same.

Trip: Do you have—based on your life's experience with him [Steven] over the last fifteen years, do you have an opinion as to whether he's a peaceful person?

Friend: Yes.

Trip: And what is that opinion?

Friend: My opinion is that Steve is extremely peaceful in character.

. . .

I will highlight Foote's cross-examination of Roger. Roger was the first of the three witnesses and Foote's cross-examination of Roger was consistent with his cross-examinations of the other character witnesses. Other than making the point that the character witnesses knew Steven but not Ward, Ellie, or Lee, I don't actually understand the purpose of his cross examination. I think it is best described as a fishing trip, but I'll let you read and decide.

. . .

Foote: Roger, you're appearing here on Mr. Gesse's behalf, is that correct?

Roger: Yes, I am.

Foote: And that's because Mr. Gesse asked you to come and testify on his behalf.

Roger: Trip asked me, yes.

Foote: Okay. And that's because you were aware that this case was pending against Mr. Gesse, correct?

Roger: Yes.

Foote: And you had spoken to Mr. Gesse about this case before?

Roger: Very briefly.

Foote: Very briefly. When did you speak to him about it?

Roger: It was in the newspaper. So I was aware of what had happened from the newspaper, but that's all really.

Foote: Okay. You read about it in the newspaper.

Roger: Yes.

Foote: So you read the news. And sometimes you come across stories in the news, like crime stories for example, is that fair to say?

Roger: Yes.

Foote: And when you come across those crime stories in the newspaper or on the TV, for example, you're pretty familiar with sometimes reporters go out to somebody's neighborhood and they interview neighbors and ask the neighbors do you think this guy could have done it? Have you seen that before in a newspaper report or a TV report?

Roger: Yes.

Foote: And you also know that the neighbors will say typically, if not all the time, no way this guy could have done it, right?

Roger: Not necessarily.

Foote: You've seen that though?

Roger: I—yeah. Yes.

Foote: And you also know that sometimes in those same cases where the neighbors say …

At this point, Trip objects. The two lawyers move to the bench. Basically, the judge sustains Trip's objection saying, "You can argue that in closing." But Foote persists.

Foote: Roger, you would agree with me that sometimes people do things out of character when they're intoxicated, would you not?

Roger: Yes.

Foote: So you may have somebody that's normally a peaceful person, but once they get intoxicated they could be not peaceful anymore.

Trip objects.

Foote: And then you spoke to Mr. Gesse.

Roger: He told me he couldn't talk about it.

Foote: Okay. So all you know is by this short blurb in the newspaper what this case is all about, is that fair to say?

Roger: Effectively, yes.

Foote: You've never spoken to Ward?

Roger: No.

Foote: Never spoken to Ellie?

Roger: No.

Foote: Lee?

Roger: No.

Foote: You haven't heard any of the evidence that's been presented in this courtroom?

Roger: No.

Foote: But by implication isn't it the case that you're saying that Mr. Gesse is a peaceful guy, so there's no way he could have committed this particular offense?

Roger: His character is peaceful.

Foote: And by implication there's no way he could have committed this offense, is that what you're saying?

Roger: That's not what I was asked, no.

Foote: Well, is that what you're saying?

Roger: By implication, I presume that would be what I'm saying.

Foote: Okay. So you're also saying that you think better—you know better than this jury about what happened in that case?

Trip's objection is overruled.

Foote: Go ahead.

Roger: No, I'm not saying I know what happened at all.

(Note: The above comments are from the transcript. I am not making this up.)

Chapter 53

Tuesday Afternoon, October 27: In the Courtroom

And then it was my turn. I assumed I would be calm. In my consulting activities, I regularly stand in front of large groups to teach. I have spoken or taught to groups as large as fifty to seventy-five people without a bit of nervousness. Here I was, getting ready to answer questions truthfully to a box filled with twelve individuals whose decision would have a huge impact on my life, and I was terrified. My voice actually cracked in the beginning, though as Trip and I got our rhythm going, it got easier.

I was called into the courtroom and like all the other witnesses, sworn in, asked to spell my name, asked about my occupation, and my relationship to Steven. In the beginning, Trip's questions walked me through two large poster board exhibits. The first was a layout of our property and its relationship to our neighbors; the second was a schematic of the entranceway to our house, including the downstairs family room and the overhead walkway. He walked me through the early part of the evening when Ward first arrived, when Tom arrived, and when Ellie arrived.

. . .

Trip: Now, shortly after Ellie arrived, did you hear your husband say anything inappropriate?

Me: When—when she had come upstairs and sat down and he had poured her a glass of white wine, he tried—he complimented her by telling her she looked really good and she looked very nice that evening and said, you know, your students are probably flirting with you all the time, or something to that effect. Ellie said no, they don't,

I'm a married woman. And Steven said I'm not saying you're not a married woman or you're not happily married. I'm just saying that they're probably imagining you in a thong and thinking that you look really good.

Trip: And what is your reaction to that?

Me: My husband tries to compliment people. Sometimes he's better at it than other times. That was not a very successful attempt. It was not well received. But it was his effort to try to compliment somebody.

Trip: Okay. And how did everybody respond when he did say that?

Me: Nobody responded at all. Everybody just kept eating and drinking. That was when they first sat down. And nobody made a move to leave, or I had no inclination that anybody there was seriously offended by anything that was said.

. . .

Trip's questions then walked me through an account of the evening—the remainder of the time in the kitchen, preparing leftovers for Ellie to take to Lee, walking folks out, cleaning up, and starting the tub—until the doorbell rang. Then Trip asked me about Ward's appearance at our door.

Trip: So tell us what happens after you walk up the stairs. First of all, is he in front of you, is he behind you?

Me: No, he walked behind me up the stairs. And when you walk into our kitchen, you turn into our kitchen and the sink is like here. And so he turned this way. The island with the stove is here.

And Steven actually was still washing dishes. He had apparently not heard the doorbell and not heard me let him in. And Ward walked up then, like right behind him, as Steven was standing at the sink. And Steven turned around, and he was holding a dish cloth and—a wash cloth and was—looked surprised to see Ward there.

And Ward then said don't ever talk to my mother like that again. And she was terribly insulted. And the part of the conversation I remember is he said if you ever talk to her like that again, I will rip your neck off and—rip your head off and shit down your neck.

Trip: And how did Ward appear as he said these things?

Me: At that point he was moving up and down in front of the stove island, and Steven was standing there. And it was like something had been unleashed. He was—he was not like he was at dinner, and he wasn't like he was at the front door. He was active, he was angry, he was—it was almost like there was a rage there or something, I mean.

Trip: How would you describe the tone of his voice when he said that?

Me: Oh, it was serious, like he wasn't booking any—any hesitation or any resistance. He was—you were going to do what he said at that point in time. And what he said to do was you're coming with me right now and you're going to apologize to my mom.

Trip then walked me through Steven's departure with Ward, my waiting, Steven's return, the remainder of the evening, Steven's arrest, and finally Ainsworth's arrival. My testimony as I read the transcript was terse. I answered questions, but didn't volunteer any additional information. In hindsight, there were a lot of things I would have liked to have said that I didn't.

Excerpts from Foote's perhaps more interesting, but most certainly less predictable, cross-examination follow.

. . .

Foote: Ms. Gesse, you talked about and obviously you know that your husband is a hunter?

Me: Yes. We both were. He still is, but I was also.

Foote: And you're not anymore, but he still is?

Me: Right.

Foote: Avid hunter?

Me: No. When we moved to Colorado—we used to go deer hunting and antelope hunting. And we moved to Colorado, we had so many deer in the back yard that were bigger than anything we ever shot, we kind of just gave up on the deer hunting and still went bird hunting.

Foote: Okay. And you've also talked about there are guns in the house?

Me: Correct. There were guns in the house.

Foote: Okay. And as you know, if he's convicted of menacing he can't own those guns ever again?

Me: Correct.

Foote: Can't go hunting with any kind of firearm, correct?

Me: Correct.

Foote: And you know that wouldn't make him very happy, would it?

Me: Well, we haven't gone hunting in a number of years. But I assume it would not.

(Note: I was totally confused at this line of questioning. During the last seven months I have been terrified of Steven being found guilty. I have been terrified of having him go to jail. I have been terrified about how this event would change him, me, our marriage, our lifestyle. I worried about what it would do to our reputations, to our business. I worried about having no protection if attacked by Ward or someone like him. I worried about all sorts of things. But I never worried about whether or not we could go hunting again or about whether or not we could move the guns back into the house. I should have simply said that. "I'm sorry Mr. Foote, but in all the time since that incident, neither my husband nor I have discussed or even considered whether future hunting trips would be affected." I should have made that simple statement. So why didn't I say that? Trip said to answer the question. But how could I answer a question when I had no idea what the question really was? My confusion increased as Foote continued his cross.)

. . .

Foote: Now, these walls here on Defense Exhibit E, and I'm pointing to walls that seem to be outside of the house? [He is pointing to the exterior walls on our house.]

Me: Correct.

Foote: And those aren't open walls, are they?

Me: No. They're walls.

Foote: So you can't see from the front porch into this room?

Me: There's not a front porch. It's a front—there's a cement area here, but it's not a front porch.

Foote: Okay. So the bottom line though is that if somebody is standing right there on this front they can't see into inside this room?
Me: That's correct.

. . .

Foote: Going back to the comments that your husband made to Ellie, you said there was a comment about a thong, which you thought he meant to be a compliment.
Me: Um-hum.
Foote: But it wasn't?
Me: She didn't take it that way.
Foote: Did you take it that way?
Me: I didn't really focus on it that much I guess. I didn't—I asked myself since then if somebody told me that, how would I take it, and I think I would probably take it as compliment.

(Note: When we watch a witness on TV, the honest witnesses are always believable. The ones who are lying get flustered and can't answer questions. I assumed I would be cool and competent, but the truth is that I was nervous and got flustered as the following transcript shows. I will also confess to not understanding where Foote was going with this line of questioning. I knew from Trip that one good thing was Eric Witte's written report stating that I kept saying I should never have let Ward into the house. Witte was scheduled to be a witness the next morning, so I assumed Foote knew that. I guess reading a transcript is like seeing a bad photo of yourself. You just can't believe you look like that. I couldn't believe I sounded like this.)

. . .

Foote: Since the night of April 5th after you guys talked about it and then took the bath and then went to bed, you obviously have talked about this event many other times, fair to say?
Me: I think that's fair to say.
Foote: Talk about how things went down, talked about what your husband did down at their house and things like that, is that fair?

Me: We talked about it that night about what happened that night, yes.

Foote: And then also subsequent days you also talked about what happened on that night of April the 5th?

Me: Yes.

Foote: And it's also fair to say that you had a chance to review over all the police reports that have been submitted in this case?

Me: I don't think I reviewed all of them. I looked at some of them last week.

Foote: Okay. And which ones did you look at?

Me: I think one of them was Officer Witte, who was the officer who stayed with me while I was there. And another one was one of the— one of the officers who was outside when I came out of the house. But I don't remember his name.

Foote: And those are the only reports you've read?

Me: Um-hum.

Foote: And you were, in preparation for this trial, given some kind of an idea of what kind of questions you would be asked, were you not?

Me: I went over some questions, yes.

Foote: And possible questions you would be asked on cross-examination?

Me: Yes.

Foote: Now, you mentioned Deputy Witte's report. I think you said that you read over that, correct?

Me: Yes.

Foote: And Deputy Witte was one that spoke to you that evening?

Me: He was the one who babysat me for the three hours while we were waiting for the search warrant.

Foote: Okay. And it's fair to say while you were with Deputy Witte during those three hours that you wanted him to know what had happened that night?

Me: Yes.

Foote: Based on what you saw?

Me: I suspect I didn't intend to talk too much. But we were there for three hours, so I talked a lot. And I talked about the events of the evening, yes.

Foote: And were you talking the entire three hours, or was it just kind of bits and pieces?

Me: Well, I don't know. We were there for a long time. I was pretty nervous. He talked about a lot of things that were personal for him. And a lot of things we talked about weren't related to the events of the evening. But we talked about the events of the evening also.

Foote: Okay. And at that time you told him that Ward and Tom arrived somewhere around 4:00?

Me: I don't—

Foote: Fair to say?

Me: I don't think I—I wouldn't have said that they arrived at the same time because they didn't arrive at the same time. I told him they were both there, but I didn't tell him that they arrived simultaneously because they did not.

Foote: So you're saying you did not tell him that?

Me: I told him they were both there, but I didn't tell him they arrived together because they didn't.

Foote: Okay. And you even told Deputy Witte that you had given Ward some kind of a gimlet to drink that night?

Me: Yes.

Foote: So you went into that particular detail?

Me: Yes.

Foote: You told him that Tom had a glass of wine?

Me: I told him there was a lot of wine that was drunk that night.

Foote: Right. And in fact, you—you really encouraged him to go take pictures of all the wine bottles that were in the storage area or by the recycling bin.

Me: I told him there was a lot of wine that was drunk. And I showed him the wine bottles for the wine that was drunk that night, yes.

Foote: Okay. You wanted him to take pictures of all those wine bottles.

Me: I didn't want him to take pictures. He asked me if he could take a picture, and I said yes.

Foote: Okay. And then you also told him that those people left, Tom and Ward and Ellie, and that you and your husband were doing the dishes.

Me: Correct.

Foote: Then you proceeded to say that Ward came back and had requested to speak with your husband?

Me: Correct. And I said I let him in the house.

Foote: Okay. And you also told the deputy that you had heard Ward make some kind of a threat about ripping your husband's head off?

Me: Correct.

Foote: You also told the deputy you heard some kind of a threat about breaking knee caps?

(Note: All previous statements made by Steven used "legs," not knees.)

Me: I said he threatened to break Steven's knee caps, but I did not say that I heard that directly. I was repeating what Steven said he [Ward] told him as he walked out of the house and up the hill.

Foote: Okay. You also told the deputy then that you allowed Mr. Gesse to leave the house and go apologize, correct?

Me: I felt very responsible for what had happened that night because I thought if I had had better sense I would have never let my husband walk out of the house with that man.

Foote: Okay. So the answer to the question is yes or no?

Me: Yes.

Foote: Now, during that time that you were talking to Deputy Witte over those three hours, isn't it the case that you said nothing about Ward coming up to the kitchen?

Me: I said I let him in the house.

Foote: You said nothing about him coming up to the kitchen?

Me: I don't know if I said specifically that he came up to the kitchen. I said I let him into the house.

Foote: Well, you read over Deputy Witte's report, right?

Me: I said I let him in.

Foote: And he—

Me: I only know what he wrote in his report. I don't know what I told him in the three hours. He did not write in the report that I said he went up to the kitchen. That doesn't necessarily mean that I didn't say it. It means he didn't write it in his report.

Foote: So you think that there's things that Deputy Witte just left out?

Me: I don't know. Three hours is a long time.

Foote: You just don't know if you told him anything about letting Ward into the kitchen?

Me: No. I said I let him into the house. Don't know if I specifically said that he followed me up into the kitchen.

Foote: Okay. You also never told Deputy Witte anything about how Ward was kind of walking, pacing back and forth and there seemed to be something unleashed, I think you said?

Me: I—my intent was not to go over the events in detail without benefit of counsel or something there. I just was nervous and talked about some things.

Foote: Well, you did go into some details though, didn't you, about the gimlet, about the wine that was drunk, about some of the comments and so on?

Me: That's right.

Foote: Right, okay.

Me: I think—

Foote: You didn't go into any kind of comment about Ward's demeanor was to your husband?

Me: No.

Foote: Okay.

Me: He didn't ask me specific questions, and I wouldn't have answered them probably.

Foote: Okay. And you also never told Deputy Witte about the fact that Ward came and demanded up in the kitchen that your husband was to apologize.

Me: I think if somebody says that they're going to rip your head off and shit down your neck that would be considered a demand to go with them.

Foote: So the answer to my question is yes or no?

Me: If I—I said that, if I said that that's what Ward said, then I—I guess I was saying that he demanded that Steven go with him.

Foote: So you don't remember specifically saying that to the deputy though?

Me: I don't remember saying the word demanded.

Foote: Okay. And you don't remember telling Deputy Witte that you and Steven were doing the dishes?

Me: I don't know if I said that or not.

Foote: Okay. You don't remember telling the deputy any of this detail about how Ward was holding the door as your husband was walking out back towards the residence, correct?

Me: No.

Foote: You did not tell the deputy that?

Me: I don't remember talking about that.

Foote: Okay.

Me: It wasn't an interview.

Foote: Okay. Now, at this time though it's—you think it's important to talk to the police and tell them the truth about what happened?

Me: Then—

Foote: Is that fair to say?

Me: At that point?

Foote: Sure.

Me: With Officer Witte I had no idea what was going on, no. All I knew—

Foote: At any point?

Me: We had a nice dinner party and somebody left and came back and threatened my husband and he had to leave. Then we had the police at the door. So I didn't know what was going on. So I wasn't in the context of making statements or anything. I was just more suffering from a serious case of disbelief that this was happening.

Foote: Do you think it's important to tell the police the truth?

Me: Now, yes, absolutely.

Foote: You didn't at the time?

Me: No. I wasn't in the mode of interview of telling anything. It wasn't an interview with the officer.

Foote: So are you saying that you have to be in some kind of interview mode in order to tell the officer the truth?

Me: No. I'm saying we were sitting there waiting for the search warrant. I may have volunteered information. I wasn't being asked direct questions. Nothing I said was a lie, but it wasn't—I wasn't answering specific questions about a timetable or what had happened in a specific order.

Foote: You just left out big details though it sounds like. For example, you left out details about walking up the driveway, how you met Mr. Gesse up the driveway, correct?

Me: I don't know if I left that out. I wasn't recounting the events of the night. I was just marveling at the fact that people who had been to our house eating and drinking and supposedly having a good time were doing something like this to us.

Foote: We understand that Ms. Gesse. But I just would ask you to answer the question if you don't mind.

Me: Could you repeat the question?

Foote: Well, the question was you didn't say anything to the deputy about you walking out and meeting your husband halfway up the driveway?

Me: I wasn't giving a detailed account of the evening time by time or event by event.

Foote: So that would be a no?

Me: Correct.

Foote: And Deputy Witte was not the only deputy that you spoke to about the events of that night?

Me: He was the only one who sat there for—with me in the evening while we were waiting for the search warrant. I don't remember having conversations with a lot of other people other than to say they can walk through the house and to ask them what was happening.

Foote: You don't remember trying to tell another deputy what had happened that evening?

Me: Not directly, no.

Foote: A female deputy?

Me: There was a female deputy there who walked through the house with us. But I don't remember being asked specific questions or answering questions about the evening.

Foote: Do you remember talk—trying to talk to that particular deputy about what had happened, you were volunteering information?

Me: Might have said the same thing that I've been saying before, that I didn't know what was going on, the people had been to our house having a nice dinner.

Foote: And you went into some detail again with this female deputy about the dinner party and the gimlet?

Me: Could be.

Foote: Correct? Okay.

Me: I don't remember that in detail.

Foote: Well, would something refresh your memory about that, the report of the deputy for example?.

Me: I could read the report of the deputy. I can also tell you that one of the reports that I read earlier had a lot of errors in it. So I don't know, I haven't read this one. I'd be glad to read it and tell you if it's accurate or not.

Foote: Well, Deputy—let me just ask—tell you her name and see if you recognize it. Bryarly?

Me: There was one female deputy there. The only name I really recognize is Eric Witte because he was there with me for a long time.

Foote: And when you were talking to the female deputy, again you never said anything about Ward coming into the kitchen.

Me: All I remember about the female deputy is that she was one of three people who walked through the house. And earlier when I went outside she was one of the people who tried to pull me away from the front door.

Foote: So was that a no?

Me: I don't remember saying that.

Foote: In fact, to that particular deputy you didn't even say anything about Ward coming into the house, correct?

Me: I don't think anybody asked me a question about it, so I didn't volunteer it, no.

Foote: So the answer would be no?

Me: I didn't volunteer it, correct.

And that was the end. In hindsight, I think Foote's strategy was to try to convince the jury that Steven and I had similar recollections of the evening because we had rehearsed and coordinated our stories. In reality, there are certain evenings whose details you never forget—because of the strong feelings they generated. The night of April 5, 2009, was one of those evenings. I remember the details of that evening including what we ate, who said what when, and every other detail. I will always remember the details of that evening. I think Foote wanted to discredit me as a witness. At the time, I had no benefit of knowing what the prosecution's witnesses had said, but it appears that "I don't remember" was a more reasonable answer for Foote's questions when given by Ward than it was when given by me—even though Ward's "I don't remember" involved details of events that should have been clear in his mind.

At the end of the cross-examination, I was feeling like I had failed my husband. There was so much I wanted the jury to know that I had not said. Did they understand that we thought it had been a nice dinner party that night? Did they understand that the reason I remembered so many details of that evening was that no other evening in my life had ever ended that way? Did they understand that Ward had walked into our house and forced my husband to leave with him? Did they understand that not only would Steven never do what he was accused of doing, but that he had absolutely no opportunity to get a gun? Did they know that I thought one of the officers had looked at the gun in the case in the family room before they got the search warrant? If only I could have said all of this. I didn't feel like I had accomplished what I wanted to do. I wanted them to understand that my husband was a good man who wanted to help Ellie and Lee and be nice to their son by inviting them over to our house. They were the bad people, not us. I didn't think I got my message across.

Excerpts from Trip's redirect:

Trip: Does that refresh your recollection? [Upon giving me a copy of Eric Witte's report to read]
Me: Right. I did say we were doing dishes, and I did say that I let him in the house.
Trip: Okay. Would you lie for your husband?

Me: No. I've thought about that question, because I assumed someone would ask me that. And the one thing I thought about is the only person I spend more time with than him is myself. And I couldn't live with myself if I had to lie. And so, no I wouldn't lie for him, not under oath.

Once the lawyers are done with the witness, the jurors can actually give the judge written questions that they would like to ask. As long as neither lawyer objects, the judge then asks the questions submitted by the jurors. I actually thought the juror's questions were better than most of Foote's. There was a moderately long discussion at the bench as the two lawyers either agreed to allow questions or objected to them. A reading of the transcript seems to indicate that Trip had no objections and the judge read most of the questions.

Judge: Where would your husband get the jacket when leaving with Ward?

Me: It was one of possibly three places. Can I step up here? [Indicating the poster board with a diagram of our downstairs]

Judge: Sure.

Me: It would have either been on the railing where we put it when we came back, or it would have been in the coat closet right here, or it could have been on the hook in the garage right there. It would have been in one of those three places.

Judge: All right. And you said you didn't know what was going on. Did you ask the police why they were taking your husband away?

Me: I did. And they said somebody had accused him of having a gun and pointing it at them earlier in the evening. I'm not sure when they said that. I think it was after they took him away.

Judge: Okay. When you went back into the house to get your husband some sweats, did anyone accompany you?

Me: No. I just ran upstairs. I don't think they did. I ran upstairs and ran downstairs.

Judge: When did Mr. Gesse put his coat on prior to going over to apologize?

Me: He did not have it on when he was doing dishes or walking down the steps. But when Ward opened the door and he came out, he was wearing his coat.

Judge: All right. Did Steve leave your sight at any time before taking off his coat?

Me: No.

Judge: Before undressing?

Me: No.

Judge: When Steven and Ward left, where did Steve go to get the jacket?

Me: I don't know. I know that he didn't have it on when he went down the stairs. And then when Ward opened the door and looked at the stairs Steven had his coat on. So I don't know if the coat was on the— on that—you know, the bottom of the railing or it was in the closet or if he grabbed it out of the garage.

Judge: Okay. Is there a second way down to the front door from the kitchen?

Me: No.

Then I was excused. I went and took a seat in the benches behind Steven and next to his brother, Gregg. Afterward, Diane insisted that some of the jurors were surprised to see me sit down in the courtroom. They wouldn't have known by watching Ward or Ellie or Lee that dismissed witnesses could stay in the courtroom.

The judge discussed the dour weather warnings for the following day. The forecast was that "travel will become difficult or impossible by Wednesday afternoon. Residents should prepare for a long duration of winter storm." Jurors were given a phone number to call in the morning to find out if the Justice Center was going to be open. As of Tuesday afternoon, we were hoping this would all be over by Wednesday … but that now depended on the weather.

Chapter 54

Tuesday Afternoon, October 27: Outside the Courtroom

Upon exiting the courtroom, Steven and Trip moved to their conference room to prepare for Steven's testimony the next morning. Gregg and I encouraged our friends to drive carefully and head home quickly, as it had begun to snow. I also told them not to worry about coming the next—and hopefully final—day of the trial if the weather was really bad. Though I really wanted all of them to be there with us, I didn't want to be responsible for any accidents or injuries to our cadre of close friends. Art headed for the airport and a return flight home.

Gregg and I sat and waited. He assured me that I was "good" on the stand, that the jurors looked different as I answered my questions.

I complained about not knowing where Foote was headed with his questions and commented that, "I thought the jurors' questions were better than his!"

I told Gregg, "I tried to make eye contact with the jurors. No one told me to do that, but I wanted them to know I was a real person and was answering the questions honestly and to the best of my ability."

"You were fine," he assured me. I'm not sure I believed him.

When the three of us got back to our house, we made the decision to get hotel rooms in Boulder so we wouldn't have to deal with chains, plows, snow, etc. the next morning. That meant picking out our wardrobes for the probable last day of the trial. I chose black pants, a red turtleneck, a black sweater-jacket, the same small gold earrings as day one, and a black and red scarf that Diane had bought for me on our trip to Italy in April— so long ago. Steven went with a black sport coat, charcoal grey pants, a white shirt, and muted pink tie. We drove down the hill to the Holiday Inn Express at the corner of Broadway and Lee Hill in heavy snow.

Once again the evening was quiet. We spoke more about the weather than we did about the trial. More than any night since the incident, I found myself wishing I could have had at least one glass of wine. Steven had mentally gone someplace during the trial. I'm not sure where that place was, but I wasn't being invited in. All I could do was make sure he knew I was outside waiting for him to either invite me in, or to come out and join me. It was a very disquieting time—like no other during our marriage. I recited my litany of prayers during the quiet.

Chapter 55

Wednesday Morning, October 29: Outside the Courtroom

Steven was up at 3:00 a.m. He was going to be on the stand today. Lawyers all tell their clients that testifying is a big risk. One of the rules of defending a client is never let them take the stand. But he was the only one who could put a motive (if you can call it that) behind Ward's accusations. His statement to Ward that "If you ever come to my house again and threaten my wife and me again, I will shoot you. And if I can't shoot you, I will ruin your career," gave Ward the motive for his accusations. Besides, Steven asserted that this would be the first time anyone besides Trip or me would hear his version of events.

I slept late—4:15 a.m. There wasn't much snow in downtown Boulder yet. We knew that there wouldn't be once we decided to stay in town. But there was more snow on our mountain and it was still snowing. If I wasn't so wound up I would have thought it pretty.

Assuming the weather was not any worse than it looked from our hotel room, this could be over today. Of course, they were predicting ten to twenty inches in Denver, so who knew. Now I began to ponder whether jurors who wanted to get home were more likely to convict or acquit. Our jurors seemed to laugh when they were on breaks, or so I was told. Was that a good sign? Jurors ready to condemn someone would be more serious, wouldn't they?

I called in the big guns the previous night—our favorite Irish priest (okay—he's the only Irish priest we know) and gave him a brief description of what was happening and asked for his prayers. He said he might try to come down the next day, but I suspected that with the weather, he wouldn't be able to do so. I thought that in a serious situation such as this, asking someone on a first-name basis with God to add his prayers to ours would be an excellent idea.

We arrived at the Justice Center early. Shortly after we arrived, Trip and Ann walked in. While Trip and Steven were in their conference room, John and Barry arrived. I was surprised to see them, given how bad the weather was. But as John said, "I wanted to see this through to the end— to the conclusion—hopefully the right one." Barry said that his dad, Don, and Patricia didn't know if they should try to come down. I called them and advised them not to drive down the mountain. They live close to us, and according to Barry, the roads were treacherous. I assured them we would keep them posted. They assured me they would be praying. Phone calls to Jimmy and Roger were also made to advise them not to make the long trip to the courthouse. The snow was worse south of Denver where they lived. Despite these phone calls, I was surprised and pleased to see Diane, Roger's wife, arrive shortly before the trial began.

As we sat outside the courtroom waiting for 9:00 a.m. and the court to resume, I saw Deputy Witte. He had arrived early to meet with Trip. He walked up to me and, extending his hand, said, "I bet you don't remember me."

He had to be kidding—of course I remembered him. I smiled and said, "Of course I do. How's that new baby?"

"He's growing fast. I can't believe he is seven months old. How are you doing?"

I knew exactly how old his baby was since he had been born only shortly before the night of the incident. "Okay, given the circumstances," I replied. I found the short exchange comforting, as he was the first and only officer to acknowledge me or to appear friendly.

As 9:00 a.m. approached, we all entered the courtroom. I sat in the first row on the aisle next to Gregg. Barry, Diane, and John were in the row behind me. At promptly 9:00 a.m., the Court was called into session.

Chapter 56

Wednesday Morning, October 28: In the Courtroom

The first order of business was for the judge and the two lawyers to agree on the wording for the instructions to the jury. This is something you don't see on TV and something you don't realize can be argued. There are, I learned, a variety of "templates" for jury instructions. This conversation did not seem either prolonged or argumentative to me in this situation. It was also something that, in all honesty, I didn't understand or appreciate.

The judge's final comments before calling the jury were directed to Trip. "I just want to keep things moving along at a good clip in terms of the instructions, et cetera, understanding we're in the defendant's portion of the case. So I'm not trying to rush you, in terms of the presentation of the defendant's evidence. But this is really just to protect the trial so that we don't run the risk of mistrial due to the weather."

She was worried that the weather would close the Justice Center and force her to send the jurors home. When the jurors were in the courtroom she told them, "We are going to try to move things along. And the expectation is that you will get the case today to begin your deliberations.

"And I'm aware of the weather situation, and we're monitoring it. And we figure we'll just deal with things as they develop. I'll keep you posted on that."

Office Witte was called to the stand as a witness for the defense. Excerpts from his testimony follow.

Trip: But your purpose was not to interrogate her, was it?
Witte: No. No.

Trip: In fact, you were specifically avoiding any effort to ask her questions, is that true?

Witte: Correct. The only questions I may have asked her were in a personal nature once we began speaking.

Trip: Nevertheless, she made some comments to you about the evening?

Witte: She did.

Trip: And specifically she made comments about Ward, the alleged victim, leaving the residence and then returning a short time later.

Witte: Correct.

Trip: And what did Ms. Gesse tell you happened after Ward left the residence and returned a short time later?

At this point Foote objected on the grounds of hearsay.

(Note: I found this interesting, as no one objected when Ellie described what Ward said had happened outside her house or when Lee described what Ward and Ellie said happened at our house. But *this* was hearsay. Go figure.)

Trip was ready for this objection. In the sidebar with the judge, he immediately cited cases and precedent for allowing the question. The judge ruled in his favor. Trip repeated the question for the witness.

Witte: She told me that Ward returned to their house and requested to speak with Mr. Gesse regarding some comments made to his mother over dinner.

Trip: And did she tell you what she and Steven were doing when Ward returned to the house?

Witte: She did. She said they were washing dishes when he returned.

Trip: And did she tell you when Ward requested to speak to Steve, what did Michelle do at that point? Did she let him in the house?

Witte: Correct.

Trip: And she told you she let him in the house?

Witte: Yes.

Trip: Okay. She didn't give you any more specifics than that, right?

Witte: No.

Trip: Other than they had previously been doing dishes?

Witte: Correct.

Trip: And you didn't know how far—she didn't specify how far she let him in the house, right?

Witte: Correct.

Trip: Didn't get into any of those details. And you weren't asking for details, were you?

Witte: Correct.

As he left the courtroom after being excused as a witness, Officer Witte stopped next to me, shook my hand and whispered, "Good luck." I started to cry. No one afterward knew for sure if any of the jurors had witnessed that exchange, but it meant a lot to me.

Steven was called to the witness stand. The judge first asked him questions intended to confirm that he knew he did not have to testify but could choose to testify. He answered in the affirmative. He wanted to testify.

Trip began his direct. After describing the events of the day leading up to Ellie's arrival at our house, he was asked about his comments to Ellie.

. . .

Trip: What happened when Ellie arrived?

Steven: I went downstairs and let Ellie in. She had a red rain coat and a black knit dress, and she looked very good. She had—Ellie had been in a little ill health the last three or four, five years. And I told her she looked really nice.

And she said the rain coat she'd just gotten at the PX in San Diego. And we walked upstairs, I put the rain coat over the—this railing right here [pointing to the easel with the diagram of our house], and we walked upstairs.

Trip: Now, when you got upstairs did you make inappropriate comments to her?

Steven: I offered her a glass of wine. I told everyone she looked really nice, and she objected a little bit. And to the best of my knowledge what I said was—best of my recollection was I'll bet the male students in your art class find you very attractive. And she said I'm a happily married woman. No. No. No. She said no, no, I'm a very happily married woman. And I said Ellie, I didn't mean anything about that. I did not mean that you were—that you were unhappily married.

And I regret saying the next thing I said, but I said I'll bet they're all—they all think you would look very attractive in a thong.

Trip: And what do you think about that comment now?

Steven: It was in very poor taste. I regret saying it. I'm sorry. And it will affect the rest of my life at this point.

Trip: What was her response to that comment?

Steven: I don't really remember. She might have said that, you know, I shouldn't say that, and it was over. I said I apologize. I probably apologized again right then. And I don't think she was near as upset about that comment as she seemed to be about the first one, about the male art students thinking she was attractive. But it was done.

(Note: I had prepared myself for Steven's testimony so I was doing okay with this. Everything he was saying was just an explanation of what had happened that night. There weren't going to be any surprises in his testimony. I tried to watch him objectively to see if he was coming across as honest and sincere. I thought he was. But no one was going to accuse me of being impartial. So far, I was doing okay with Steven on the stand, though I still found myself holding onto Gregg's hand.)

Trip then walked Steven through the events prior to Ward's return and Ward's actual return. The surprise for me and, I assume, for everyone else in the courtroom, was Steven's testimony regarding the walk up the hill to Lee and Ellie's house.

. . .

Trip: And what happened as you start up the hill?

Steven: Well, I made it to the blacktop right here, and I told him I really thought it was a bad idea. I said we should wait until tomorrow morning.

Trip: Now, do you have a gun with you?

Steven: No.

Trip: Okay.

Steven: No.

Trip: And when you tell him it's a bad idea and we should wait until tomorrow morning what's his reaction?

Steven: He said let's go. He said—he said we're going over to my mother's or something to that effect. He said we're not going back.

Trip: Did he touch you?

Steven: He tapped—he was right on my left side. He stood about a foot, two feet behind me all the way, my left shoulder. He might have tapped me then.

Trip: And what was the tone of voice he used when he said let's go?

Steven: I would say it was still forceful. It was still forceful.

Trip: And how did you feel about him at this point?

Steven: I was getting a little scared.

Tri: Okay. Then what happened?

Steven: I walked about five or six more steps, and he poked me in the back and said let's go. He said I can break both of your legs before you can turn around.

Trip: What's his tone of voice?

Steven: It was more—I would say it got more forceful, very forceful at that point.

Trip: How are you feeling now?

Steven: More scared.

Trip: Okay. Then what happened?

Steven: Walked up the hill. This is a hill up here. We got about two-thirds of the way up, and I slipped. Remember it had been snowing that night. And he grabbed my shoulder and held me up. He didn't say anything, he just grabbed my shoulder, helped me up.

Trip: Okay. What happened?

Steven: Got a little farther, and I slipped again to my knees. And he tapped me on the shoulder and said you might as well crawl.

(Note: At this point, not only was Steven emotional, but he was crying. I had never heard this portion of the story and Steven's fear and humiliation were evident. I was crying and squeezing Gregg's hand at this point. I can't imagine that walk up the hill. My husband must have been terrified. The fact that Steven had never discussed this with me told me a lot. It was one of those private things that you don't even discuss with your spouse. Steven looked so embarrassed and pitiful that I wanted to run up to him and hug him. At the same time, I wished Ward was there so I could run up to him and hurt him. I could do neither. I felt useless.)

Trip: What did you do?
Steven: I crawled.
Trip: For how far?
Steven: From here to Detective Ainsworth.
Trip: And then what happened?
Judge: There's a Kleenex box to your left . . .
Steven: I got up.
Trip: Is it hard for you to admit that you crawled?
Steven: witness nodded his head.
Trip: Why?
Steven: Well, it's humiliating.
Trip: Your wife is in the audience. Has she ever heard this before?
Steven: No.

. . .

Steven's response when asked by Trip about his comments to Ward after his apologies to Ellie and Lee:

Steven: I turned around to him and I said—I said I really appreciate your military service, and I thanked him for the fact that he served all these years. And I said but you're a lousy drunk and a bully.

And I said if you ever come into my house again and threaten me or my wife again I will shoot you. I never said kill, I said shoot you. I said I will have you arrested. I will sue you, your wife, your family, the navy. I will make your life miserable. If you have a career left at that point, I will wreck your career in the navy. I said never, never, come on my property again, never.

And I—and he said okay. He said it twice, okay, maybe even three times. And he turned around and walked away. And I turned around and hustled away myself. And I never saw him go in his house. So I just made a beeline to get out of there before I lost my courage and get back home.

Trip: Did you have a gun?

Steven: No.

(Note: I hate to admit this, but even then at the trial I found myself thinking, *Why did you have to say that? Why couldn't you just let it drop?* My anxiety level had decreased since Steven's earlier revelation about having to crawl partway up the hill, but I was still very anxious. Was he doing a better job of convincing the jury of his innocence than I had?)

Foote's cross continued with his effort to discredit me and Steven, and to imply that we had jointly crafted our statements.

. . .

Foote: Mr. Gesse, you have obviously spoken with your wife quite a bit about this case, is that fair to say?

Steven: Yes.

Foote: That night you spoke to her about what had happened?

Steven: First night?

Foote: That first night.

Steven: Yes.

Foote: And also obviously when you came back after being arrested, you spoke to her about the case, correct?

Steven: I don't—I don't recall talking that first or second night about the case that much.

Foote: So you just came back and just ignored it, didn't talk to your wife at all about it?

Steven: We—when I got released from jail we went to the attorney's office. And he said, you know, you probably should let it sit for a few days.

At this point Trip asked for a sidebar with the Court and made the point that Foote appeared to be violating spousal privilege as well as attorney/client privilege. The Court agreed.

Foote: You also know if you're convicted here of menacing then you lose all your guns as we talked about yesterday, correct?

Steven: I have not focused on that. But if you say so, yes.

Foote: You don't know that that's the case?

Steven: I have not focused on that. But if you say so, yes.

Foote: But you know it's the case that you'll lose your guns if you're convicted of menacing, correct?

Steven: If you're saying so, yes.

Foote: And so this is obviously an important case for you?

Steven: Its occupied seven months of my life.

(Note: At this point my frustration with Foote was overcoming my concern for Steven. Where was he going with this line of questioning *yet again*?)

. . .

Foote: Do you remember, Mr. Gesse, what you had for dinner on April the 4th, 2009?

Steven: No.

. . .

Foote: What at the time made you think that the thong comment—or let me back up—the thong comment would be an appropriate comment made to Ellie?

Steven: I tend to be a little playful at occasion. Just way off base I guess at that point. Certainly regret saying it. I'm sorry I said it. Didn't seem terribly wrong to me at the time, but it was I guess. I'm sorry.

Foote: You had no idea then they would take offense to that?

Steven: No—they—no.

Foote: Okay. And so it was—it sounds surprising to you that at some point Ward would show up at your door and tell you to apologize to his mom? Is that fair to say?

Steven: Yes.

(Note: I really disliked Foote by this point in Steven's testimony. My anger at him and my feeling that he was inept and unprofessional had grown. What did any of this have to do with the charges, or with proving Steven either guilty or innocent? He seemed like a nasty man to me at this point; small and with prejudice.)

. . .

Foote: How did it go from there being no offense from what you perceived to Ward saying he was going to rip off your head and shit down your neck?

Steven: I can't answer that question. You'd have to ask him.

. . .

Foote: You didn't want to apologize that night, correct?

Steven: I just didn't think apologies with alcohol probably had much effect. Everybody was tired and had effects of alcohol. And I think probably we could straighten it out later. I have to live with those people, and so I wanted it straightened out.

Foote: You thought at the time the alcohol was really affecting your judgment, then, is that why you didn't want to do anything that night?

Steven: No.

Foote: So you on the one hand didn't think that apologies and alcohol should be mixed, but on the other hand it sounds like you're saying alcohol was not affecting your judgment at all?

Steven: I didn't think it was affecting my judgment. I thought it was affecting Ward's.

Foote: So you thought he was intoxicated?

Steven: Absolutely.

Foote: But not you?

Steven: Absolutely.

Foote: Even though he had less to drink than you did?

Steven: I don't believe that's the case at all.

. . .

Foote: So you don't remember telling the sheriff's deputies that you were
actually the victim that night, not anybody else?

Steven: I said that. I said that twice.

. . .

Steven: I went up to Mr. Smith [at the jail the night of his arrest]—
Deputy Smith and I said do I have the rights to press charges against
Ward. And he said no, go sit down.

. . .

There is a lengthy dialogue between Foote and Steven about what Steven
may or may not have said to one or more deputies while he was waiting to
be charged at the jail. This is interrupted by Trip and sidebars between the
lawyers and the judge with the judge finally addressing Foote with the following comments: "Well, then just ask those questions, what did he volunteer and that's it. I mean, he testified he asked for a lawyer. He can assert
those rights. Big deal. We're done with it." I think even she was beginning
to lose patience with Foote's aimless fishing expeditions. Though we can
read the conversations in the sidebar in the transcripts, no one except the
two lawyers and the judge were privy to them during the trial.

. . .

Foote: You did not show any guns to anybody?

Steven: Absolutely. The guns were never out. I don't believe I can remember a party that had alcohol where those safes were open or any guns
were out. I cannot remember a party we've had at our house when—
and we've had many—where we let guns out of those vaults or we
even opened the vaults when there's alcohol present.

Foote: And so you know for a fact that Ward has never seen that Thompson Contender?

Steven: He has seen that Thompson Contender.

Foote: That night? Not that night?

Steven: '97 he saw it.

When Foote asked Steven to list every gun we own, the judge asked, "How much longer is your cross-examination going to be?" and Trip asked to approach the bench. Trip asked about the relevance of his line of questioning. Foote said, "The relevance is none of them look like a flintlock." The judge said, "Well, he just—why don't you just ask him that question instead of him reciting the fifty different guns he has."

Foote's final questions (finally!)

Foote: Flintlock has a long barrel though, right?

Steven: Some have long barrels. Some are very short.

Foote: So some flintlocks have long barrels, correct?

Steven: Some could, yes.

Foote: Longer than you would consider on an ordinary barrel of a pistol, fair to say?

Steven: Well the Deringer that killed Lincoln was a flintlock that long.

Foote: Well, you're saying that long. How long are you saying?

Steven: Six inches.

Foote: Okay. But some can be as much as fourteen inches?

Steven: A Blunderbuss is probably twenty-eight inches, thirty inches. They can be in all sizes. There's no magic to fourteen inches.

Foote: Okay. So any of those pistols you mentioned, were any of the pistols in your house that you haven't mentioned, none of those look like a flintlock?

Steven: No.

Foote: You're saying not even the Thompson Contender?

Steven: I don't think it looks anything like a flintlock, the Contender.

(Note: I could have told Foote not to talk guns with Steven unless he knew the answers. I would like to remind the reader of two things. The first is that the dialogue is directly from the trial transcript so I am not making it up. The second is that although the above exchange can be humorous, it is not funny when your future is hanging in the balance. Sometimes I wonder why Foote didn't know that lawyers are never supposed to ask questions unless they already know the answer!)

The Court adjourned for a ten-minute break before Trip's re-direct.

I felt exhausted at this point, but unsure of why. Steven was on the stand, not me. I couldn't catalog my feelings, as they were mixed. Did he do well? Well enough? I couldn't tell despite the fact that I had spent much of the morning examining each of the juror's faces for hints of their reaction to Steven's testimony. How could twelve people have faces that were all so unreadable to me?

Chapter 57

Wednesday Morning, October 28: Outside the Courtroom

Steven and Trip went off to their conference room. The rest of us scurried to bathrooms and clustered outside the courtroom.

"What do you think Foote is trying to do?" John asked. "I couldn't figure out where he was going with his questions."

"Give me a break," Diane said. "I can't tell you what I ate last Tuesday night, but I can tell you what I had at certain meals last year that were memorable."

"I think he just wants the jurors to think that you and Steven are lying because your stories are consistent. Ellie and Ward and Lee are telling the truth because their stories don't match on almost anything," Gregg said.

"Shit," was all I could say at that point. I was tired and scared and could no longer figure out whose strategies were better. Was Trip's strategy not to push Ellie and make her even more sympathetic correct? Was Foote's strategy to make us out like liars going to work? Was Steven going to be convicted of a felony because we drank nice wine and he made a remark that one out of a hundred women would find offensive. We would soon find out.

"Have you noticed Trip and Steven using the hand sanitizer on their table?" Diane asked.

"Not really. Why?"

"The bottle was full when the trial started on Monday. I think it's a nervous thing. But they keep using it and rubbing their hands."

"I suspect the strain of listening to a lot of this is taking its toll on both of them. And Steven is supposed to not show any emotion on his face, which I suspect is hard. It's been hard for me to remain passive in expression and I've only been in the courtroom for a while," I replied.

"Plus you have to know they are both wound up tighter than a top," added Gregg.

"I guess it gives them something to do," Barry said.

By the end of the trial that Costco-sized hand sanitizer bottle was almost empty.

Within minutes, we were back in the courtroom.

Chapter 58

Wednesday Morning, October 28: In the Courtroom

Trip asked Steven to read Officer Bonafede's report. Then the following:

Trip: Does that refresh your recollection as to what you might have said to Deputy Bonafede regarding the guns that night?

Steven: Yes.

Trip: What did you say?

Steven: He asked if all the guns were in the vaults. And I said no, there were those guns, the ones in the silver case were out of the vaults, they were in the family room.

Trip: So you said they were out?

Steven: Out of the vaults, yes.

Trip: And by that you meant not in the vaults?

Steven: Yes.

(Note: We had earlier suspected that the use by both Steven and me of the term "out" with regard to the guns would be an issue. When we said the guns were out, we meant just what Steven said—they were not in the vaults where they are typically kept. We realized at some point that the word "out" would be interpreted by some to mean out of the cases, being handled or passed around at the dinner party or something worse.)

There was another short recess to finalize the instructions to the jury before the closing arguments. The instructions to the jurors were given to them and read by the judge prior to the closing arguments. The prosecution would make its closing argument then the defense, and then the prosecution would get to make a rebuttal. So Foote would get to talk twice, but Trip only once. I don't remember that on TV court dramas. But I have found myself much more critical since "our" trial of trials on TV.

Excerpts from Foote's initial closing argument:

Think about this as far as memory goes. Say that you and a friend go to a movie. You watch the movie. You sit through it for about two hours. At the end of the movie of course you probably are walking out saying what did you think of the movie, was it a good movie, bad movie, do you remember this part, do you remember that part?

All the time people have different recollections of what that movie— what happened in that movie. People will say—you'll say, well, do you re- member this part and your friend will say, well, I don't really remember it that way, I remember it this way. Do you remember when this character said this thing? And you'll say well, yes, or maybe I remember something else.

You and your friend just got out of that move, and you are remem- bering things a little bit different because of how you were affected by those things, how you remember those things. You're not lying to each other. You're not trying to trap each other in some kind of untruthful statement. You're just remembering what you remember.

. . .

And you also have to wonder what makes sense as far as motive goes. Where is the motive for Ward to be not telling the truth in this case? And I think I'll just put it right out there, you will probably figure it out in all of your minds, somebody is not telling the truth here. Is it Ward or is it the Gesses? And that's the decision you're going to have to make.

But what's the motive for Ward completely making up this story? Be- cause that's what you would have to believe, that he just made up this story out of nothing.

. . .

Now let's look at Mr. and Mrs. Gesse on the other hand. Obviously he's the defendant, he's the accused. And as you heard he has quite a bit to lose if you were to find beyond reasonable doubt in this case.

He has his hobby of hunting that he would lose if you were to find him guilty. He has all of those guns that he were to lose that he's had for years and years and years being a gun collector, gun connoisseur perhaps. That's gone. He has all of that to lose.

So when you look at the different stories here that people have said, you have to look at the motive or lack thereof of motive. It doesn't make any sense for Ward to make this up. For Mr. and Mrs. Gesse it sure does.

. . .

How do you determine credibility? Well, of course, like anything in law you can put words to it. But really what it comes down to is what's your feeling on credibility. I mean is it you look at their demeanor on the stand, you look at what they have to gain and lose, you look at these different things. But what's the demeanor, and how do the stories add up or how do they not add up? All of those different factors you'll read about in the credibility instructions if you chose.

And the contrast between the two sets of witnesses really couldn't be more clear. On the one hand we have Ellie, Ward, and Lee. And they testified, and you saw how nervous they were on the stand. And Ellie even couldn't identify her neighbor when he was in court at that time, that's how nervous she was.

And you heard them talk several times and ask several times when I was asking the questions if I could state it some other way or they didn't really understand what I was asking, they didn't really know the answer to the question.

You could see also that they would think before they answered those questions because they were searching back in their memory. This was seven months ago about by the way. They were searching back to try to remember the answers to those questions.

So let's compare it to the Gesses on the stand. Virtual simultaneous recall apparently of every single thing that happened during that day seven months ago. Ms. Gesse has virtually encyclopedic knowledge apparently of the ingredients that went into her appetizers that night. They apparently remember exactly everything that they drank down to the last ounce and they remember it exactly the same. They remember all of these details virtually exactly the same.

And when you heard them answer questions, it was questions from the defense attorney; question, answer, no pause like they knew it was coming, question, answer. Never anything like well, let me think about that until it got to cross-examination occasionally, but still question answer, question answer.

. . .

When you—everybody has seen this before, or probably everybody, but think of it like an infomercial. You're up late at night, you can't sleep, somebody is trying to sell you a Bowflex or something like that, some kind of fitness equipment, a person standing there and they're smiling at you and they're saying you can look just like this person here with the six-pack abs if you use Bowflex twenty minutes a day three days a week just like him.

And then let's start talking. Sir, have you used the Bowflex three times a week twenty minutes a day and that's all you've ever done? Yes, that's all I've ever done.

And when you're looking at that you're like yeah, right, of course that's what he's going to say because they're trying to sell you the Bowflex. Look at it like that. They're trying to sell you the machine.

. . .

But ladies and gentlemen, you are the jury. And you have the last word. And you can tell Mr. Gesse that that is unacceptable to pull a gun on somebody, whether it be loaded or unloaded, point it at them, cock it back and threaten their life. It's unacceptable.

. . .

When you look at the elements, this isn't the kind of case, this is a question of whether or not the elements are met. It's a question of credibility and who you believe.

(Note: Though I had always felt we were both on trial, Foote's closing argument that attacked my veracity as well as Steven's really made that apparent. Mr. and Mrs. Gesse were jointly going to be found guilty or not guilty. We were both on trial. Foote's closing argument came to be called the "Bowflex" argument among me and our friends.)

An excerpt from Trip's closing argument follows. Remember that he does not get a second chance to argue anything further.

Ladies and gentleman, first I want to thank you for your time and attention. This process that we have here is the most democratic process that we have. This is truly government of the people by the people.

And ever since he's been taken from his home and hauled off to jail, you've heard him testify that he has wanted somebody to listen to the evidence. Somebody please listen to me.

And so we are very thankful to you for giving us this time. We realize it's an inconvenience. Obviously it's a matter of importance. We thank you for listening to the evidence.

The burden of proof is on the prosecutor, this man here [pointing to Foote]. In order for him to win his conviction he has to prove Mr. Gesse guilty beyond a reasonable doubt.

The standard here isn't who made more sense. That's not the standard. His whole argument was nothing more than not what makes more sense. He has to prove it beyond a reasonable doubt.

. . .

This man [Steven] had no reason to get a gun before that [confrontation with Ward] because no harsh language was used. And once face to face with the Navy Seal he had no opportunity to get a gun. Does that make sense? When and how and why would he get a gun? That doesn't make sense.

And also what about the fact that then after they're face to face, now the Navy Seal says he's going to rip his head off. If you ever talk to my mom again like that I'm going to rip your head off. He threatens his life in his home, in or at his home.

If you have a gun, is that not the time? Is this not self-defense? Is this not defense of your home? If you truly are armed, is this not the time you would pull it out? Oh no. No.

The prosecution's theory, and it's nothing more than a theory because it's not been proven, is that he arms himself, conceals a weapon this size on him, a man who has plenty of other guns, even a .38. Of course they're locked up. But he's going to pick this huge weapon, which apparently is stuck down the back of somebody's pants. But he's going to do that and first go apologize before he gets even for the threat.

. . .

Well, which version did Ward give to the commanding officer? Do you think the commanding officer would be we're okay, this is not going to affect your career if he heard Mr. Gesse's version, his version about how he by threat of force and threat forced this man out of his own home, make him crawl with threat of force?

Why is it that—why is it that the captain is so insistent he didn't go into the house? The one thing you know for certain, one thing you know for certain is that Michelle Gesse, they've just hauled her husband off to jail, she can't even be alone in her house. Deputy Eric Witte has to stay with her until they get a search warrant.

And the one thing you know for certain, she has no idea of the importance of telling Deputy Witte I let him in the house. At that moment in time that's proof. That's the kind of proof he should have. And he doesn't have that kind of proof, but I do. There is no reason she would know it would be important to tell Eric Witte I let him in. Who is telling you the truth here today?

She had no way to know on that evening as her husband sat in a jail in Boulder County that telling that officer that insignificant detail, I let him into the house, who does that confirm is telling the truth? Ms. Gesse.

She would have no way of knowing the importance of that because it's not until we get here that he starts denying it. And that's the only time she can possibly figure that out. That's corroborating evidence.

. . .

He [Steven] said I will ruin your career. And the lightbulb must have gone on in Ward's head. Ward was not afraid of this man twenty years older than him and half his size.

But he felt compelled to tell his commanding officer. Why? Because he had to. And now the light goes on. My gosh, he recognizes what he just did, and that's enough to make a man white as a sheet. That's enough to make a man like Ward who is going to seek promotion with congressional approval to conceivably become an admiral, his entire career flashed—must have flashed in front of his eyes at that moment.

And when you're drinking, you know, and when you're upset because your father has gotten so incredibly upset that it's brought you to the boiling point and you've had too much to drink and your career flashes in front of your eyes, how easy is it to add that extra detail he had a gun?

He did say he threatened to shoot me and he had a gun. Well, it's really easy in the heat of that moment to add that extra detail given how scared he was. And it's uncontested that he was scared about what he had done to Mr. Gesse that night. But once you do that, it's not so easy to describe that gun and it's not so easy to stick with all the details exactly right.

. . .

Again, dispatch—he's [Ward] on the phone with dispatch. How far apart when he pointed it at you? Three feet. Three feet? Yes, sir. That was the testimony. And again, then later in the evening he tells his dad we were about three feet apart. We were pretty close. I thought I could take him down.

But when the detectives start talking to him about describing the details of that gun that changes from three feet to ten feet. You know, at three feet that gun is right in front of his face and he has no excuse for not seeing any of the details on that gun. Ten feet, that's not a little mistake for any person, much less a Navy Seal. Ten feet is across the room.

First it was ten feet. Then he paced it off at home and it was eight feet. But then when we came in court he said it was twelve and half feet.

. . .

And let me talk a little bit about Mr. Gesse's testimony. Regarding his testimony, he's presumed innocent until proven guilty beyond a reasonable doubt. The burden does not shift to him. He does not have to prove he was being truthful. He doesn't even have to testify. It's the prosecution that has to prove their witnesses beyond a reasonable doubt.

This case—the question in this case is not whether he's selling something. He doesn't have to sell anything. He doesn't have to prove anything. The person who is selling something that doesn't have the proof is Mr. Foote.

. . .

If this case is proof beyond a reasonable doubt, then there is no defense against a false accusation because this case has more hesitation in it upon hesitation.

And there is no defense to a false accusation if this is proof beyond a reasonable doubt. He hasn't done it. He hasn't proven it.

And by the way, you don't—you're not—you don't have to find— along the lines of that presumption of innocent and proof beyond a reasonable doubt, you do not have to make a finding that the captain was being untruthful. You do not. Not guilty says not proven. That's what that says. You don't have to make a finding about the captain.

. . .

Ladies and gentlemen, the prosecutor has not met its burden. And you should find Mr. Gesse not guilty. He didn't have a gun. He's not guilty of anything. Thank you very much.

Following is Foote's rebuttal—excerpts from his second closing argument after Trip's closing argument was completed.

Ladies and gentleman, trying to imagine a scenario that this would affect Ward's career is simply ridiculous.

. . .

So ladies and gentleman, I would ask you—of course you have to apply the reasonable doubt standard. But of course also, unlike what the defense said, it can be something where you believe somebody, one person, you believe what they have to say, and that can be beyond a reasonable doubt. Otherwise ladies and gentlemen, whenever it's a one-on-one crime it could never be proven, ever. A sex assault, domestic violence, none of that could be proven if that were the case.

You have to look at reasonable doubt as a puzzle. You look at it like you have a thousand piece puzzle. Let's say it is of a house. You take all the pieces of the puzzle, you start moving them around, you start putting the puzzle together. Some corners first, probably other pieces that obviously fit together.

As time goes on you're starting to to put more and more pieces of the puzzle together. Now, at some point in time you realize that the puzzle resembles that house. Is it at 750 pieces? Is it at 900? You just don't know. But at some point you realize the house that that puzzle was supposed to represent.

So when you reach that point you've reached beyond a reasonable doubt. You don't have to have all pieces of the puzzle in place to reach beyond a reasonable doubt. You just have to have enough to see the picture and know beyond a reasonable doubt what happened that night. And that's what we ask you to do. Thank you very much.

. . .

It was about 12:45. The judge advised the jurors that she would have lunch brought into their deliberation room. One of the jurors, the priest, asked who was paying for lunch. The judge smiled and said she was, but actually he was as a taxpayer. It was still snowing.

The bailiff was sworn in and the jurors were escorted to the jury room.

The judge said, "With the weather being as bad as it is, I usually permit the parties and counsel to leave the courthouse, of course just so long as you're within ten minutes.

"So if you'd be so kind as to stay. Plus I don't want anybody to get in a car accident, then having problems there. So if you'd just stick around, and then we'll get a sense of where things are as the afternoon goes on, I'd appreciate that."

Both lawyers left their cell phone numbers on the bailiff's desk and we left the courtroom to wait for the verdict. I was numb. I wanted this to be over ... but only if it ended well. I wasn't emotional at this point. I was just numb. It was over, or soon to be over. This was what we were waiting for and whatever the results, it would be over. Just a little bit longer.

Chapter 59

Early Wednesday Afternoon, October 28: Outside the Courtroom

We all agreed that none of us were going to leave the building.

Trip said, "There's lunch—sandwiches, chips, and sodas—back at the law firm, but I don't think we should leave the building. Hopefully this will be a short deliberation."

"Let's ask Chris to go get them. Is there enough for everyone?" asked Steven. He meant was there enough for Trip, Ann, Gregg, Barry, Diane, John, Chris and I.

"Chris is the partner in charge of our law firm," Ann said. "I'm not going to ask him to run and pick up sandwiches."

Chris had been in the courtroom for almost all of the trial since Monday morning and was still there with us waiting for the verdict.

"We've known Chris a long time," Steven said. "I don't think he'd mind. I'll ask him."

And sure enough, Chris drove back to the law firm and picked up the lunches for all of us to share. The conference room that Trip and Steven had been using became lunch central for a while. I managed to eat half a sandwich and drink a diet soda, but my stomach was too tight to do more than that.

"Amazing," Ann said. "Our chief partner is an errand boy for lunch. You must be more important than even I realized."

"He's just a good friend," replied Steven.

As you might imagine, the stress was palpable in the air, and increased as the jury took longer. We sat in small groups in various seating areas in the corridor outside the courtroom. We fielded calls from the friends who had not made it to the courthouse that day. And we prayed silently each in our own way.

And we began to discuss the case, the testimony of various individuals, and our impression of jurors. Folks who had been in the courtroom for jury selection had strong, totally unqualified opinions about the various jurors. As time went on, they began to hypothesize about which ones were holding out for a guilty verdict. But none of us knew anything. We were all Monday morning quarterbacks at this point. We had hoped it would be a short wait, but two hours later we still had no news.

"Bowflex?" Barry said. "What was that all about?"

"Who knows?" replied Diane.

"What did you think?" I asked Trip. His opinion meant a lot more than ours. I had never been to a criminal trial.

"It sounded like a generic closing argument. You could have used most of it at almost any trial. That doesn't mean some jurors won't find it effective. It's just that I don't think it was directly applicable to this trial."

"I was glad you said that finding Steven innocent wasn't finding Ward a liar—even though we all know he is. I just think some folks have trouble thinking an officer would lie about something. If they are finding Foote ineffective, that may be a more comfortable conclusion for them to reach," I said.

"What's with the 'If you don't find Steven guilty, sexual assaults and domestic violence will run rampant' argument?" John asked.

"I don't know. Wasn't it Nazi Germany where people were sent to concentration camps and murdered if their neighbors accused them of something, despite the fact that there was no evidence?" Gregg asked.

"Yeah, I seem to remember that from the history channel," Diane said. "But we don't live in Nazi Germany. Hopefully in America there has to be some proof before you get sent to jail."

"Hopefully," I replied weakly.

Diane had taken detailed notes during the trial. Since I wasn't in the courtroom until I testified and no one was supposed to discuss other testimony with me, she took the time that afternoon to give me a replay.

We discussed jurors' body language. We kept reassuring one another that there was just no way that they could come back with a guilty verdict. There was no way Foote had proven his case beyond a reasonable doubt. But there was no phone call to return us to the courtroom. What could be taking them so long? The correct decision was obvious to us. We began to evaluate the jurors. Maybe engineers on the jury were not a good idea. Maybe, maybe, maybe ...

It was strange, but I found myself avoiding Steven. I couldn't bring myself to sit or stand next to him or really to talk to him. I don't know why. I don't know if that was my decision or if I felt that was what he wanted. At some point, Gregg came over and sat next to me. "You know, you are both really lucky," he said.

At my totally perplexed look, he continued. "I don't think I would have this many friends in court supporting me if that was me on trial. I know this whole thing is awful. But you should take a lot of comfort in knowing that you have all of these good friends here with you, calling to see how things are going, and maybe most important, praying and rooting for you."

Since I was once again tearing up, the best I could do was nod in agreement.

At 3:00 p.m. Trip's cell phone rang. It might as well have been a gunshot. Not good news. The jurors had a question. None of us thought that was good news—not even Trip. The judge said the Justice Center was being officially closed at 3:30 and all non-essential personnel were being asked to leave. She also said the jury had asked for copies of the police reports. She was going to send them a note telling them about the closure, but also telling them she would let them deliberate until 5:00 p.m. If they thought they would have a decision by then, they could keep going. If not, they could recess and come back tomorrow. She also said they could not be given any police reports that had not been entered into evidence. (The police reports are written, but they are not necessarily accurate. One of them indicated that Steven had decided, on his own, to go to Lee and Ellie's to apologize.)

We went back to waiting and speculating. Was taking more time a good sign or a bad sign? Even Trip started second guessing himself and his strategy. I went over, sat next to him and said sincerely, "Trip, whatever the outcome—I know you have been really vested in the case—and I know you worked long and hard on our behalf. You've done the best possible for us. I truly mean that. Whatever happens, I know you did the best."

"I really appreciate that," was all he said.

More waiting. It was like an emergency room or an intensive care waiting room. There were jokes made and we laughed about some things, but it was most certainly not festive. No one would leave despite the snow. Our friends wanted to be with us. When I suggested leaving because of the weather, John said, "It would be like losing a book before you read the ending. I'm not going. I want to know what happens. Besides, you need us." He mumbled the last few words. He was right. We did need our friends at this point.

One reoccurring topic was how strange we all thought it was that the supposed victims were not here. Though Lee had cried profusely, and said that Steven had verbally raped his wife, and Ward had saved his life by coming to our home, he wasn't here. We wondered how vested in the outcome they were if they didn't care enough to be present for the trial.

I actually found myself feeling momentarily sorry for Lee and Ellie. They have lived in their house for much longer than us (thirty-plus years, I think.) But there were no friends or family here to support them, despite Lee's testimony that the whole incident and the last seven months had been emotionally traumatizing to him. I felt fortunate to think that we did have family and friends who were really suffering through this with us.

Finally, at approximately 4:30 p.m., Trip's phone rang ... the jury had arrived at a verdict.

Chapter 60

Late Afternoon, Wednesday, October 28: In the Courtroom

I sat in the first row of benches behind Steven and Trip, with Gregg to my right. As Diane began to move into the row behind us, I grabbed her hand and pulled her into the first row to my left. I grabbed Gregg's hand tightly with my right hand and Diane's with my left hand.

We watched the jurors walk to the jury box. They were not smiling or making eye contact with Steven or any of us. I knew instinctively that this was not a good sign. Jurors who convict don't look at the defendant. Jurors who acquit do. Jurors who acquit smile. Jurors who convict don't. Everyone knows these simple truths. I tightened my grip on Diane and Gregg's hands.

Judge: When I read the verdict, I know this has been an emotional case and there are people here who have been watching the trial as it progressed. So I'm going to ask to make sure that there are no undue displays of emotion no matter what the verdict is. Thank you.

Judge: Has the jury reached a verdict?

Juror: We have.

Judge: Would you please give the verdict forms to the bailiff?

The Court will now read the verdict forms. Count No. 1. We, the jury, find the defendant, Mark Steven Gesse not guilty of Count No. 1, Menacing.

Count No. 2. We, the jury, find the defendant, Mark Steven Gesse, not guilty of Count No. 2, Prohibited Use of a Weapon.

Is this your verdict?

Juror: Yes.

The Court then polled the jurors to confirm that they had all agreed to this verdict. The judge proceeded to advise the jurors that they were now free to discuss the case with anyone, including the lawyers if they were contacted by them. The decision to speak or not speak to any attorney regarding the case or their deliberations was their's and their's alone. The judge then asked them to join her in the jury room to receive her personal thanks and to receive their certificates. The judge asked Foote and Trip if there was anything else, and upon being assured we were done, left the courtroom.

Chapter 61

Wednesday, October 28: In the Courtroom after the Trial

If the three most beautiful words in the English language are "I love you," the two most beautiful words must be "not guilty."

I released my death grip on Diane and Gregg's hands and, crying, jumped up as soon as I could. As I was jumping up toward Steven, he was standing and turning around toward me. We hugged and kissed and then hugged one another once more. I then moved to Trip and hugged him (without the kiss). We were surrounded by our friends—some were crying. I assume they were tears of happiness and relief like mine. Everyone was hugging, kissing and saying, "It couldn't have gone any other way."

"I knew it had to be not guilty."

"There's no way they could have done anything else."

"You're the man, Trip."

"If I ever get arrested, I'm calling you."

I didn't know who was saying what. I said to Diane, "Call Roger," and to Barry, "Call your dad." I added, "Someone should call Art." The friends who had been there on the first two days of the trial needed to know the good news.

"Did you see the judge?" asked Trip.

"No. What do you mean?" I rejoined.

"She smiled at Steven as soon as she read the verdicts. She tried to make eye contact with you," he said, directing his comment to Steven. "But you were looking at Michelle and didn't see her. She thought it was the correct verdict. You don't see that very often in a judge," Trip said.

"It was the right verdict," Steven and I replied in unison, and then both of us started to laugh—a real, honest to god laugh.

I can't explain clearly the difference in how I felt before the verdict and after the verdict. I did not believe there was any way the jury could decide "without a reasonable doubt" that Steven had done what Ward said he did. But then, I didn't believe the charges would be considered credible enough for us to be prosecuted for seven months. Though I know on the level of reason that I looked the same after the verdict, my body felt different ... lighter ... like things could move through it ... centered ... in the present. All of these terms describe the feeling, but none of them do it justice.

Steven looked younger to me. He was laughing without any of the reservation that had been behind his laughter in the last seven months. He looked handsome to me—and sexy, too. His green eyes were crinkled at the corners with happiness. My husband was back. He had stepped out of that place he had gone and was joining me. Everything was going to be okay again.

As our jubilation subsided, we remembered the bad weather outside.

"What do you need us to do?" Steven asked Trip, pointing to the boxes of briefs and notes and posters.

"I'll pull the truck around and maybe you could help Ann take the boxes down in front," he said.

"No problem. We'll get everything downstairs."

"Do you want to stop for a beer? Or a glass of champagne? You can do that now," beamed Trip.

"Yes, but I'm worried about the weather and everyone getting home safely. Michelle will plan something. We'll plan something for this Friday or Saturday and we can celebrate without worrying about everyone having to drive home. I think the best thing right now is to get everyone home safely," Steven said.

You could tell that Trip was "wired." He had truly been vested in the outcome of this case and worried like us during the longer than expected deliberations that things were not going to turn out well. But our celebrations would have to wait.

I turned to Gregg and said, "The gifts. Can you go out to our car and give everyone who was here today their 'trial gifts'?" I had bought and wrapped key chains to distribute to everyone who supported us during the trial. They had a gear on them that had the Latin aphorism, "ILLE-GITIMI NON CARBORUNDUM" on one side, with the English translation, "DON'T LET THE BASTARDS GRIND YOU DOWN" on the other. When I saw the key chains in a catalog, they seemed like a most appropriate way to remember the trial.

"Sure, I'll go," Gregg said, as he put on his coat and headed to our car in the Justice Center parking lot.

Barry said, "I'll go plow your driveway so you can drive in okay." Something else to be grateful for.

As the three of us headed home, we realized there was nothing at home for us to eat, so we stopped at a neighborhood restaurant for dinner. Delaying our return would also give Barry some time to plow. It was Steven's first drink in almost seven months. There were numerous phone calls on our cell phones while we were at the restaurant—one from a friend as far away as New Zealand. We don't even know how some of these folks found out about the verdict. It was great! The hamburger I had tasted better than anything I had eaten in the last seven months. We were celebrating!

Chapter 62

After the Trial

The next morning, there were lots of sentimental e-mails, lots of phone calls, and lots of snow—forty inches or more. I sent the following e-mail to Trip and Ann:

I am having some sort of delayed reaction here. We slept for more than ten hours last night. I could swear that my body actually felt different after the verdict than it has in the last seven months.

Just wanted to say again (for what I can promise you is not the last time) THANK YOU. In one of our first meetings you said, "I am fighting for your life." That could not have been more true, though I don't think I realized it at the time. I know that the jury reached the right verdict, but my recent experience did leave me with concerns about whether or not that would actually happen. So right now I think I'm dealing with some sort of post-traumatic thing because I am more emotional than I was last night thinking about what could have happened. Steven and Gregg are outside dealing with our three feet of snow. Good thing we don't have to come down the mountain today!

I am sure we will speak to you today, but I wanted you to know how grateful both of us, but perhaps especially me, are. Thank you again.

This was Trip's reply:

Seldom have I ever been so emotional about a case. I have handled much bigger cases in terms of charges, but none of them seem as important as this one. I know this is because Steve was/is innocent and wrongfully prosecuted by our government. Representing an innocent man is much more stressful than representing the guilty. As a result I, too, am dealing with some sort of post-traumatic thing.

Furthermore, you looked physically different after the verdict. I will never forget my memory of you and Steve as I drove away from the court-house. With large snowflakes floating everywhere, you and Steven strolled arm-in-arm away from the courthouse with your heads held high, your shoulders relaxed and back, and with an expression of con-tentment and happiness that I have not seen before. The change is ob-vious. I am very happy for you, and I am very relieved that I did not let you down.

Chapter 63

Lessons Learned

Weeks after the trial, Trip spoke to one of the jurors. She was pleased to speak to him. She said she took the judge's instructions very seriously and assumed that Steven was innocent and that it was the DA's job to prove him guilty beyond a reasonable doubt. She said she was ready to find him guilty if she was convinced of his guilt, but she did not assume he was guilty. When the jury convened on the third day of the trial, she assumed that it would be a matter of minutes and that they would all agree that the DA had not proven Steven guilty beyond a reasonable doubt. She was surprised to find that most of the jurors (she said all but three) assumed Steven was guilty of something. They wanted something that supported that conclusion and tried hard to find evidence, facts, anything that would allow them to come back with a guilty verdict. That's why the jury was out so long. But despite their efforts for over four hours, they could not find that the DA had provided sufficient evidence or arguments to support the conclusion they wanted.

Think about that conversation. Not only do the police assume you are guilty because you have been arrested; not only does the "investigating" officer assume you are guilty; not only does the DA assume you are guilty; not only does the judicial system assume you are guilty; but perhaps scariest of all, the majority of the jurors assume you are guilty. You are truly assumed guilty as soon as you get enmeshed in the U.S. criminal justice system. We were fortunate to have the resources to fight the charges, but if you don't have the resources, no one is ever going to find you innocent. In fact, a lot of people even right now probably assume that Steven was guilty, but was just lucky to get acquitted.

So what lessons have I learned that I would like to share? Here they are.

- You should be the first one to call the police.
- Be prepared.
- Have the name and number of a criminal attorney.
- Know your rights. TV is correct—you do not have to talk to the cops or detectives or anyone else without your attorney present.
- No one can search your house without a search warrant.
- Understand that the system assumes guilt. You are PRESUMED GUILTY. Don't kid yourself into thinking that the police or the detectives think you are innocent, or that they want to investigate. I know this isn't what it's like on TV—but trust me, in the real world, once you are arrested you are guilty.
- And most important, never have anything to do with someone who has no sense of humor.

Epilogue

October, 2011: Two Years after the Trial

Two years after the trial, we look and act to every observer the same as we did before that fateful day when Ward came to dinner. What's happened since then? A lot and nothing.

We had a very nice celebratory dinner at Laudisio's, our favorite Italian restaurant in Boulder, on the Saturday after the trial ended. Everyone who attended the trial and lived in town, along with our legal council, attended. It was our first social meeting with Trip and his wife, Sue. Though we celebrated Steven's acquittal, Trip was the much-toasted guest of honor.

That evening was the start of a great friendship between Steven and me and Trip and Sue. Trip often says, "The best thing to come out of that trial was our friendship." My reply is always the same. "Yes, but someone could just have introduced the four of us!" By association and success, Trip and Sue have also become friends of our good friends who supported us during the trial.

Sue continues to say that she has never, during his whole career, seen Trip so vested in a case, nor so stressed about the outcome. Trip says, "It's a lot harder to defend an innocent man than one who you know is guilty. If your client is guilty, your work on his behalf is to get him the best deal possible. But if your client is innocent, you are trying to prevent injustice from being done. It's not often that I have to defend an innocent man." I don't think it's something he wants to do frequently, as it did take a toll on him.

Steven was not able to recoup any of our financial expenses or get any legal revenge, though that realization was slow to come to him. You aren't allowed to sue the prosecuting attorney or the county, which in hindsight makes some sense. Though we investigated the possibility of legal action against Ward, Ellie and/or Lee, the advice we received was that the expense would never justify the possible reward—even if we did succeed.

As someone once said, "A good life is the best revenge." So "having a good life" has been our goal. We are trying to enjoy ourselves, although we are very cognitive of the fact that life can be taken away from you in a minute. I don't mean life as a doctor would define it—by your heart beating and your brain functioning. I mean life as defined by living—by being able to do the things you enjoy that harm no one. We are back to entertaining, traveling, and vintage car racing—and enjoying a few glasses of wine with dinner most nights! Though the dogs still get groomed, they are nowhere as well groomed as they were during our ordeal. Steven and I have both regained the weight we lost between his arrest and the trial. Steven has also regained his sense of humor. He can still be heard occasionally making mildly crude comments to our friends. In fact, the comment, "I do think you would look good in a thong" has become a standing joke among some of our friends.

Steven doesn't like to talk about his arrest, the period leading up to the trial, or the trial. He says it's behind us and there is no reason to talk about it anymore. As you might expect, the topic comes up frequently, especially as I move toward publishing this book. The book for me is closure. I want Ellie and Lee to know that their son walked into our home, walked upstairs into our kitchen, and threatened Steven. I doubt that they will believe this fact, but I want to introduce doubt into their minds about what their son did that night. It is the truth. Since they were not at the trial except during their individual testimonies, I want them to hear this. I want Jean to know that I called Tom that evening in a desperate cry for help when I was frightened and alone. I want her to know that he denied knowing what was happening and did nothing. I don't know if she knows this. I would be ashamed of my husband if he acted that way toward a friend.

We still live in the same house. Ellie and Lee and Jean and Tom live in the same homes on our lane as they did in 2009. As you might expect, we have never spoken to Ellie or Lee and rarely see them on the road or in the driveway. We wave to Jean and Tom when we see them in the driveway or on the road, but haven't had any social contact with them since the night of the incident. I, probably more than Steven, missed Jean and Tom and their supposed friendship for a long time after the trial. But the void has since been filled with real friends like Trip and Sue.

Some folks have said they would have moved. "How can you stand to live close to Ellie and Lee?" they ask. "Why do you want to stay there?" My answer is simple. I refuse to let anyone else dictate my agenda. This is my home. I like my home. I like living here and I am not going to move because of anyone. Both Steven and I made a very conscious decision not to change our lifestyle because of what happened. Although both of us have most certainly been changed by what happened, we have tried very hard not to let it change our activities or actions. I have tried even harder to retain my sense of humor and a perspective on life.

Even though Steven was finally acquitted, after seven months and a lot of legal fees, we would not have been the "winners" if we made changes to our lifestyle or where we lived because of these individuals. I was damn sure that after everything we had been through, I wasn't going to lose the rest of my life. If I did that, they would have won something more precious than money.

As for Steven and me, we celebrated our fortieth wedding anniversary in July 2011. We survived and our marriage survived. I'm not sure whether it is stronger than it would otherwise have been, but it is an exceptionally good marriage from what I can tell. No regrets—except perhaps inviting Ward to dinner that fateful night in April 2009. Not bad for forty years!